ECONOMIC REFORMS AND SMALL SCALE INDUSTRIES

About the Author

Prof. M. Soundarapandian is the Head of the Department of Rural Industries and Management, Gandhigram Rural University, Gandhigram. He has the additional charge of the Director of the Centre of Entrepreneurship Development (CED). He did his post-graduation in Economics, Business Administration and Education from Madurai Kamaraj University, Madurai and obtained a Doctorate in Economics from the same University. He has published 81 papers in various national and international journals of repute. He has also to his credit 22 books in various fields of Rural Industries and Management, Economics and Entrepreneurship Development.

Prof. Soundarapandian has conducted 15 minor and major research projects with the financial assistantance of UGC, ICSSR, Ministry of Rural Development, BGVS, New Delhi and State Resource Centre for Non-formal Education, Chennai. Under CED many skill development training programmes are conducted for the promotion of women self help groups in Tamil Nadu. At present, he is undertaking a action project on "Entrepreneurship Development in Tsunami affected area of Tamil Nadu" funded by International Labour Organisation (ILO), Geneva.

ECONOMIC REFORMS AND SMALL SCALE INDUSTRIES

Dr. M. Soundarapandian

Professor and Head
Department of Rural Industries and Management
Gandhigram Rural University
Gandhigram

CONCEPT PUBLISHING COMPANY, NEW DELHI-110059

ISBN : 13-978-81-8069-449-3 **ISBN : 13-10-81-8069-449-6**

First Published 2009

Published and Printed by

Since 1974

Concept Publishing Company

Regd. Office:

A/15-16, Commercial Block, Mohan Garden

New Delhi-110059 (India)

Phones : 25351460, 25351794, *Fax* : 091-11-25357109

Email : publishing@conceptpub.com,

website: www.conceptpub.com

Editorial Office:

H-13, Bali Nagar, New Delhi-110 015, India.

Cataloging in Publication Data--*Courtesy:* D.K. Agencies (P) Ltd. <docinfo@dkagencies.com>

Soundarapandian, M. (Mookkiah), 1960-

Economic reforms and small scale industries / M. Soundarapandian.

p. cm.

Study conducted at Dindigul and Madurai districts of Tamil Nadu, India.

Includes bibliographical references (p.).

Includes index.

ISBN 13: 9788180694493 ISBN 10: 8180694496

1. Small business--Government policy--India--Dindigul (District) 2. Small business--Government policy--India--Madurai (District) 3. Industrial policy--India. 4. India--Economic policy--1991- I. Title.

DDC 338.642 095 482 22

PREFACE

In the year 1990-91, the New Economic Policy was implemented in India based on the Structural Adjustment Programme (SAP) and Stabilization Policies of International Monetary Fund (IMF) and World Bank. The 4 D Formula is the conditionalities of IMF. They are : (i) Deregulation, (ii) Deflation, (iii) Denationalisation, and (iv) Devaluation. These economic reforms were initiated by year by year and stage by stage in all sectors of economy. All sectors of the Indian economy have the tremendous changes only after implementation of New Economic Policy. An attempt has been made to analyse the impact of New Economic Policy in Small Scale Industries sector in Tamil Nadu State of India. The analyses and the findings of the project is useful to the policy-makers for the effective implementation of New Economic Policy in developing countries like India.

I am very much thankful to the Indian Council of Social Science Research (ICSSR) for providing the financial assistance for conducting the present major research project. I am grateful to the Gandhigram Rural University authorities – (Vice Chancellor and Registrar) for permitting me and for providing facilities to complete the project within the stipulated period. My sincere thanks to the Organizations, Departments, Ministries and the SSI entrepreneurs for providing the necessary data for the use of research project analysis. I am happy to thank Mrs. A.Chandra Prabha who served as Research Assistant in the project. It gives me a great pleasure in thanking my family members – Mrs. S.Indumathi (Wife), S. Diwakaran (Son) and S. Vidya (Daughter) for their cooperation in completing the project work.

PREFACE

Contents

1. Introduction

1. Statement of the Problem

The term globalization has been used widely in recent times. Though often without consideration of its precise epistemological connotations. Industrial globalization refers to an evolving pattern of cross-border enterprise activities relating to international investment, trade and strategic alliances for product development, production sourcing and marketing. To what extend small and medium enterprises have achieved globalization is a question.

The major branching of economic theory-best suited to industrialized countries and the other one called Development Economics, perfect for the experience of the less developed countries, is becoming less relevant in this era of globalization. While the world today is richer than ever, disparities are increasing: 75 per cent of the world's population enjoys only 16 per cent of its income, while the richest 20 per cent have access to 85 per cent of global income. This situation prompted an enquiry at the international level, especially at the instance of the ILO.

The structure of industrialized economies gradually changed, as well as the objectives of economic policy, in a way which made difficult for a rapid growth of production and employment. The mounting levels of unemployment in the industrialized countries led them to protectionist measures, with obvious implications on the demand for imports from developing countries.

In order to safeguard incomes and employment amidst these dramatic changes in the world economy, the developing countries, in varying degrees, had adopted structural adjustment policies. The worst victim of these policies were the traditional policy thrusts of these countries, such as, basic needs and growth with equity.

At least in developing countries, most discussions on globalization are comparatmentalised. For instance, Government agencies and business associations confine their discussions to areas such as industrial organization and policy. Attention in areas such as trade regime, WTO, etc., has been very recent. In the industralised countries on the other hand, academic enquiries on developing countries have been confined to their overseas development policy.

Any discussion on international cooperation in the area of small enterprise development has to be made against the background of the official development policy in industralised countries during the past five decades. Official development policy in industraised countries, in relation to developing countries, has undergone a sea change. The shift from aid to trade was a major one. During the 1980s and 1990s, aid itself has undergone a metamorphosis. While during the 1960s and 70s aid was largely directed through official development channels, during the 1980s and 1990s, international NGOs started playing a key role in development cooperation. However, the role of international NGOs has traditionally been concentrated in some areas like women employment, conscientization programmes and reduction of glaring forms of poverty. Some of these have also entered into the area of human rights.

This tradition has undergone substantial changes in the recent past. Germany and Netherlands are two countries which have attempted major innovations in the area of international cooperation, wherein small enterprise development has found a significant place.[1]

Small is beautiful. Small Scale Enterprises (SSEs) play an important role in recovery and increasingly recognized as having a permanent role as a seedbed for future growth. Their activities span a wide range in both the formal and informal sectors and these provide a good source of non-public sector employment. Even for some in public sector employment, small scale enterprises provide a substantial supplement to their incomes as second job.

An important feature of the small scale enterprises, whether urban or rural, is that they make better use of factors of production than large scale enterprises. The small scale enterprises usually labour intensive and the amount of capital invested is small. The Small Scale Industry (SSI) sector has emerged as India's engine of growth. In 2000, the SSI sector accounted for nearly 40 per cent of gross value of output in total exports from the country through over 32 lakh units of the SSI sector provided.

The present economic scenario in India has created an excellent climate for the development of SMEs. Although the Indian Economy traditionally has been agro-based, with a sizeable part of its gross domestic product (GDP) being contributed by agriculture, a notable contributor to the nation's gross domestic product is the small scale industrial sector. The SSI sector was dominated in the earlier years by village and cottage industries, and small industrial units with very low capital base, with the increasing pressure of population, which has grown from 350 million in 1947 at the time of Independence to over 985 million as of now, there has been a perceptible shift towards industrial economy which provides gainful employment. Larger industrial undertakings came up in core sectors, such as, steel, cement and petro-chemicals. During the paradigm shift in economy, the small scale sector has remained a very active participant in India's growth.

To illustrate :

- Over 95 per cent of total industrial units are in the SSI sector numbering 2.7 million.
- SSI has 15.3 million work force, representing 80 per cent of the total industrial workforce.
- Over 40 per cent of turnover of the manufacturing sector comes from the SSI sector, i.e., Rs.3,40,650 million out of Rs.21,19,680 million.
- Over 40 per cent of industrial exports are contributed by the SSI sector.[2]

In India, the New Economic Policy (NEP) is a set of policy (ies) and administrative procedures introduced in July 1991 to bring about changes in the economic direction of the country. It has got two major components — stabilization and structural reforms.

Stabilization part has again three components :

1. Management of Balance of Payments.
2. Control of Inflation
3. Fiscal Correction.

Structural Reforms part has seven components :

1. Exchange rate adjustment.
2. Liberalization of imports.
3. Rationalization of tariff structure.
4. Delicensing/removal of licensing restrictions.
5. Financial sector reforms.
6. Disinvestment of public sector shares.
7. Foreign Direct Investment.[3]

In the process of liberalization of the industrial sector, the Government of India announced New Industrial Policy (NIP) in August 1991 which reiterate the importance of small units and announced different measures for the promotion of small tiny and village industries. Definition of SSI was also revised. To encourage modernization and upgrading of technology, equity participation by other industrial undertakings including foreign collaborators was permitted upto 24 per cent.

Presently, the Government is implementing various promotional schemes to encourage the small enterprises. Important schemes are:

(a) Excise Concessions available for both registered and

unregistered units on a graded scale depending on turnover upto Rs.300 lakh.

(b) Integrated Infrastructure Development Scheme to strengthen infrastructural facilities in the rural and backward areas.

(c) Quality Certification Scheme to improve SSI product quality and financial support to acquire ISO 9000.

(d) Seven Point Action Plan to improve credit flow to SSI sector.

(e) To support expansion, modernization and technology upgradation, the scope of National Equity Fund Scheme is enlarged to cover the entire country except metropolitan areas.

(f) Technology Development and Modernisation Fund Scheme for the modernization and adoption of improved and upgraded technology.

(g) A scheme for creation of Technology Development Fund in the States with the involvement of State Governments and Industry Associations.

(h) Priority Sector Lending.

(i) 40 per cent of advances to SSI sector reserved for tiny sector and village and cottage industries.

(j) Refinance facilities and special schemes of Small Industries Development Bank of India (SIDBI).

(k) Concessional/fixed rate for loans upto Rs.2 lakhs in two slabs.

(l) Single window scheme of SIDBI for project outlays upto Rs.50 lakhs.

(m) Prime Minister's Rozgar Yozana (PMRY) for loans to micro-enterprises.

(n) Infrastructural support to Entrepreneurship Development Institutes to augment their training capacities.

(o) Joint programme with the State Bank of India and SIDBI for modernization and technology upgradation of industry customs.

(p) Assistance to industrial associations and voluntary agencies to set up Quality Testing Centres.
(q) Special programmes on render development, quality awareness and pollution control.
(r) Reservation of products for exclusive manufacture by the SSI.
(s) Government priority for purchase and price preference for items from the SSI sector.

Under the integrated production programme of the small and large scale industries, the number of products reserved for the SSI have increased from initial 47 in the First Five Year Plan to 836 (as on March 1996). About 409 items have been reserved for the exclusive purchase by the Government from the SSI sector. Thus the Government of India has been adopting various protective and promotional policies for the development of SSI in the Country.[4]

New Economic Policy play a vital role on the economy in our country. The Industrial policies announced by the Central and State Governments, have been providing various incentives for accelerating the growth of the SSI sector. However, the rational of State intervention in the promotion of SSI was questioned in some studies. Most of the studies were focused on the performance of SSI at the national level while, the issues related to size, growth, structure and productivity have received inadequate attention at the State level. The process of restructuring Indian Economy through liberalization and decontrols has put the small enterprises at a critical juncture of intricacies concerning their future. Therefore, for any change in policy related to small industries there is a need for elaborate studies on the growth and performance of SSI. This study is based on the entrepreneurs of small scale enterprises under liberalization.

Small Scale Enterprises (SSEs) play an important role in the recovery and are increasingly recognized as having a permanent role as a seed-bed for future growth. Their activities span a wide range in both the formal and informal sectors and they provide a good source of non-public sector employment. Even for some in public sector employment, SSEs provide a substantial supplement to their incomes as second job. An important feature of the SSE, whether urban or rural, is the belief that they make better use of scarce factors of production than large scale enterprises. The SSE is usually labour intensive and the amount of capital invested is small.

A number of problems have been identified with the SSEs in India. These include shortages of capital, raw materials, spare parts and machinery competition from large scale industries and complicated procedures which must be followed in order to start or expand a small business shortage of imported raw materials, spares and machinery has been an added problem mainly due to the difficulty of import licenses for these imputes. This has been a function of the preventing shortage or foreign exchange.

The structure of Indian economics is currently undergoing a period of transformation under the aegis of structural adjustment policy packages negotiated with the IMF and the world Bank, Government in all corners to the continent are effecting programmes after radically the nature and orientation of their national economics. In most cases their involves a substantial degree of economic liberalization with the role of the Government in the management and regulation of economic activity having much reduced. Since the inception of the New Economic Policy (NEP) in 1990, within the broad set of structural adjustment programmes, certain policies have affected the activities of SSEs.[5]

The on-going programme of Economic Reform based upon the principle and the changes at the international economic scene including the emergence of brought certain challenges and several new opportunities before the SSI sector is that of growing competition both globally and domestically. At the same problems which relate to credit, infrastructure, technology, marketing, delayed and regulations etc. In order to enable this sector to avail the opportunities and to address to these problems effectively and urgently. At attempt has been made to analyse the impact of economic policy on the small scale industry in India.

2. Objectives of the Study

The main objectives of the study are two fold :

(i) To assess the impact of the New Economic Policy on Small Scale Enterprises through a sample survey in India; and
(ii) To identify the measures to promote and develop the small scale industrial sector under the liberalization policy.

The specific objectives of the study are :

(i) To identify the macro-economic policy measures of the new economic policy on the promotion of small scale industries;
(ii) To study the impact of economic reforms on the production, employment and earnings level of the small scale enterprises in the study area;
(iii) To analyse the institutional and financial arrangements under the New Economic Policy for the development of small scale enterprises;
(iv) To review the role of legislation in the promotion of small scale industries after liberalization in India;
(v) To review the problems faced by the small scale entrepreneurs after implementation of New Economic Policy; and
(vi) To suggest the concrete measures for the development of small scale enterprises during the liberalization period.

3. Concepts

A clear definition of the concepts used in this study of New Economic Policy on Small Scale Enterprises would help to understand the different issues dealt with the present study. Hence before proceeding with the actual discussion and analysis, an attempt is made to define the various concepts used in the present study.

Small Scale Industry

Industry is generally understood to mean a manufacturing process or activity resulting in production of goods or articles. These manufactured goods may be either for human consumption or used as sinputs for intermediary goods in the form of half finished products or ancillary products, for final processing and production.[6]

The definition of small scale industries differs from country to country. All the definitions are based upon certain factors like number of persons employed, amount of investment, power, input, production/turnover, location, technology etc. In most cases 'number of persons used' and 'investment' are taken as the basis for defining the concept of small scale industry. For example in U.S.A. and U.K., employment is taken as the basis for defining small industry. Similarly 'investment' in India, Indonesia and Malaysia; 'investment and employment' in Japan, Korea, Philippines and Indonesia, 'Turnover' in China are taken as the basis for making distinction between small and big industry. A small scale industry is defined as follows in various countries:

U.S.A.

No official definition exists but generally taken to mean less than 100 employees.

U.K.

A manufacturing unit employing less than 200 employees, in retail trade having a turnover less than 50,000 Pounds, in wholesale trade below 200,000 Pounds turnover. In case of construction unit employing less than 25 employees and in transport units having less than 5 vehicles is taken as a small unit.

Japan

In Japan, the definition varies depending on the nature of the unit.

In manufacturing unit the investment limit is 100 million Yen and employing below 300 persons. In mining and wholesale trade, the investment ceiling is 30 million Yen and employing less than 100 persons whereas in retail trade the investment limit is 10 million Yen and employing less 50 persons.

Korea

In the case of a manufacturing unit, the investment limit is 500 million Won and employing more than 5 persons but less than 300, in construction unit 500 million Won and persons employing more than 5 but below 50.

Malaysia

A small industry is defined as an unit employing investment less than R.M 250,000 and there is no ceiling on the number of persons employed.

Philippines

In Philippines, no specific definition is given. The small industry is referred as an industry employing assets between P 100,000 and P1.0 million and employing workers between 5 to 99 persons.

Indonesia

The small scale unit is one which employs an investment in plant and machinery not exceeding Rp 150 million and investment per person employed does not exceed USS 100.

Sri Lanka

A small scale unit is defined as an unit which is mainly run by power and employing investment not exceeding Rs. 2 lakh.

Table 1.1 : Definition of SMEs in Asia and Other Countries

Country	*Category of Industry*	*Criteria/Country's Official Definition*
Australia	Manufacturing	Small enterprises < 100 employees
	Services	Medium enterprises < 200 employees
Belgium	SME	Annual staff average of 50 employees
Canada	Manufacturing	Independent firms having < 200 Employees
China	SME	Depends on product group usually <100 employees Investment ceiling 30 million Yuan
Denmark	Manufacturing	<500 employees Production units with more than 5 employees
France	SME	10-499 employees
Germany	SME	< 500 employees
Greece	Small Enterprises	< 50 employees
	Medium Enterprises	50-500 employees
Indonesia	SME	< 100 Employees
Ireland	SME	< 500 employees
Italy	Small Enterprises	< 200 employees
Japan	Manufacturing	<300 employees or asset Capitalization <100 Million Yen
Korea	Manufacturing	< 300 employees
	Services	< 200 employees
Malasiya	SMEs	< 75 full time workers or with a shareholder fund of < RM 2.5 million
	Sis	Manufacturing establishments employing between 5 and 50 employees or with a shareholders fund up to RM 500,000
	Mis	Manufacturing establishments Employing between 5 and 50 employees or with a shareholders fund between RM 500,000 to RM 2.5 million.
Mexico	Micro	< 15 employees and gross income/ Sales <US175,000
	Small	15-99 employees and gross Income/ sales <USS17500
	Medium	100-249 employees and gross income/sales <USS500,000
Netherlands	Small Enterprises	< 10 employees
	Medium Enterprises	10-100 employees
Singapore	Manufacturing	< SS 12 million fixed assets
	Services	< 100 employees
Sweeden	SME	Autonomous firms with < 200 Employees

(*Contd.*)

(**Table 1.1** : *Contd.*)

Switzerland	SME	No fixed definition
Thailand	Labour Intensive Sectors	< 200 employees
	Capital Intensive Sectors	< 100 employees
United Kingdom	SME	No fixed definition
United States	Very Small Enterprises	< 20 employees
	Small Enterprises	20-99 employees
	Medium Enterprises	100-499 employees
Vietnam	SME	No fixed definition, generally < 200 Employees

Source: SIDBI Report.

In India, in the beginning both investment and labour employed are taken into account to define the concept of small industry. The definition has undergone changes periodically. Over the past five decades, Government policies have been formulated to develop a framework for the revival and development of cottage, tiny, agro and small scale industries. With a view to determining the type of industrial units which needed special support, it was considered necessary to develop an appropriate definition for small scale units under the Industries (Development and Regulation) Act, 1951.

There has been many changes in the ceiling limit of investment in plant and machinery over the years. The periodic revisions in the definition of Small Scale Industries as made by the Government of India is given in Table 1.2.

Table 1.2 : Periodic Revision of SSI Definitions in India

Year	*SSI*	*Remarks*
1950	Gross investment in fixed assets not exceeding Rs.5 lakhs	Employing less than 50 workers per day (with the use of power) or less than 100 workers per day (without use of power)
1958	Gross investment in fixed assets less than Rs. 5 lakhs	Same as above, except the criteria based on the employment per day was henceforth replaced by a per shift provision

(*Contd.*)

(**Table 1.2** : *Contd.*)

1959	Gross investment in the fixed assets value of machinery (original)	Same as above, except that the criteria based on the employment per day henceforth replaced by a per shifts. provision
1960	Gross investment in the fixed assets value up to Rs.5 lakhs	The employment condition was dropped from the definition
Original value of plant and machinery only		
1966	Up to Rs.75 lakhs	—
1975	Up to Rs.10 lakhs	—
1977	Up to Rs.10 lakhs	Units located in rural area towns with a maximum population of 50,000 (as per the 1971 Census)
1980	Up to Rs. 20 lakhs	Units located in rural areas/towns with a maximum population of 50,000 (as per the 1971 Census)
1985	Up to Rs. 35 lakhs	Units located in rural areas and towns with a maximum population of up to 5 lakhs (as per the 1981 Census)
1991	Up to Rs. 60 lakhs	(a) The location-specific condition was withdrawn. (b) The SSSEs classification was suspended in 1991 and replaced by the term SSSBEs.
1997	Up to Rs.3 crores	
1999	Up to Rs.1 crore	

Note : SSI—Small Scale Industry, ANC-Ancillary Industry, TINY-Tiny Unit, EOU-Export Oriented Unit, SSSE-Small Scale Service Establishment, SSSBE-Small Scale Service & Business (industry-related) Enterprise.

Source : Ministry of SSI and ARI, Government of India.

In 1997, the Government has increased the investment limit in plant and machinery in respect of small scale/ancillary industrial undertaking up to Rs.3 crores. Subsequently, there has been requests from individual small scale industrial units and SSI associations to reduce the investment limit on plant and machinery in respect of Small Scale Industries/Ancillary industrial undertakings. Therefore, the Government has decided to reduce the investment on plant and machinery from Rs.3 crores to Rs.1 crore w.e.f.24.12.1999.

The present definition of SSI (w.e.f.24.12.1999) is that an industrial undertaking in which the investment is fixed assets plant and machinery, whether held on ownership terms or on lease or by hire-purchase does not exceed rupees one crore.

Ancillary Industrial Undertaking

An industrial undertaking which is engaged or is proposed to have been engaged in the manufacture or production of parts, components, sub-assemblies, tooling or intermediaries, or the rendering of services and undertaking supplies or renders or proposes to supply or render not more than 50 per cent of its production or services, as the case may be, to one or more other industrial undertakings and whose investment is fixed assets in plant and machinery whether held on ownership terms or on lease or on hire-purchase, does not exceed rupees one crore.

Note 1: No small scale or ancillary industrial undertaking referred to above shall be subsidiary of or owned or controlled by any other industrial undertaking.

Note 2: In calculating the value of plant and machinery; the original price thereof, irrespective of whether plant and machinery are new or second hand, shall be taken into account.

Tiny Enterprises

A unit is treated as a tiny enterprise where the investment in plant and machinery does not exceed Rs. 25 lakhs, irrespective of location of the units.

Women Enterprises

Small scale unit where one or more women entrepreneurs have not less than 51per cent financial holding.

Condition: A small industry cannot be owned, controlled or be a subsidiary of another industrial undertaking.

Export Oriented Unit

A unit with an obligation to export at least 30 per cent of its annual production by the end of the third year of commencement of production and having an investment ceiling as prescribed for small scale undertakings i.e., up to Rs. 1 crore in plant and machinery, is termed an export oriented SSI unit.

Small Scale Service and Business (Industry-related) Enterprise (SSSBE)

An Industry related service and business enterprise with an investment in fixed assets, excluding land and building up to Rs.5 lakhs irrespective of location is treated as a Small Scale Service and Business (Industry-related) Enterprise.

The following enterprises are recognized Small Scale Service and Business (Industry-related) Enterprises (SSSBEs):

1. Advertising Agencies,
2. Marketing Consultancy,
3. Equipment Rent and Leasing,
4. Industrial Consultancy,
5. Typing Centre,
6. Xeroxing,
7. Industrial R & D Labs,
8. Industrial Testing Labs,
9. Computerized Design and Drafting,
10. Creation of data bases suitable for Foreign/Indian Markets,
11. Auto repair services and garages,
12. Documentary films on themes like, family planning, social forestry, energy conservation and commercial advertising,
13. Laboratories engaged in testing of raw material, finshed products,
14. Servicing Industry Undertakings engaged in maintenance, repair, testing or servicing of all types of vehicles and machinery of any description including electronic/electrical equipment/instruments i.e., measuring/control instruments, televisions, tape recorders, VCRs, radios, transformers, motors, watches etc.,

15. Laundry and Dry Cleaning,
16. X-Ray Clinic,
17. Tailoring,
18. Servicing of agriculture farm equipment e.g., tractor pump, rig, boring machine etc.,
19. Weigh Bridge,
20. Photographic Lab,
21. Blue printing and enlargement of drawing/designs facilities,
22. All ISD Booths,
23. Teleprinter/Fax services,
24. Sub-Contract Exchanges (SCXs) established by non-Government Industry Associations,
25. EDP Institutes established by Voluntary Association/Non-Government Organizations,
26. Studios, colour, black and white equipped with processing lab,
27. Rope-way in hilly areas,
28. Cable TV Services – Installation and Operation of Cable T.V. Networks,
29. Industrial Photography.

The following enterprises are not recognised as Small Scale Service and Business (Industry-related) Enterprise (SSSBE):

1. Transportation,
2. Storage (except cold storage which is recognized as SSI),
3. Retail/wholesale trade establishments,
4. General Merchandise Stores,
5. Sale outlets for industrial components,
6. Health services including pathological laboratories,
7. Legal Services,
8. Educational Services,
9. Social Services,
10. Hotels.

Consumer Suppliers

Small scale industries now produce a wide range of mass consumption items, over 5000 product, are being manufactured in the small scale sector.

4. Methodology

Primary data as well as secondary data were used for the present study. The study period was from 1990-91 to 2003-04 (Fourteen years after liberalization policy in India). Secondary data were collected from the office records and reports of the Ministry of Statistics and Progrmme Implementations, Ministry of Small Scale Industries and Agro and Rural Industries, Ministry of Industry and Commerce, etc.

In order to measure the impact of liberalistion on small scale enterprises, certain parameters, namely, number of registered units, production level, sales value, employment generation and earnings were used for the present study. The national level data, state level data and sample study districts data were compared to the analyse of impact of economic reforms on small scale industries.

Primary data were also collected from the sample small scale enterprises in Madurai and Dindigul Districts of Tamil Nadu. Madurai and Dindigul district are purposively selected for the study based on the concentration of small scale industries in these study district. The sample enterprises were selected based on the criteria of large number of enterprises in the study districts.

The sample enterprises include the textile and garments, wood products and furniture, food processing, motor repair and welding, leather products, metal products, electrical and electronic repairs etc. A sample of 240 small scale enterprises from the study districts were randomly selected and the sample entrepreneurs were administered with a pre-tested questionnaire. The collected secondary and primary data were analysed with the suitable statistical tools like percentage analysis, etc.

5. Profile of the Study Area

The present section explains the profile of the study area – Tamil Nadu State and the study districts – Dindigul and Madurai Districts. The profile includes the area, Demography, Topography, Agriculture, Trade, Industry, Transport, River, Soil, Minerals and other infrastructure facilities etc.

Profile of Tamil Nadu State

Tamil Nadu State is situated at the South Eastern extremity of the Indian Peninsula bounded on the north by Karnataka and Andhra Pradesh on the east by Bay of Bengal, on the South by the Indian Ocean and on the West by Kerala State.

Land and Area

The Tamil Nadu State lies between 85° and 13° 35′ of northern latitude and 76° 15′ and 80° 20′ of eastern longitude with an area of 1,30,058 square kilometres. It is the 11th State in India in area forming 4.11 per cent of the Union areas.

The Tamil Nadu State can be divided broadly into two natural divisions (a) the Coastal plains of South India and (b) the hilly western area. It can further be sub divided into coromandal plains comprising the districts of Kancheepuram, Thiruvallur, Cuddalore and Vellore. The alluvial plains of the Cauvery Delta extending over Thanjavur and part of Tiruchirapally districts and dry southern plains in Madurai, Dindigul, Ramanathapuram, Sivaganga, Virudhnagar, Tirunelveli and Tuticorin districts. It extends a little beyond Western Ghats in Kanyakumari District.

The State has an uninterrupted coastline of 922 kms. It includes the coastline of Pondicherry and Karaikkal. The coastline is a lengthy boundary on the east. Not a single natural harbour capable of accommodating ocean-going vessels can be found on the coast. Madras City has an artificial harbour. While it is a major Port and Tuticorin a medium one, several smaller ports like Cuddalore, Nagapattinam and Colochel are found.

Hills and Rivers

The Western Ghats averaging 3000 to 8000 feet height run along the western part with the hill group of the Nilgiris and Anamalai on either side of it. Palani Hills, Varushanad and Andipatti ranges are the major off-shoots of the Ghat. The other prominent hill group comprises the Javadir, the Shevaroys, the Kalrayan and the Pachaimalai. These ranges continue south of the river Cauvery. A plateau is found between these hills and the Western Ghats with an average elevation of 1000 feet rising westward. The highest peak of Doddabetta in the Nilgiris is 8650 feet above sea level. The characteristic feature of the hills of Tamil Nadu is that they have flatfish surface at the height. In general the summits are higher than those of Mysore Plateau area. The main hill ranges in Tamil Nadu are: Eastern Ghats, Western Ghats, Shevaroy Hills, Palani Hills, Anamalai, etc.

The Western Ghats from complete water shed and no river passes through them. The main stream viz., Paralliyar and Vattaseri Phazhayar are 37 and 23 miles respectively in length and fall in the Arabian Sea. All the other rivers are east flowing rivers. The Eastern Ghats are not a complete watershed and as a result the river passes through them and notable among them is the river Cauvery. The main rivers are: Cauvery, Vaigai, Thamiraparani, Palani, Poomigar, Vellan etc.

Among the small rivers worth mentioning in the context is Couralayar, which flows from the surplus waters of Kaveripakkam tank. The river runs through Chennai City and joins the sea.

Population

The provisional population of India (2001 Census) is 1,027,015,247 comprising of 531,277,078 males and 495,738,169 females. The population of Tamil Nadu stood at 62,110,839 comprising of 31,268,654 males and 30,842,185 females. The population of Tamil Nadu constitutes 6.05 per cent of the India's population. It ranks 6th among the States/UTs. The population, which was 55,858,946 in 1991, has gone up by 6,251,893 over the last ten years. This represents an increase of 11.19 per cent during the period 1991-2001 as against the growth rate of 15.39 per cent during the period 1981-91. The density of population per sq. km. is 478 in 2001 as against 429 in 1991. The population and its growth trend are important economic factors in a developing economy. As the development programme and policies depend on its growth, trend in the growth of population.

Literacy Rate

Literacy standard in Tamil Nadu State as per 2001 census is 73.47 per cent as against 62.66 per cent in 1991 Census. This shows the good growth rate in literacy. This growth rate is in tune with All India growth rates and literate population is 65.38 per cent in 2001 Census as against 52.21 per cent in 1991 Census.

Climate and Temperature

The Tamil Nadu has an equatorial, tropical climate in the inland and an equatorial, maritime climate in its coastal regions. In the inland, the temperature may go to extreme in some places while it tends to be moderate in the coastal areas.

By and large, the average temperature for most parts of the State range between 28°C and 40°C in the summer season and between 18°C and 26oC in the short-lived winter season. In the more hilly terrain, the maximum temperature may be as low as 26°C and the minimum temperature may go down to 3°C. The normal rainfall is 945.0 mm.

Administrative Division

The State of Tamil Nadu is divided into 29 administrative districts, which in turn are further bifurcated into smaller divisions and sub-division, including a total of 16,317 villages. The State capital,

Madras now renamed, as Chennai is the fourth largest city in the Indian sub-continent and 30th largest city in the world. It extends over an area of 174 sq. km.

In 1991, there were only 21 districts in the State of Tamil Nadu. In 2001, eight new districts were created by reorganizing the territorial jurisdiction. The nine districts are – Thiruvallur, Namakkal, Karur, Perambalur, Viluppuram, Thiruvarur, Nagapattinam and Theni.

The Languages

This history of Tamil Nadu dates back to Paleolithic age. The Official languages spoken in the State is Tamil, one of the oldest languages greatly influenced by its rich and colourful past. Concerted efforts have been made over the last decade or so to preserve the purity and identity of the Tamil language. More recently, there has been a steady stream of people migrating into the State from all parts of India, particularly to the State's urban centres, making Tamil Nadu truly cosmopolitan in its composition. Today, one can hear several languages such as Telugu, Malayalam, Hindi and other Indian languages being spoken in the State. Above all, the foreign visitor need have no fear of not being understood as English is spoken with considerable fluency in most parts of the State. Two prominent English newspapers and a number of economic dailies besides several newspapers in the local vernacular are brought out here.

Culture and Tradition

Tamil Nadu has a legacy of ancient tradition and rich cultural heritage. Dance forms like Bharathanatyam and various forms of music, including carnatic music, have flourished here for centuries. The awe-inspiring sculptors found in the State date as far back as the 7th century AD famous temples, which still stand in all their pristine glory in several parts of this land, speak for themselves of the rich heritage of the Tamil people. Handicrafts include the most intricately carved designs in wood, stone and metal. The exquisitely carved Bronze and Tanjore plates deserve special mention here.

Lifestyles

The people of Tamil Nadu lead, by and large, relaxed lifestyles. The urban social recreations include clubs, golf, links, beach resorts, theme parks, racecourses, art and theatre. Visits to game reserves holiday resorts, long sandy beaches, zoological and entertainment parks are the other way of social pastimes available. Tourists' spots include hill stations like Ooty, Kodaikanal, which are all time favourites.

Agriculture Profile

Tamil Nadu is gifted with 33 river basins, the largest one's being, Cauvery, Pennaiaru, Vaigai and Tamaraparani. Of the total area in the State, 59.2 per cent is under cultivation (not including forestlands). Rice and various pulses are grown extensively here. The annual foodgrain production exceeds 10 million tonnes, with Rice alone contributing average 8 million tonnes. The main cash crops grown in the State are sugarcane, tobacco, chillies, and cotton, giving rich scope for the growth and development of the sugar, alcohol-based and textile industries. Other State-sponsored schemes include the large-scale cultivation of spices and oil seeds particularly groundnut, seasmum, castor and coconut. Sunflower has become increasingly popular in recent times. The diverse Agro-ecological conditions also make this land ideal for growing fruits and vegetables. The state ranks first in the yield of mangoes and fourth in bananas and grapes.

Tamil Nadu has six diverse Agro-climate conditions and it grows partially every type of fruit or vegetable. Of late, a number of hi-tech horticulture projects are mushrooming in different parts of Tamil Nadu. Rich resource endowments base offers vast vistas of opportunities for setting up of food processing industries to produce value added products. Tamil Nadu has a large bovine population and produces about 3.9 million MT of milk per year. Also, Tamil Nadu has a large poultry population and is ranked second among Indian States. Annual production of eggs is 3,050 million. All these offer excellent investment opportunities in milk and poultry based industries in Tamil Nadu.

Resources Profile

Minerals like limestone, lignite, granite, clay, gypsum, feldspar and graphite found abundantly in Tamil Nadu. Besides these, small quantities of gold, copper, magnesite, kaolin, bauxite, asbestos, etc., are also found here. Many industrial units have been set up for optimum utilisation of these mineral resources. The total area under forest cover is 17 per cent. Of the 22,742.42 sq. km. of forest, timber and sandal wood are the main produce while tea, wattle bark and cashew are some of the minor products.

Regarding the marine resources, Tamil Nadu has a 922 km. long coastline with its equatorial climate permitting year round conducive fishery and farming. It is estimated that an offshore region of 22 lakh hectares is yet to be exploited. Tamil Nadu has 362 fish landing centres and annual fish catch is around 0.5 million MT. The State has a fairly stable presence in this sector with abundant skilled labour available, over 200 registered exporters of marine products, 29 freezing plants and 36 cold storages. Investment opportunities in this sector include, shrimp farming and processing, crab culture, seaweed culture, etc., in addition to opportunities in infrastructure like air freight services, cold storage facilities, freezing plant, etc.

Major Business Groups

The major business groups in the Tamil Nadu State is detailed in Table 1.3.

Table 1.3 : Major Business Groups in Tamil Nadu

Tittle of the Company	*Ownership/Group*	*Industry*
Ashok Leyland	Hinduja	Commercial Vehicles
Southern Petro Chemical Industries (SPCI)	Chidambaram M.A	Fertilisers and Chemicals
MRF	MRF	Tyres and Tubes
		Tractors and Farm Equip
		Tube Investment
		Amalgamation Tractors
TVS – Suzuki	T.V.S	Mopeds, Motor Cycles
Lakshmi Machine	Lakshmi	Machine Tools
SRF Fabrics	DCM	Tyrecord
India Cements	India Cements	Cement
SIV Industries	Shapoorji Pallanji	Man-made Fibre
Chemplast Sanmar	Sanmar	PVC and Chemicals
DCW	Shriyans Prasad Jain	Chemicals and Plastics
Coats Viyella India	Coats Viyella(F)	Industrial Fabrics
Titan	Tata	Watches and Clocks
Sundaram Fasteners	T.V.S	High Tensile Fastener's
Tamil Nadu Newsprint	State Government	Newsprint
GEC Althom India	GEC-Althom(F)	Switching Apparatus
Hindustan Motors	Birla C.K	Cars
Wheels India	T.V.S	Auto Ancillaries
Breakes India	T.V.S	Auto Ancillaries
Dalmia Cement	Dalmia Sanjay	Cement
Sakthi Sugars	Sakthi	Sugar and Soya Products

Source: www.tamilnaduprofile.com.

Infrastructure Development Profile

Traditionally, Government of Tamil Nadu has been according high priority to both industrial and off site infrastructure development. Government has been earmarking substantial amount of funds in its annual budgets to continuously upgrade the quality of infrastructure. As a result today Tamil Nadu is one of the few States in India endowed with fairly sound infrastructure.

Power Availabiliy

Tamil Nadu is one of the few States which is fairly comfortably placed in the power availability front. The gap between energy demand-supply is lower than all India averages. (All India Deficit:

11.5%; Tamil Nadu Deficit : 10.9%) It has made impressive strides in power generation and is comfortably placed in this sector. Against an installed capacity of 6,904 MW, the additional capacity envisaged is to the tune of 12,685 MW and to cater to this need, investment of an estimated Rs. 450 billion through 39 projects are in the pipeline. Though the availability power situation in Tamil Nadu is comfortable, the Government of Tamil Nadu does not remain complacent. The Government has recently proposed to set up 20 short gestation power projects with capacity ranging between 40-150 MW each. The total capacity proposed to be added before 2000 AD is 2,005 MW which will be sufficient to meet future demand of industry.

It is worthwhile mentioning that the State has also made pioneering attempts to harness non-conventional sources of energy especially wind power. With numerous incentives of offer, greater exploration of wind corridors are anticipated. Similarly, efforts are on to create capacity of 12,685 MW is planned through terminal power generation. This clearly indicates not only the low levels of dependence on hydro power but also that the power situation is likely to remain unaffected by the vagaries of the monsoon. Thus it can be said with confidence that power will be the least of the concern for investors. Though the State at present generates adequate power to fulfill the need of all sectors, and the Government has set in motion ambitious plans to meet its future needs the speed of implementing this as well as the capital outlay envisaged is quite formidable. Foreign investment in this sector are being encouraged.

Water Availability

The totally dynamic ground water resource in Tamil Nadu is estimated to be around 27,346 mcm/year. The Government has recommended that 15 per cent of this should be reserved for domestic use and a similar quantum for Industrial use – leaving enough ground water reserves to meet any additional new demands. The Telugu-Ganga project will be soon supplying 10 tmc of water to Chennai. Various schemes are being planned to recycle water on a large scale and secondary treated sewage water will be made available in urban conglomerations for Industrial use. Additionally desalination plants along the coast are being established. Emphasis is being laid here on the harnessing of both conventional and non-conventional sources of energy.

Port Facilities

The State has two major all-weather ports at Chennai (Madras) and Tuticorin as well as two intermediate and seven minor ports all of which are currently capable of handling over 32 million metric tonnes of cargo annually. Chennai and Tuticorin ports have the intrastructure to handle containerized cargo and are rapidly emerging as a major ports along the South-east Asian sea route. Envisaging a growing demand of cargo handling, an outlay of Rs.30 billion is being planned for upgradation of its capacity and handing with private participation. After Mumbai, Chennai (Madras) port ranks second in total cargo handled and first in terms of number of vessels handled. With increased activity in Chennai (Madras), Ennore on the outskirts of the city was developed as a satellite port which should bring down the level of congestion at Chennai (Madras) port.

Speed-link freight (container) trains-link Chennai port with Delhi and other Northern cities. For inland water transport, there are two canal systems the Vederanyam Canal and North Buckingham Canal. Government of Tamil Nadu invites investments in inland waterways improvement and operating projects. A new LNG handling terminal is proposed to be commissioned as part of Ennore satellite port to handle, storage and supply LNG.[7]

Road, Rail and Air Transport

Tamil Nadu ranks second in terms of transport network. Roads and rail account for maximum percentage of carrying goods. The State has a high percentage of surfaced roads sq more than 1,38,500 kms. (as high as 64%).

National Highways of length of about 2,000 kms. run through Tamil Nadu—ensuring easy, uninterrupted movement of goods and passengers. Major plans have been drawn up to reinforce this sector including an extensive Mass Rapid Transportation (MRT) network in Chennai (Madras), 27km. by-pass in Coimbatore, elevated road facility for freight transportation and Outer Ring Road at Chennai and widening of the existing National Highways-NH-4 and NH-5 into 4 lane. Government of Tamil Nadu invites private sector investments in roads sector. The road length per thousand sq.km. area in Tamil Nadu is 1,572 as against All India average of 663 kms. The efficient railway network accounts for a large share in movement of bulk cargo such as coal, iron ore, etc. as well as finished goods. At present, the railway route length in the State spans more than 41,000 kms. In Tamil Nadu, the rail length per 1,000 sq.km. area is 30.91 as against All India average of 19.01 km.

The presence of an international airport at Chennai (Madras) with direct links to Europe, USA and Far-East as well as domestic airports at Salem, Tiruchy, Coimbatore and Madurai, make several parts of the State easily accessible. Increased industrial activity has given rise to an increase in growing at over 18 per cent per year. Chennai airport is connected with 15 countries with more than 65 direct flights every week. To respond to the increasing cargo traffic and the emerging industrial needs, large-scale plans are upgrading for setting up an aircraft maintenance center and for upgrading existing infrastructure. Further, with the emergence of private sector airlines, the frequency of flights and their coverage will be boosted considerably. To facilitate smooth flow of air cargo, an air cargo city is proposed to be set up with private investment at Chennai (Madras). Also TIDCO has proposed to set up the second International Airport in Chennai and is looking for private sector participation in this project. A feasibility study is currently underway.

Communication

Tamil Nadu is part of the global telecom network. It has 1,603 telecom exchange with over 1.4 million lines with integrated communication facilities linking it to all parts of the world. The entry of international giants like US wheat and skycell into the market should give the much needed boost to this sector and provide basic and value added services in the State. Cellular and radio-paging services have been recently introduced in major cities like Chennai, Coimbatore etc. in the State. Given below are some important telecom services provided in the State, especially in Chennai (Madras) city. The phone services available in the Tamil Nadu State are: Operator dialed services, Toll free services for US, International telephone conference service, International data transmission service, International digital leased line service, Inamoratas service, International radio-photo and Video conferencing, International programme transmission service and International newscast service, Meteorological transmission.

Human Resource Development

Tamil Nadu can be justly proud of its valuable wealth of human resources. The manpower of the State is market for its diverse skills, professional expertise and its ability to communicate in several local languages as well as English. The total work force in Tamil Nadu is about 25 million constituting 44 per cent of State population. The organized sector employed more than 9 million people. The industrial climate in the State is peaceful with people's attitudes to work being positive and competent. The number of man days lost due to unrest is the lowest in the country (less 0.25 per cent of total man days) – all of this and much more contribute to making Tamil Nadu, the ideal platform for industry to scale greater heights. The State of Tamil Nadu invests highly on education and ranks the third highest in terms of total expenditure on education clearly indicating the thrust on creating a sound Human Capital Base. The literacy level of the State is 62.6 per cent and

44 per cent of the State population is economically active. At a stage when the emphasis is gradually shifting to knowledge and technology-based industries, this human resources base combined with a favourable labour climate offers ideal conditions for economic growth.

There has been a rapid growth in the number of Institutions imparting education at the college level. Today there are 19 universities; in addition, there are 102 Engineering Colleges, 135 polytechnics, 526 Industrial Institutes, 244 Arts and Science Colleges, 27 Colleges of Education, 15 Oriental Colleges, 5 Physical Education Colleges and 2 Schools of Social Work. Of late, all universities offer courses in management science. Besides a host of other educational institutions. The total number of engineering graduates produced every year in different disciplines is well over 23,000. Apart from this, skilled labour produced is 65,000 every year. Hence, there is no shortage of skilled manpower.[8]

Recognising Technical Education as a crucial link in the development process, the State Government has bestowed special attention in this direction. The State has 102 engineering colleges and 135 Polytechnics and 526 Industrial Training Institutes.

The existing set up of institutions imparting skills in various specialization dental college, 2 physiotherapy colleges, private medical colleges and 6 private dental colleges. In addition to these, the State Institute of Road Transport runs a medical college at Perundurai.

Industrial Parks and Complexes

Government of Tamil Nadu has promoted more than 120 Industrial Parks/Estates all over Tamil Nadu. Developed Industrial plots endowed with sound infrastructure support like, water supply, electricity, road link, communication facilities etc. besides social amenities are available to investors. Further, Government of Tamil Nadu provides an attractive package of incentives to investors locating their projects in these industrial estates/parks.

Integrated Industrial Parks (IIPs) concept originated with "Guindy Industrial Estate" in 1956. The Tamil Nadu State has at persent SIDCO Industrial estates, SIPCOT Industrial complexes, TACID growth centres and parks, Chennai Export Processing Zone (MEPZ), Co-operative Industrial estates, etc. Of Industries industrial estates, many are private Industrial estates. Total area developed so far for the industrial estate is about 15,000 acres.

The TIDCO's New Industrial Parks are 4, such as Petroleum Park at Ennore, Auto Ancillaries Park at Maraimalai Nagar, Floriculture Park at Housur, Hitech Industrial Park in Tirunelveli district. The ELCOT Information Technology Parks are two – one at Chennai and another at Coimbatore. The TACID's New Industrial Parks are three. They are: (i) Orgadam Industrial Park near Chennai, (ii) Gagaikondan Growth Center; and (iii) Cholavaram Industrial Park near Chennai.

There are 8 New Industrial Parks — New SIDCO Industrial Estates. They are located at near Channai are Avadi, Manali (Vichoor) and Thirumudivakkam, Bargur, Valathur (RK Pet), Vathiyoor (Uthangarai), Malummichampatty and Nanjilkottai.

There are also seven New SIPCOT Industrial Parks.They are: Irugattukottai Industrial Park, Export Promotion Industrial Park, Sriperumbudur Industrial Park, Cheyyar Industrial Park, Hosur Industrial Complex Expansion (Phase III), Ranipet Industrial Complex Expansion (Phase II), Cuddalore Industrial Complex Expansion (Phase II).

Good scope for setting up Naphtha Cracker, Refinery and Power generation projects invites Foreign investments: US $ 300 million for establishment of Industrial Park. TICDO will assist project implementation with Equity Participation, Technology Sourcing and Escort Services (Procedural Facilitation).[9]

Maduri District Profile

Location of Madurai

The geographical position of Madurai is situated principally between 9°30′00″ and 10°30′00″ of North Latitude and between 77°28′00″ and 78°28′00″ of East Longitude. It lies entirely within it is bound by Thiruchirappalli, in the East by Sivaganga, in the south by Virudhunagar and in the west by Theni and Dindigul districts. It is situated on the banks of the river Vaigai.

Origin of Madurai

The term 'Madurai' means 'sweetness', derived from another legend which says, "On the day the city was to be named, Lord Shiva is said to have appeared and drops of nectar from his hair fell on the town". Yule and Burmell say that the term Madurai was given to this city referring to the place Mathura, 30 miles away from Agra, situated on the banks of river Yamuna, one of the oldest Hindu pilgrim city.

There is another legend which says that Lord Shiva, fascinated by the various architectures such as palaces, temples, mandapams, houses, etc., built by the Pandya kings around his statue, spread nectar on these structures and hence Madurai is called 'the place of honey nectar (Mathuram). So the place was named Madurai, from the word Mathuram meaning 'Sweetness' in Tamil.

Ancient Tamil literature such as *Kadampavanam Mathurapuri Naanmada Koodal* refer to Madurai in its puranas. It is also said that some of the plays of Lord Shiva *(Thiruvilaiyadals)* took place in Madurai. For became prominent in Madurai in the light of the story of the wedding of Goddess Meenakshi, the sister of Vishnu. This contributed to the growth and development of Hinduism in Madurai. Madurai became a religious city and was later called *'Meenakshipattanam'*.

Administrative Set-up

It is said that Madurai is the second largest city of Tamil Nadu. The old city was laid around the temple with most of its streets running parallel to the walls of the temple. The now separated districts such as Dindigul, Theni, Ramanathapuram and Sivagangai were once part of Madurai district. Madurai and Usilampatti are the two revenue divisions of Madurai district. The seven revenue taluks are (1) Madurai North; (2) Madurai South; (3) Melur; (4) T. Vadipatti; (5) Usilampatti; (6) Thirumangalam; (7) Periyur. There are 51 revenue Firkas comprising of 670 revenue villages. In this district there is one corporation (Madurai) and one Grade II Municipality (Thirumangalam) and two Grade II Municipalities (Melur and Usilampatti), 15 Town Panchayats and 431 Village Panchayats.

Population

According to the Census 2001, the total population in Madurai district is 25,62,279 of which the male population is 12,95,124 (50.55%) and the female population is 12,67,155 (49.45%). Approximately 70 per cent of people in Madurai district are literates. The urban population in Madurai district is 14,33,251 (55.94%) and the rural population is 11,29,028 (44.06%). The male population in the urban area is 7,25,136 (50.59%) and the female population is 7,08,115(49.41%). The male population in the rural area is 5,68,988 (50.48%) and the female population is 5,59,040 (49.52%). Madurai is known for its Tamil heritage. The languages spoken in this district are Tamil, Sourastra, English, Telugu, Malayalam, Hindi and Gujarathi.

Occupational Distribution

Of the total workers (10,81,686), male workers are 7,37,871 and female workers are 3,43,815 according to the Census 2001. The rural workers constitute 53.57 per cent of the total workers. The non-workers are 14,80,593 in the Madurai district.

Humidity and Rainfall

The rainfall season in Madurai district stands from August till November by the influence of both South West and North East monsoons. The winter season starts from end of November and lasts till February. The summer season begins in March and continues upto June.

The maximum temperature recorded in Madurai was 38.7 (June 2002) and 38.2 in May 2003. Madurai district also experiences high humidity between October and February.

Land Utilization

As per the information taken since 1999, the forest regions are predominant in Madurai district which covers 13.46 per cent of the landscape (50,452 hect). The barren and uncultivable uses of land covers 3.53 per cent (15,799 hect). 19 per cent of the (64,831 hect) put to non-agricultural use and 1.52 per cent (5387 hect) are cultivable wasteland. The net area sown in Madurai district is 32.58 per cent. The total cropped area is 16,511 hect., of which 12,419 hect. land is sown more than once in the financial year 2002-2003

Transport

The road length of the National Highways in Madurai district is 145 km. out of 3865 km. in Tamil Nadu (2001-2002) and the length of State Highways is 114 km. The road length of Corporation and Municipal roads is 364 km. and the road lengths of Town Panchayats/Panchayat Unions is 1349 km. As per the 2002-2003 records, the commercial registered motor vehicles are 9503 and the non-commercial registered motor vehicles are 57,339 in Madurai district. The Government public transportation in Madurai district was formed in 1972 (T. N. S. T.C) which owns 924 motor vehicles of which 549 city buses, 116 tour service and 259 moffussal service.

The total railway route length in Madurai district is 145.54km. of which broad gauge length is 62.95 km. and meter gauge length is 81.59km. There are 11 railway stations in Madurai district.

There is only one domestic Airport in Madurai district that transported about 47,215 passengers to various parts of the country in the financial year 2002-03.

Communication

During 2002-2003 there were 411 post offices. Out of which 19 post offices handled both postal and telegraphs business as well. There were 61 telephone exchanges which served 1,49,181 customers in Madurai district. There were 6551 public call offices (PCO) in Madurai district.

Madurai Corporation

There are 72 wards in Madurai Corporation. The total population of Madurai Corporation is 10,46,000 (2001 Census) of which 3,66,937 are males of above 18 years and 3,41,617 are females of above 18 years. The literacy rate in Madurai Corporation is 88.18 per cent (Census of India, 2001).

Agriculture

Agriculture is the main source of economy in this district. Out of the total cultivated area of Tamil Nadu 1.95 per cent of the cultivated area are in Madurai district. Out of net area sown in Tamil Nadu, 22.85 per cent of the land are sown in Madurai district at least once a year. The main crops cultivated in Madurai district are paddy, millets, cholam, ragi, cambu, kora, maize, pulses, sugarcane, coconut, groundnut, gingelly and cotton. Cattle, buffalo, sheep, goat and poultry are commonly reared in the district.

Factories

Out of the 25,457 factories in Tamil Nadu, 1306 (5.13%) factories are in Madurai district. 101.5 lakhs of people are working in these factories in the district. There are 37 large scale industries, 548 medium scale industries, 700 small scale industries and 21 cottage industries in Madurai district. The chief industries are textiles, toys, matches, handloom and software.

Education

In the educational system, there are 33 Arts and Science Colleges affiliated to Madurai Kamaraj University. There are 9 professional colleges that include medicine, engineering, agriculture and law in the district. In terms of Children's education, there are 109 higher secondary schools, 94 high schools, 218 primary schools and 1034 middle schools in the district. It is estimated that more than 80 per cent of the children in the district are going to school. About 2,51,366 children are benefiting through noon meals scheme in 1421 centers in the district. According to the information from the District Employment and Training Department 3,72,920 students from below 10th standard to technical qualification have registered for employment out of which 18,734 candidates did not renew their seniority (as on 31-3-03).[20]

Dindigul District Profile

Historical Background

Dindigul, which was under the way of the famous Muslim Monarch Tippu Sultan, has a hoary past. The historical Rock fort of this district was constructed by the Famous Naik King Muthukrishnappa Naicker. It is located between 10°.05″ North 10°.9″ Latitude and 77°.30″ and 78°.20″ East latitude. This district is privileged to have one of the six celebrated hill abodes of "LORD MURUGA" at Palani Hills, where the famous Dhandayuthapani Temple is situated on the hilly rock at a height of about 450 metves Dindigul district was carved out of the composite Madurai district on 15-9-1985.

Besides the famous Palani Murugan Temple, there is also another Murugan temple at Thirumalaikeni; 25 km. away from Dindigul Town which is becoming a growing pilgrim centre.

Abiramiyamman Temple in Dindigul Town and Rajakaliyamman Temple at Tethupatti 20 km. away from Dindigul are the other important Temples worth mentioning and which attracts several thousand pilgrims.

Kodaikanal, a popular summer resort, located at an altitude of 2133 metres in the Western Ghats is the princess of hill stations. A notable feature of this Hillock is "Kurunji" flowers blooming once in 12 years. It is also famous for potato cultivation. Peranai and Sirumalai are two fine picnic spots of this district.

Location and Administrative Set-up

This district is bound by Erode, Coimbatore, Karur and Trichy districts on the North, by Sivaganga and Trichy district on the east, by Madurai district on the south and by Theni and Coimbatore distirct and Kerala State on the west. It is spread over an area of 6266.64 sq. km. It comprises 3 Revenue Divisions 7 Taluks and 14 Panchayat Unions.

Education and Population

Educationally Dindigul is a well developed and popular city. It has got many higher secondary schools to its credit. St, Mary's Higher Secondary School, a well disciplined Institution is one of the oldest institutions in this city. The district has the credit of having two universities, viz, Mother Theresa University for Woman at Kodaikannal and Gandhigram Rural Deemed University at Gandhigram.

The total population of Dindigul District was 11,81,746 in 2001. The proportion of the urban population is 35 per cent, although the rural population constituted 65 per cent of the total population.

Rainfall and Irrigation

The district has a unique advantage of rainfall in all the seasons except in the winter period. The rainfall is generally high during

North-east Monsoon period. The success of agriculture operation in Dindigul district depend mainly on the fair and good rainfall. It benefited by both South-west and North-east monsoon. 61.3 per cent of the rainfall received during North-east monsoon season and remaining 38.01 per cent of the rainfall received during South-west monsoon. Dindigul district has achieved agricultural prosperity during the last two decodes due to the development in irrigational facilities and important in modern technological methods of cultivation. Palar, Porandalar, and Parappalar are important irrigation schemes.

Area Under Major Crops

Paddy, Cholam, Cumbu, Groundnut, Cotton, Sugarcane are the major crops cultivated in Dindigul district. The details of area under various crops cultivated in these regions and their respective percentage to the total area shows that the area of important crops in Dindigul was 84366 hectares. Cholam is a major crop cultivated in this district occupies 53798 hect. land area. Other minor crops like Paddy, Cumbu, Groundnut, Cotton, Sugarcane etc., also cultivated.

Popular in Dindigul District

For a long time Dindigul town has been associated with iron locks, iron safe of good quality and durability. A lock manufacturing unit under co-operative sector is functioning here. Another famous industry in Dindigul is noted Leather Training. The widely known Angu Vilas scented Tobacco and "Roja Supari" are produced in this town area are being sent to various places in our State and out side. It is flourishing Industry gives employment to vide section of people.[11]

The district is having a flourishing Handloom Industry at Chinnalapatty, which is located at 11 kms. away from Dindigul on the Madurai, Dindigul Road. Art, silk sarees and sungudi sarees produced in Chinnalapatty are famous through out India. More than 1000 families are engaged in this Industry.

Dindigul district city which is an important wholesale market for Onion and Groundnut. It has the network of Inter-district roads connecting Coimbatore, Erode, Trichy, Karur, Madurai and Sivaganga district.

Porandalar, Varathamanathi, Parappalar in Palani Taluk and Maruthanathi in Dindigul Taluk to augment irrigation facilities to agricultural fields in this district. Nilakottai town is famous for Brass Vessels and Jewellary. Nilakkottai Taluk is famous for the growing and marketing of flowers and grapes

The profile of the study area would guide the researcher to undertake the study with the proper understanding on the impact of the New Economic Policy on the SSI in Tamil Nadu State.

REFERENCES

1. P.M.Mathew and Hentrysandee, "International Cooperation for Small Enterprise Development", *Small Enterprise Development*, Oxford & IBH Publishing Co.Pvt.Ltd., New Delhi, 2000, pp.229-244.
2. Prahlad Sabnani, " WTO Development Managing Transformation by Indian Banking Industry", *The State Bank of India Monthly Review*, April 2003, pp.169-172.
3. M.Soundarapandian, "Economic Reforms and Public Distribution System: A Micro-lavel study in Tamil Nadu", Serials Publication, New Delhi, 2003, pp. 3-4.
4. Hina Sidhu, *Structural Changes and Productivity in Small Scale Industries*, Mittal Publication, New Delhi,1998, pp. 7-9.
5. Prahalad Sabnani,"WTO Developing Managing Transformation by India Banking Industry", *State Bank of India Monthly Review*, April 2003, pp.169-172.
6. J.C. Verma and Gurpal Singh, *Small Business and Industries: A Handbook for Entrepreneurs*, Response Book, New Delhi, 2002, PP.11.
7. Department of Economics and Statistics, Chennai.
8. Department of Economics and Statistics, Chennai, 2004.
9. *www.tamilnadu profile.com*
10. Madurai Statistical Record, 2003.
11. Dindigul District Industries Centre Record, 2005.

2. Review of Literature

The past studies related to the present research aspect have been reviewed in the chapter. The chapter has been divided into three parts. The first part deals with the studies on New Economic Policy and Economic Reforms in India. A few studies on Small Scale Industries are reviewed in the second part of the chapter. The third part gives a brief account of past studies on the impact of Economic Reforms on the Small Scale Industries.

1. New Economic Policy

The article of Ramaswamy R. Iyar[1] brings together in a broad synoptic overview a diversity of concerns relating to the NEP. These include the dangers of a deepening of the dualism that already exists in India. The possibility of the erosion of some of the strengths and capabilities built up during the last four decades; the need for wariness in dealing with MNC; and the importance of safeguarding national interest in the face of the inequities of the global market and the pressures of the global political configuration. The article argues against a feeling of helplessness and in favour of a constant endeavour to enlarge the space for independent decision-making.

Rajesh Chadha[2] concluded that the success or failure of the EXIM policy announcements now depends on how promptly and ingeniously the Government reforms these weaknesses. Obviously, India has to learn lesson from China's success. Given the differences between the political regime of China in 1980 and that of India in 2000. This should not be difficult task. However, it will not be worth spending so much time and resources in re-christening ceremonies, unless the fundamentals are on currently reformed. Not only should we expect these zones to be economically efficient and growth promoting, even through they are 'special' the whole economy needs to follow these traits. The country needs to take a bold stand and do away with the various policy induced weaknesses that have plagued our economic system with in efficient and corrupt practices.

Manisha Lodha[3] pointed out that the liberalization of external trade formed an important aspect of the economic reforms programme launched in July 1991. Although, Policy efforts directed towards external liberalization can be traced back to late seventies and mid-eighties, it is only during the nineties that such measures received a momentum as well as definitive direction.

According to Manfred B. Steger,[4] the new market ideology rejects the notion that we find ourselves at the end of ideology and that democracy has won instead, Steger argues that the opening decade of the 21st century will constitute a terming battlefield of clashing ideologies the chief protagonists the dominant neoliberal marked ideology Steger calls "globalism". Although globalism constitutes little more than a gigantic repackaging of old *laissez faire* ideas, if deserves the label new market ideology because its advocacy have been able to link their quaint free market concepts with cutting edge global talk. Steger offers an overview of the counterclaims made by anti-globalist forces.

David Held[5] and Mathias Koening, Archibugi focused that the globalization discuss the economic, political and ethical implications of global economic integration. They assess the benefits and the costs of globalization and suggest strategies for reconciling it with the interests and aspirations of the people in all regions of the world. The contributors understand globalization not as a uniform process that should be praised or condemned in its entirety, but as a complex phonemenon that can and must be shaped and steered towards socially desirable goals. Taming globalization offers a fresh look at a much debated topic and sets out ideas for curtailing and overcoming the negative aspects of global economic change.

Gaur[6] concluded that the percentage of employment among males has gone down and it has increased among female workers in both public and private sectors. Public sector provides the highest employment in community, social and personal services with an increasing rate and primary sector remain on the lowest rank on the other hand, and secondary sector occupies the highest position in providing employment in private sector during the study. India is a populous country jobs in public and organized sector are sinking present policy of URS in organized sector provides fuel of fire. The Government cannot shift its responsibility of employment generation to the private sector/informal sector or institutions shoulders.

Nagesh Kumar[7] explained that the most developing countries now offer a welcoming attitude to FDI. After following a some what restrictive policy towards FDI, Indian has liberalized her policy regime considerably since 1991. This liberalization has been accompanied by increasing inflows and also by changes in the sectoral composition, sources and entry modes of FDI. The increasing recognition of India's locational advantages knowledge-based industries among MNCs has led to increasing investments in software development and global R&D centres set up in India to exploit these advantages.

A study of Abhijit Banerjee [8] found that the embarking on all these policy initiatives will surely be a challenging task in the short run. Our hope is that they will help define the main directions or economic policy in the medium to long-term. Considerations of administrative and political feasibility have played and important role in our thinking. The policies we have suggested are already being undertaken in some other Indian States and other developing countries. We have also tried to make suggestions that have the prospect of commanding a reasonable consensus within the State. This may mean that we are sometimes stating, the obvious.

The paper of Romesh Diwan[9] contends that the on going "Economic Reforms" are a political ideology to shore up support for the use of power of the ruling resident non-Indians (RNI). To understand an ideology one has to understand the power behind it. The existing power base is shifting from industrial to financial capital. As finance defines the power loss, it promotes the ideology that makes financial capital respectable and desirable. Only minimals changes in the economy were needed. Hence, real functioning of the economy has not changed while its performance has become more depressing. A positive change will need a paradigm shift of ideas. It's underlying priniciple has to be integrative and not divisiveness.

The view of J.Mohan Rao[10] is that the potential for economic growth based on existing technologies growth can not only serve to raise living standards but also provide the means for redressing environmental ills. The transition to a substainable scale of economic activity at which population is stabilized and incomes are sufficient to meet at least the basic needs of the whole population, is very far from being assured.

Vijay Joshi,[11] IMD little stated that the rate of growth of 5.5 per cent per year in the 1980s could not be sustained without major reforms. It was based on a mountain of pubic borrowing which erupted in 1991. A much reduced rate of growth of output for sometime was the unavoidable consequence of the essential crisis measures. The critical questions are whether the stabilization measures, together with the structural reforms already made this rate of growth sustainable and if not what further measures and reforms are needed for low inflation and indefinite expansion at 6 per cent or more. He discussed the relevant issues under the headings of fiscal adjustment, inflation and balance of payments management. India's industrialisation policies since independence biased development towards capital intensity and against employment the exception, at least in intention, has been a package of programmes and measures favouring small industrial enterprises. These progrnmes were never given large public resources, but a wide range of incentives have been enacted, the most important of which have been tax exemption and product reservation.

Pankaj Ghemawat, Murali Patibandla[12] observed a three pronged effect of the reforms implemented in India so far, first reforms such as devaluation of the rupee have enhanced India's competitive advantage in labour and skill intensive Industries, second allowing free imports of raw materials, intermediate goods and capital goods has reduced the dependence of competitive industries on inefficient domestic producers of input and technology and thereby contribute to the growth of exports. This has also contributed the increased domestic consumption and exports liberalisaiton appears to have made domestic production of critical inputs more efficient by enhancing domestic competitive conditions. One consequence is reduced prices of final products. This has not only enhanced exports competitiveness, but it is also generating and expanding domestic demand, which was marginal in major product segment of these industries prior to the 1990. The reforms have contributed not only to an increase in export volume but also to a moderate shift into higher quality.

Rangarajan,C.[13] stated that the risks of an open economy are well known, we must not nevertheless, miss the opportunities that the global system can offer. As an eminent critic put it, the world cannot marginalize India. But India, if it chooses, can marginalize itself, we must guard ourselves against this danger. More than many other developing countries, India is in a position to wrest significant gains from globalization. However, we must voice our concerns and in cooperation with other developing countries modify the international barding arrangements to take care of the special needs of such countries. At the same time, we must identify and strengthen our comparative advantages. It is this two-fold approach which well enables us to meet the challenges of globalization which may be the defining characteristic of the new millennium.

2. Small Scale Industries

Neela Mukherjee[14] pointed out that the present setting one can comprehend three main policy objectives for SME's. They are (i) creating space for SME's to co-exist and providing enabling environment for a level playing field, (ii) providing them with a reasonable period of time and pace for adjustment; and (iii) providing adequate safequards against 'unfair' trade direct assistance to SME's. Rather, some of the financial and tax measures undertaken by the Government to assist SME's are : (i) provision of subsidies for R&D costs; (ii) guarantee of loans when extended by the Credit Guarantee Association; (iii) provision of ventre capital funds; tax reductions for capital investment, (iv) credits for machinery leasing.

Mahalingam[15] revealed Small Scale Enterprises (SSEs) in many areas of the service sector are fast emerging as providers of employment and contributors to export development which necessitates reconsiderations of the view that the policies for Small Scale Enterprises (SSEs) development should concentrate on the manufacturing sector. It is thus necessary to address the need for reforms in the existing policies and design new policies for Small and Medium Enterprises (SMEs) development which will facilitate the growth of viable, value adding and efficient enterprises that can adjust the technological charge and remains internationally active. In this context, he fully endorsed the view of Abid Hussain, Chairman, and Expert Committee on small enterprises. "As efficient Industrial System should be so organised in India that the industrial linkage between the small, medium and large sector become mutually reinforcing and not competitively erosive".

Danish, A. Hashim[16] suggests that India needs to focus on cost reduction if it has to compete with Asian textile giants like China and Indonesia and neighbours such as Sri Lanka, Pakistan and Bangladesh. It argues that while China remains the undisputed leader with cost advantages in al! factors of production. India is fast losing its traditional advantages in homegrown cotton and low labour cost. The study noted that in cotton textiles, besides technology, costs of raw materials, energy, dyes and chemicals, and wages are crucial for India to stay cost competitive. In garments, India's last competitiveness is restrained by the limited scale of operation and the use of traditional technology, as this sector was till recently reserved for Small Scale Industries.

Anuradha Seth[17] found that the small firms to be relatively cost inefficient in all the industries. Prime costs were found to be more significant than fixed costs. Curiously, the difference in fixed costs between small and large firms was not of much significance of the costs directly associated with production, material costs were quite a substantial element affecting the relative cost efficiency of a firm. The relative cost efficiency of small firms also depended in part on their ability to trade productivity differentials with wage differentials. The data show that small firms were not even half as productive as large firms. Their technical inefficiency stems in large part from their technology of production and their inability to capture economics of scale. Small firms in the diesel and PVC pipe industries were not even 25 per cent as capital intensive as large firms and small leather firms were not even half as capital intensive as compared to the large firms in the industry.

Sundar *et al.*[18] pointed out that the role of Small Industries Development Bank of India in providing financial assistance is generally commendable both in terms of number of schemes sanctioned and the quantum of loans disbursed over a period of 8 years. The Bank is mainly financing to SSI through "Refinance" and "Bills Financing" schemes. But Bank's performance in providing promotional and development assistance is not so impressive, similar is the case so for as project related and equity financing are concerned. Therefore it is suggested that the Bank should widen its horizon of loan assistance to cater to diverse credit requirements of small scale units.

B.Krishnamurthy[19] concluded that in the earlier periods, the SSI sector was protected by the Government because to some of its inherent advantages. Wide publicity had also been given to develop the sector. But now due to liberalization and entry into World Trade Organization, the small scale industries have to be strong enough to compete not only the internal market but also the enterprises of foreign countries. The Government determined to withdraw the protective measures and leaving them to stand on their own legs. So now the time has come to exhibit their experience in the field. Therefore the SSI's have to improve the quality. Update technology and administrative ability. Thus the Government of India has become only a passport agency for SSI enterprises.

G.K.Chadha and P.P Sahu[20] revealed that the agro-industry occupied an important place in India's manufacturing sector. The post-reforms pace and pattern of its growth throws of a mingle of cheers and setback. For example, the share of agro-based manufacturing enterprises in the number of Industrial units increased sizably between 1994-95 and 2000-01. Also, the rate of growth of the number of agro-based production units, as also the number of workers employed by them, was remarkably higher during the post-reforms years compared with the pre-reform decade. Infact, it was a switchover from varying levels of negative growth rates, during the post-1994 year, with for the number of enterprises as well as employment, from the viewpoint of agro-industry as a whole, these post-1994 changes could be interpreted as cheering spots, although some of these changes may as well be interpreted as distress drives.

Rajshri Jayaraman and Peter F. Lanjou[21] pointed out the small-scale enterprises have generated a surge of interest among policy-makers and development agencies in recent years. The World Bank and the International Finance Corporation (IFC) have been particularly active in promoting small-scale enterprises, setting up a separate department for them in 2000 and allotting $ 1.5 billion toward their development in 2002. This emphasis is not unwarranted small-scale enterprises are dominant employers in much of the developing world. In Ecuador, for instance, 99 per cent of firms have 50 or fewer employees. In northeast and southeast Brazil, 71 per cent of workers are employed in firms with fewer than 20 employees. Despite forming the economic bedrock of most low-income countries, small-scale enterprises operate in difficult business environments and weak institutional settings and with little access to physical and human capital. Improving the investment climate faced by small-scale enterprises is therefore increasingly viewed as pivotal to promoting economic growth in low-income countries.

A study of Rana Bijoy Deb[22] found that the 41.8 per cent sample rural units employ 43.9 per cent of the total sample workers while 58.2 per cent urban units could employ only 56.1 per cent of the workers. The density of employment in rural units is 19.4 person as against 17.8 person in urban ones. A rural based unit investing fixed capital within the range of Rs.1 lakh to Rs. 2 lakh generates employment for 48 persons on an average, while for employing 43 persons, an urban based industrial unit requires fixed capital investment of above Rs.5 lakh. Operating at more than 50 per cent of the installed capacity, 13 per cent of the rural units employ 23.2 per cent of the workers employed by the sample rural units, while 40.6 per cent of the urban units operating all the same level employ only 45.3 per cent of the sample urban workers. Only 7.2 per cent of the skilled workers employed in the rural units get monthly wages above Rs.1,140 the maximum fixed for a skilled worker as against 18.9 per cent in case of urban units.

Neelam Jain[23] found that number of problems have been conformed by the SSI sector following the process of globalization. There is no alternative to accept the situation arising from globalization by SSI India. Sickness in small scale sector is always a matter of debate. Large number of units is sick with little scope for improvement in near future. The number of sick units in 1995 are declined to about 2.2 lakh by 1998. Instead of following the approach of rehabilitation of sick units isolation, restructuring of small scale sector by way of amalgamation and reorganization of the activities is required. BIFR approach needs to be evaluated for developing a new restructuring method based on the Japanese model.

A study of Chinnaiyan and Nandagopal[24] found that type of ownership of the firm, age of the units and socio-economic groups significantly influence the accessibility of bank finance. It is suggested that apart from financial documents, selective entrepreneurial traits could also be considered for sanctioning loans. It could also be of help for many of the first generation entrepreneurs who need the institutional support without having their own financial back up.

Pradip Singh Shehrawat and Labaria[25] had revealed that

majority of entrepreneurs were in medium age group, well educated without professional attainment, had not attended any training belonged to families having farming as their occupation and medium level of annual income. They were found to have medium to high level of innovation proneness, cosmopolitans, risk preference, extension contact, mass-media exposure, motivation but high degree of commitment for promotion of viable agro-processing units. It is suggested to organize more number of motivational skill oriented, entrepreneurship programmes to improve the managerial competency of the entrepreneurs. It is time that entrepreneurship be a part of education at college or University level in addition to the other entrepreneur development programmes organized by different developmental agencies, which in turn can help in minimizing the unemployment among youth, because it is not possible to provide job in Government as well as in private sector to a huge number of unemployed.

Rasul[26] revealed that the large corporating cannot do both production and marketing in an efficient way. But can concentrate on international marketing of products only. Large corporations may develop horizontal network through ancillarisation. Small units may be brought under sub-contract. The small and medium units may concentrate on production only without any worry about marketing of their products. Wherever feasible, large international companies may function as assembling units and small medium enterprises may produce intermediate products or ancillaries to the principal assembling units, there can be technology fit up between the principal units and ancillary units. This joint venture production will take care of the equity problem of small-scale units.

Soundarapandian M.[27] analysed that the labourisation in Small Scale Industries had found that the SSI provide an opportunity to achieve national goal of growth with equity and growth with efficiency. Regional development could be achieved through effective worker's participation which is desirable for attaining balanced development and for raising the standard of living and investment habits of the rural masses.

Valasamma Antony[28] pointed out that the multifarious kind of schemes and programmes are available to assist sick SSI units. But the fact remains that most of these schemes are not working out as planned and are proving incapable of serving their objectives. The reason for this rests largely on the fact that the "Government and the RBI bureaucracy and their convoluted rules and regulations have given rise it a situation where delayed sanction. Unhelpful attitudes and official corruption have become the rule.

The analysis of Dinish Awasthi[29] suggests that consolidation of the restructuring process wherein shifting from micro to relatively larger size classes with the SSIs; from rural to urban locations and from non-cluster to cluster units in associated with better productivity and growth. It is likely that these core activities trend to gravitate towards product and/or spatial clusters. The review, therefore argues for adopting a product specific policy and a cluster-based approach to foster growth among MSEs which would help strengthening the ongoing processes of restructuring.

Papola[30] reveals that the recent years, of course certain specified service activities which are related with industry have been brought within the purview of SSI policy and units having upto Rs.5 lakhs (raised to 10 lakhs in 2002) of fixed assets (excluding land and buildings) have been made eligible for the benefits under the SSI policy. The SSI Cencus of 2001-02 recorded service sector units making up the largest category, accounting for 44 per cent of units, manufacturing accounting for 40 and repair and maintenance for 16 per cent. Of the service sector units, 10 per cent were registered, the proportion being higher at 21 per cent for manufacturing but low at 1.7 per cent for repair and maintenance units. In terms of the access to facilities under any promotional scheme, the service units seem to be much more disadvantaged than those in manufacturing.

Rajarshi Majumder[31] emphasized that the contribution of Small Medium Enterprises (SMEs) to the economy is being questioned on improving labour productivity through technological upgradation. In a developing economy, this is a costly proposition due to capital scarcity and the effect of technological changes on productivity levels has to be estimated before taking up such policies. However, for the SME, technological diffusion is more important and the modernity of the technology itself. It is found that in about 70 per cent of the situations where indeed there has been some technological improvement, technological diffusion has by for outstripped the role of pure technical progress. A combination of better technology and wide diffusion is they recommended for productivity rise.

Vandana Parashar[32] has analysed on the current status of Micro and Small Enterprises (MSEs) and found that most of which fall in the unorganized segment, in terms of number of enterprises, employment and output. It looks at the growth of these three variables as well as productivity of workers. The period covered is 1979-2001, but the emphasis is on the more recent period, i.e, 1994, 2001. Finally, the problems of and policy towards, MSE are analysed on the basis of the scenario emerging from the 56th round of the NSSO on unorganized segment pertaining to the year 2000-01.

The results of the study of Sambit Kumar Mishra[33] show that female ownership, informality and sole proprietorship have negative effects on enterprise productivity, however increases with entrepreneur's age educational achievement and membership in business support groups. Rural based enterprises and those that are irregularly operated are less productive than those that are urban based and regularly operated traders do not produce as much as entrepreneurs involved in other business activities and productivity generally increases with the age of enterprise.

K. Nageshwara Rao[34] found that the employed workers in mining of limestone is of two types; casual labour or labour hired on adhoc basis and staff consisting of different grades employed in the office, mining pit, sorting plot, etc. Most of the workers are paid on piece rate for the work turned out by them. Total piece rate wages are equal to the wages per tonne multiplied by the number of tonns of output turned out by the labour. The working conditions and the health environment at the mining sites are deplorably poor with dust, mud etc. The medical facilities available are not satisfactory. The ESI staff should visit the work sites periodically and extend the much needed medical facilities to the mining workers.

Hrudanand Mishra[35] analysed the labour productivity and incomes in the micro and small enterprises, which employ as much as 93 per cent of Indian labour force, are low because of bad working conditions and outdated technology used by item. The poor working conditions and other problems faced by the workers need to be changed for the better through suitable institutional supports based on cooperation among employers, workers, Government organizaitons and civil society organizations. In this connection there is need to learn from the positive experiences with respect to labour and productivity if any, in the western context such as in Germany, Italy etc.

Sarthi Acharya and Niru Acharya[36] revealed that the problem stated was non-availability of skilled labour. High technology firms require highly skilled personnel, which are not so easily available to small firms, due to their incapacity to pay, and limited upward mobility offered by them to the workers. The relatively larger firms in the small sector say those having fixed capital of Rs.5 million upwards are able to attract skilled manpower; others find it difficult. Thus, with the proposed restructuring when ancillaristation takes full shape, the relatively large with (in the small-scale category) would have better change of survival on this count, compared to the relatively small ones. In essence, in a country of high illiteracy and overall low skills, the rent on high skills is too high for the small units to afford. This discussion refers to the industry in general.

According to Ragurama[37] and Hala Naik Small Scale Industries must survive and grow for which marketing is of vital importance. But Small Scale Industries are faced with marketing problems. Marketing problem is not an independent one, it is a related issue and its is a complex problem of marketing, Finance, marketing infrastructure like forward and backward linkages, products decision, pricing decision, promotion policy, selection of distribution channel problems and to like. It requires a well devised future marketing strategy to overcome this problems. The problems of marketing of small scale units in future can be tackled if all engaged in the process realize their responsibility and both converted efforts with commitment, dedication and real win to solve the problem.

Sree Ramulu[38] pointed out the Industrial Policy Resolution (IPR) 1948 accepted the importance of small scale industries in Industrial Development. These industries are particularly suited for the utilization of local resources and for creation of employment opportunities.

Rajendra Prasad[39] emphasized that the small scale industry occupies an important position in the country's industrial economy and continues to enjoy priority in view of the sizeable contribution to industrial production, exports creation of employment opportunities and under-geographical dispersal of industrial activities. As on March 2000, there were over 32 lakh small scale units in the organized sector manufacturing about 7500 products. Some of them are based on local craft, skills and raw materials, while others employ highly sophisticated technologies to twin out products that compete even in international markets. The contribution of small scale sector (including traditional sub-sector) to gross domestic product, export earning and employment generation has been consistently prominent with the estimated production of Rs. 6,88,814 crore constituting 37.94 per cent of GDP, export valued at Rs. 1,08,666 crore (70% of exports) and providing employment avenues to over 570 lakh persons in 1999-2000.

Karmakar and Banerjee[40] explained the Agro-based industries have been providing the missing link between the agricultural and industrial sectors. Agro-based industries relate to food processing, vegetable oil production, horticultural products, dairy and livestock products and consumer goods. Conventionally, agro industries are often considered as enterprises that process agricultural raw materials.

Raj Kishore Barik[41] concluded that the development of small scale sector depends on the coordinated efforts of Government, financial institutions and entrepreneurs. Entrepreneurs have the added responsibility of running the unit viably. This is possible only if the entrepreneur thinks in turns of constantly improving the productivity of his unit. Productivity is an attitude research for means and ways of increasing production and decreasing costs. Small scale units should periodically undertake productivity studies which should ensure the viability of the individual units and this in turn, would contribute to the development of SSI sectors.

Rashid, R. Pansare[42] explained that the SRI (Small and Rural Industries) sector traditionally occupied a promise position in the national economy in terms of its size, spread production, employment and exports. The steady growth of small scale industries has been one for the most significant features of planned economic development. The small scale sector has grown phenomenally duing the last three decades and the sector has played and has the potential to play a vital role in the fulfillment of our socio-economic objectives. According to a recent estimate there are about 31 lakh SSI units throughout the country employing over 167 lakh workers providing Rs.51,150 crore of revenue to the Government and Rs.44,000 crore of export earnings. SSI sector contributes 44 per cent of the total industrial production and 35 per cent of Indian exports. The SSI sector is non-homogenous in structure and includes divine types of production units ranging from traditional crafts to high tech industries of the total number of SSI working units in the country referred above in terms of ownership, the vast majority of them are propriety concern (80.5%) with only 16.8 per cent functioning as partnership and private limited companies.

B.Krishnamurthy[43] concluded that in the earlier periods, the SSI sector was protected by the Government because to some to its inherent advantages. Wide publicity had also been given to develop the sector. But now due to liberalization and entry into World Trade Organization, the small scale industries have to be strong enough to compete not only with the internal market but also the enterprises of foreign countries. The Government determined to withdraw the protective measures and leaving them to stand on their own legs. So now the time has come to exhibit their experience in the field. Therefore the SSI's have to improve the quality, update technology and administrative ability. Thus the Government of India has become only a passport agency for SSI enterprises.

V. Padmanand and V.G. Patel[44] (2004) concluded that the managing India's small Industrial Economy is an indepth and pragmatic guide to the changes that needed to help the small industries sector to survive. Examining the role of industrial counsellors and policy-makers at both the operational and policy levels, this book presents a step by step roadmap to tackling challenges through professionalism, better management, technology upgradation and innovation. The authors maintained that intervention from industrial counsellors and consultants is the key for maintaining a healthy and profitable small industrial sector.

3. Economic Reforms and Small Scale Industries

Rakesh Basant[45] pointed out that the industrial policy did not encourage competition but contributed to inefficiencies. Bureaucratic determination of plant capacity, product mix and location resulted in ignoring the market processes. Industrial licensing and other controls led to severe entry and exit barriers and encouraged rent seeking and lobbying. Besides, trade in scarce materials became more lucrative that efficient manufacture. Further, licensing and product reservation for small-scale sector inhibited firms from reaping economics of seeds. Finally, pronounced pro-labour stance restricted workforce rationalization.

Another article of Raghurama[46] explained the Industrial Policy of 1991 with the emphasis liberalization, privatization and globalization of the economy with the opening of the economy, the small scale sector which has been whether to protected and operating in a secured environment has started whethering they are faced with stiff competition from similar products. Unless they are competitive and financially vibrant they will not be able to withstand competition and survive in the global environment.

Bhavani[47] focused on the on-going changes in the business environment and the analysis of their implications for small scale units, specifically it looks at possible way of improving. The competitive strength and commercial viability of small scale units in the changing context for this substantial improvement will be needed in technology. Such as mechanization, organization and information and the revamping of policy measures to encourage the growth of small units through collective efforts, ending their isolated mode of operation.

Anbumani, V.[48], based on the SIDBI Report of 2003 revealed that the small scale industries happened to be significant component of Industrial Sector, and therefore Government has initiated several schemes and projects for the development of these industries, which cover almost every major aspect of the operation such as finance, technology, marketing etc. Small scale industry employs 45 per cent of the industrial work force and account for 40 per cent of the total manufacturing output and 35 per cent of our exports.

Sudip Chaudhuri[49] concluded that a basic reason behind the disappointing performance is the adverse impact of import liberalization and the decline in the role of the Government on demand. Poor export growth since the mid 1990s has made it worse. If import liberalization results in higher efficiency, higher exports, higher production, higher employment, one understands its rationale. But if import liberalization (and other policies) result not in more efficient production but lower demand and hence lower production and employment, then the policy needs to be seriously re-examined rather than being blindly followed. Try to export more but if export demand is not high enough then generate demand through other means for example, through import substitution and more Government expenditure.

Nanjundan, S.[50] suggested that the considerable expansion of ancillary relationship has ensured providing more profits to big industry and increasing the dependence of the small and large; there have been parallel development; a number of small enterprises manufacture independently for the replacement market. Some of them even spurious and unsafe products; more important a middle sized sector entrepreneurs by graduate engineers and MBA. As been successful in producing and marketing technologically oriented, skill and knowledge oriented products in electronics, computers, chemicals, engineering, food processing etc. The informal sector in urban areas and rural cottage household enterprises in the non-farm sector have had varying experiences; rich markets for differentiated products and services for the low income groups, agro-processing and some other industrial activities moving away from prosperous rural area causing migration and growth of the urban informal sector.

Goldar and Ranganathan[51] (1998) revealed the evidence of declining trend in R and D in the corporate sector in 1990s. R and D to sales ratios in the Indian corporate sector is either stagnating or declining. Neglect of R and D is a matter concern because R and D activity is an important determinant of long-terms productivity growth, competitiveness and hence sustainability of growth of industry.

Thamarajakshi[52] reveals that it is time that efficiency considerations prevail in public spending in agriculture and market signals are allowed to come into full play so that changes in agricultural investment and production prices, Government should focus on productive investment, technology and research, marketing and storage and agro-processing facilities and provision at food safety nets for the vulnerable poor development of a diversified agriculture in time with emerging demand patterns.

The Indian Economic Survey[53] the broad-based industrial

recovery has been supported by continued reforms in industry, trade and financial sectors, which have helped industry to improve its efficiency, productivity and international competitiveness. Recent liberalization of foreign investment policy would encourage further industrial investment output and employment. However, further reforms are necessary in the financial system and labour markets to import dynamism to the overall growth process and promote industrial employment. There is an urgent need to carry out legislative reforms to facilitate rapid redeployment in today's fast changing international and domestic economic environment. The support of the SSI sector needs to emphasize increasingly promotional policies, rather than protection additional areas where reforms would promote greater efficiency include restructuring of public enterprises and improvement in corporate governance, infrastructural constrains in roads, power and telecom need to be removed by creating higher capacities for sustained industrial growth. Although Y2K problems have been tackled efficiently. India will have to face and surmount. The challenges posed by new technologies and market places such as internet and e-commerce.

Gupta[54] attempted to study the impact of the economic reforms measures on the poor by looking at (i) the effect of these measures on income and consumption in agriculture and the informal small industry sector, (ii) the performance of safety net programme to protect the new poor exposed to the adverse impact of reform in the short run, (iii) the direct and indirect effect of the Government social services and human development programmes in the pre- and post-reforms periods, and (iv) the employment picture of the country in the post-reform period. The results of the study are mixed, but in general they show that the social cost of reforms. While they may have been low as compared to these in many other developing countries are never the less high enough to demand a corrective course.

Neela Mukherjee[55] suggested that the Government role is that of facilitators of SMEs preparing a road map for SME's constructing incubators, providing SME's with enabling conditions to access technology including information technology and providing the kind of protection which is WTO compatible. As regards technology, policy-makers must focus on technological capability building as an essential element for sustained competitiveness and productivity of SME's in an increasingly technology-intensive global economy. The foreign direct investment can accelerate the process of technological upgrading but it cannot be a substitute for local technological capabilities.

Ravindra H. Dholakia, Deepak Kapur,[56] pointed out the year 1991-92, India has undertaken widespread policy reforms in order to integrate its economy with the rest of the world. In this fact finding study, the balance sheet data of 557 private sector companies are considered with several ratios and indicators of performance and trade behaviour. The companies are divided into exporting and non-exporting groups, on the whole exporting companies are found to be performing much better than non-exporting ones. The policy reforms have however helped the latter to improve their margins; through they have been pushed to the lower end of the domestic markets.

G.K. Chadha[57] concluded that the post-reforms year have thrown bare the sectors/activities that can be confidently looked at as future sources of rural employment expansion. A wide range of manufacturing activities (e.g. food processing and beverages, textile, wood, leather and metal products and basic metal industries) construction, retail trade, hotel, restaurant, transport-storage-communication and some activities under community, social, personal services (e.g. education and scientific personnel, medical and health services etc.), stand out as the most likely thrust areas.

Ritu Dewan[58] revealed that the gendered labour process as well as employment patterns and trends in urban Small Scale Industries (SSIs) need to be analysed in the context of declining formal manufacturing job opportunities and the emergence of captivity now being imposed on SSI units through the putting-cut and sub-contracting system initiated by big companies. The fundamentals are examined in relation to the existence of the reality of workers in small-scale units specifically those located in Industrial Estates (IEs). Analysis of detailed results of the primary survey focuses on several aspects including sectoral distribution of manufacturing industries, nature and conditions of work activities, extent of permanency and benefits and history of job changes. Also examined are impacts of health hazards and lack of occupational safety of workers employed in small units even in such controlled and controllable conditions as those existing in IEs.

S.N. Rajesh Raj and Malathy Duraisamy[59] analysed the employment, investment and growth in real value added in the unorganized manufacturing sector across 13 major Indian States. The study revealed wide variations over space and time in the number of enterprises, employment, capital formation and real gross value added. During the period 1984-85 to 2000-01, the Indian unorganized manufacturing sector as a whole witnessed a decline in number of enterprise, employment and capital formation while at the same time the real value added by the sector increased.

G. Somayajulu and V. Venkataramana[60] analysed that the recent EXIM Policy for 2001-02 dismantled quantities a commitment to the WTO. The possible impacts of removal of QRs on imports are: (i) The QRs removal can result in higher import bill thereby putting pressure on the balance of trade; (ii) Since QRs are currently imposed on some specific product categories mostly concentrated in agriculture and small-scale sector. It is expected that the effect of removals will be pronounced in these sectors. (iii) Higher level of competitions through imports can also act as a catalytic agent for enhanced. Indian industry has been worried that lifting of QR will lead to sudden surge imports. However, statistics prove otherwise. This does not mean India can relax. The Anti-dumping Directorate in India will have to ensure that no unfair imports flood the country and wreck the domestic industry.

S.Vaidehi[61] *et al.*, explained that Government has given the crucial importance to the SSI sector in the economy with 40 per cent share in the total industrial output, 35 per cent in exports and over 80 per cent industrial employment, it deserves all the policy support the Government can offer. What the small entrepreneurs need is not production but institutional support to fund modernization and technology upgradation, infrastructural support and adequate working capital finance from the banking sector. There is also a need for small entrepreneurs to keep pace with the structural and technological changes taking place in large industries. The accent should be on a much greater degree of ancillarisation and on providing services as the large companies are keen on of loading a number of job work to smaller units. Hence, there is an urgent need to refraction the policies governing the sector so as to improve its competitive strength and long-term outlook.

Vilasini G. Patkar[62] examined the technological input and innovative marketing endeavours have brought about promising prospects to the village industries by improvement in the quality of goods and services. With the necessary and timely intervention, tax and non-tax concessions, liberal definition of village industries covering seven major groups, namely, mineral-based industry, forest based industry, agro-based and food industry, polymer and chemical based industry, engineering and non-conventional energy, textile industry (excluding Khadi) and service industry has created variety of income generating activities in the rural areas. There is no doubt that the village industry sector would continue to flourish in the post-liberalization era through its policy of production by masses and growth with a human face.

Nilajan Banik[63] analysed the two broad objectives, first, identify a set of factors that appear to be responsible for a significant decline in India's export growth during the post-reforms era, and second an examination of the possible impediments for high exports growth in a sustained manner, the decline in Indian exports during 1996-97 was due mainly to a fall in the growth rate of export volumes. This analysis brings out the nature of demand side factors as against supply side bottlenecks that have restricted the growth of exports. However, the supply side constraints too would have aided the revival of exports growth.

Mubarak Ali and Mohamed Sindhasha[64] revealed that the light of globalization and the impact of WTO on agriculture and agro-based industries, the use of IT based services in this field has become imperative. The immense scale and diversity of Indian agriculture provide the ultimate challenge to the potential of information technology. The rapid strides that the country has registered in the IT field will remain incomplete unless IT is fully utilized to ensure more efficient and productive Indian agriculture. Practically there is no area in agriculture in which IT has no role to play. It can be argued that the next revolution in urgent need of focus is IT revolution in Indian farming. As far as India is concerned, textile exports earn substantial foreign exchange and provide employment opportunities. It utilizes cotton cultivated in India and indirectly, it contributors to the growth of agriculture activities in India. Textile sector has to meet challenges related to product quality, pricing and overall competition in the world market after 2004, i.e, after abolition of quota restrictions and the emergence of trade blocks call for a change in the garment export strategy for facilitating the environment to increase and improve the production of readymade garments and other higher value added items.

Vasudeva[65] revealed that the removal of the remaining QRs would lead to an anomalous situation in the case of the products reserved for the SSI sector as the resented items could be imported freely. It would not make sense therefore to continue with reservation of product lines alongside free imports. What is not understood is the Government's continuous reluctance to do away the reservation of items from the SSI sector even when the items in the reserved list will face open competition from imports. Once QRs on imports are lifted reservation of items for the SSI sector would become meaningless.

Balu, V.,[66] examined the existing policies and programmes concerned with the development of small enterprises, the reservation policy and observed that SSIs sectors has to be made highly competitive to face the challenges of liberalization and globalization and also there should be no restrictions on SSIs to grow. Today, there is an imperative need for technological upgradation and modernization and adoption of cluster approach for quick and effective delivery of inputs SSI sector to study tariff/ non-tariff barriers under WTO, review of labour laws to make them SSI friendly and enhancing capacity-utilization of SSI units.

4. Studies of International Institutions

The World Economic and Financial Surveys explained the two clear priorities to help the potential risk arising from institutional globalisation while maximising its benefits. First, supervisors need to colloborate ever more closely in the oversight of cross-border institutions. Second authorities need to continue improving crisis management procedures with the counterparts with whom they share the greatest overlapping responsibilities and interests. While the jurisdiction of supervisors and regulations remains predominantly domestic, at odds with the scope of activities of global institutions, there practical steps can go some way toward addressing the challenges to financial stability posed by institutional globalisation[67].

Michael Deppler and G.Russell Kincaid[68] emphasized forestalling such as adverse scenario entails three policy priorities. Safeguarding budgetary stability while tempering demand; raising supply capacity and improring competitiveness; and keeping the financial sector strong. Institutional mechanisms for fiscal discipline at all levels of Government need to be strengthened. Competition enhancing efforts should be stepped up and backed by political commitment. Worthwhile pending economic legislation should proceed forthwith. While agreeing on the nature of the underlying risks, the authorities assigned lesser probability to adverse scenarios, and thus less urgency to staff's recommendation, which they nonetheless generally shared.

Mick Silver[69] revealed that the unit value export indices compiled from returns to customs authorities are after used as surrogates for price indices in the measurement of inflation transmission, terms of trade (effects), and to deflate import and export value series to derive volume series. Their widespread use is mainly due to their relatively low use is mainly due to their relatively low cost compared with establishment price surveys. The evidence of substantial bias in their representation of such price changes. Their continued use would mislead economic analysis. It considers the efficacy of alternative strategies for their improvement, and argues for a more to establishment-based price surveys.

Rita Babihuga and Kal Wajid[70] analysed the relationship between selected macro-economic and Financial Soundness Indicators (FSIs) using a newly assembled panel dataset of FSIs for 96 countries covering the period 1998-2005. The analysis covers key macro-economic indicators and FSIs of capital adequacy, asset qualiy and profitability. The paper finds that FSIs fluctuate strongly with both the business cycle and the inflation rate, short terms interest rates and the real exchange rate also emerge as important determinants. There is also a considerable degree of heterogeneity in the relationship between macro-economic indicators and FSIs across the sample of countries several country and industry specific characteristics including country income levels, financial depth, market concentration, and the quality of regularity supervision and found to be significant in explaining this cross country heterogeneity.

Miranda Xafa[71] discussed two opposing views on global imbalances; the "Traditional View", which regards the imbalances as a threat to global economic and financial stability, and the "New Paradigm" view, which considers that they are the natural consequence of economic and financial globalization. In terms of their policy implications, the traditional view focusses on monetary and fiscal policy decisions in the United States that need to be urgently reversed to avoid an abrupt unwinding of the imbalances involving a self-off of dollar assets, a sharp increase in US interest rates and a hard landing for the global economy. By contrast, the new paradigm view considers that the imbalances will be resolved smoothly through the normal functioning of markets. The paper argues that an abrupt unwinding of imbalance is highly unlikely and advances a number of arguments in support of the new paradigm view.

Rufus Yerxa and Bruce Wilson[72] examined the aspects of the operation of the WTO dispute settlement system during the first ten years of the WTO. It covers a representative cross-section of the issue and situations. WTO members have dealt with under the Dispute Settlement Understanding. It also includes contribution from several academics who closely follow and carefully scrutinize all that goes on within the system. It therefore provides fascinating insights into how the system has operated in practice, and how the lessons of the first decade can be applied to make the system even more successful in the years to come.

Katherine A.Hagen[73] revealed that Dialogue on Globalization is based on the premise that globalization can be shaped into a directions that promotes peace, democracy and social justice. Dialogue on globalization address "movers and shakers" both in developing countries and in the industrialized parts of the world i.e., politicians, trade unionists, Government officials, business people, and journalists as well as representative from NGO's International Organization and academia.

Stephanie Seguino and Maria Sagrario Floro[74] investigated the effects on aggregate saving and test the hypothesis that shifts in women's relative income, which can affect their bargaining power within the household, have a discernible impact on household saving and be extension, gross domestic saving, due to differing saving propensities by gender. These findings suggest the importance of understanding, gender differences in planning for savings mobilization and in the formulation of financial and investment policies.

Thiam Hee Ng[75] examined the linkage between foreign direct investment and productivity in eight East Asian Economics – China, Hong Kong SAR, Indonesia, Malaysia, Rupublic of Korea, Singapore, Taiwan province of China and Thailand. Yamamoto vession of the Granger Causality text are used to test if inflows of foreign direct investment cause productivity growth. The results show that only two countries reveal evidence of a one-way causality between inflows of foreign direct investment and total factor productivity growth, similarly, there is also little evidence that inflows of foreign direct investment cause technical change of efficiency change in the sample economics.

Peter Raynard and Maya Forstater[76] reported that the Corporate Social Responsibility (CSR) developments have been concentrated in industries that involved high health or environmental risks, activities covered by high levels of regulation, and industries that provide essential services of lifestyle products. The issue focus has moved from bribery and corruption to environmental stewardship to social issues such as labour standards and human rights current emerging issues include product responsibility, responsible downsizing and corporate influence on public policy. Civil society and consumer campaigns and media attention have focused attention on major national and international brand names, however international standards are increasingly being developed to provide a global framework for CSR and overall sustainability management.

The United Nations Development Programme[77] (UNDP) pointed out the small and medium enterprise development in direct support projects located within Government institutions have often experienced problem in reaching out to SMEs and ensuming sustainability. Careful attendion should be given to selecting which institution will manage the project and which support agencies and finance institution to work with the capacities there entities possess to make the project a success should also be identified characteristics of potentially good collaborations are good quality of services and outreach, client orientation, an appropriate pricing policy, self-sufficiency, and organizational independence. Where possible, private sector companies could be used as contractors for project activities.

M.H. Bala Subramanya[78], explained the small scale industries occupy a place of strategic importance in Indian economy in view of its considerable contribution to employment, production and exports. However since 1991 small scale industries in India find themselves in an intensely competitive environment due to globalization, domestic economic liberalization and dilution of sector specific protective measures This paper probes the implications of globalization and domestic economic liberalization for small-scale industries and analyses in growth performance in terms of unit, employment, output and exports. The paper concludes with policy recommendations to ensure the sustenance and competitive growth of small scale industries in India.

Fabio Russo[79] pointed out the several Indian States are formulating comprehensive cluster development programmes. In spite of all challenges still ahead to develop an effective and sustainable national cluster programme, the above factors are all positive signals indicating that cluster approach could become an effective new way for promoting SSI development in India.

Summary

The past studies reviewed above are summarized as below :

The implication of New Economic Policy on various sectors of the Indian Economy are analysed by Ramaswamy R.Iyar (1995), Rajesh Chadha (2000), Raj Kishore Barik (2005), Rashid R.Pansare (2005), V. Padmanand, V.G. Patel (2004), T. Bhavani (2002), V. Anbumani *et al.* (2005) Indian Economic Survey (1999).

The Impact of New Economic Policy was attempted by G.L.Gaur (2004), Anuradha Seth (1995), Vandana Parashar (2004), K. Nageshwara Rao (2004), Hrudanand Mishra (2004), T.Rajendra Prasad (2004), Neela Mukerjee (2001), G.K. Chadha (2001), Ritu Dewan (2005), S.N.Rajesh Raj and Malathy Duraiswamy (2004), G.G. Somayajalu (2002), S. Vaidehi, S. Nirmala Mary and K. Raja Mohan Rao (2003), Vilasini G. Patkar, Sanjay S. Kaptan (2005) Nilanjan Banik (2001).

B. Steger (2004), David Held and Mathias Koening – Archibagi

(Eds). (2004), Nagesh Kumar (2005) Romesh Diwan (1995), J. Mohan Rao, (1995), Vijay Joshi (1997), Pankaj Ghemawat, Murali Patibandla (1998), C. Rangarajan (2002), M. Soundarapandian (2002) Rajesh Majumder (2004), Sudip Chadhurai (2002), S. Nanjundan (1996), Goldar R.N and V.S. Ranganathan (1998), Thamarajakshi (1999), S.P. Gupta (1999), Ravindra H. Dholakia and Deepak Kapur (2001) had evaluated the status of the Indian Economy after implementation of New Economic Policy. Need for modernization of Small Scale Industries was analysed by Neela Mukherjee (2001), N. Mahalingam (2004), Danish A. Hashim (2005), K. Sundar *et al.* (2002), B. Krishnamoorthy and C.S. Yatanal (2002), G.K. Chadha and P.P. Sahu (2003), Rajshri Jayaraman and Peter F. Lanjou (2004), Rana Bijoy Deb (2004), Neelam Jain (2004), P. Chinnaiyan and R. Nandagopal (2005).

The suggestions for the changing strategies for shaping the future of SSI were focused by the Abhijit Baneerjee *et al.* (2002), Pardip Singh Shehrawat, S.N. Labaria (2000), N. Rasul (2002), Valasamma Antony (2003), Dinesh Awasthi (2004), T.S. Papola (2004), Sambit Kumar Mishra (2004), Sarthi Acharya, Niru Acharya (1995), A. Raghurama and N. Hala Naik (2001), D. Sree Ramulu (2004), K.G. Karmakar and G.D. Banerjee (2004), Krishnamurthy and C.S. Yatanali (2002), E. Mubarak Ali and A.M. Mohamed Sindhasha (2004), P.K. Vasudeva (2001), V. Balu (2001).

The past studies reviewed in this chapter are the basis for conducting the present study in the selected districts of Tamil Nadu on the Impact of New Economic Policy on the Small Scale Industrial Sectors.

REFERENCES

1. Ramaswasmy R. Iyar, "The NEP: The Dangers Ahead", *Economic and Political Weekly*, Vol. XXX, No.30, July30, 1995, pp.1913.
2. Rajesh Chadha, "EXIM Policy changes", *Economic and Political Weekly*, Vol. XXXV, No.16 April 15-21, 2000, pp 1345.
3. Manisha Lodha, "Liberalisation and Trade Policy", *Southern Economist*, Vol.42, No.9, September, 2003 pp. 19-21.

4. Manfred B. Steger, *Globalisation – The New Market Idelogy,* Rawat Publications 2004, New Delhi.
5. David Held and Mathias Koening–Archibagi (Eds) *Taming Globalisation: Frontiers of Governance,* Rawat Publications, 2004, New Delhi, p.3.
6. G.L. Gaur, " Impact of Liberalization and Globalisation on Employment in Inida", *Southern Economist,* November 1, 2004, Vol. 43, No.13 p.14.
7. Nagesh Kumar, "Liberalisation, Foreign Direct Investment Flows and Development Indian Experience in the 1990s", *Economic and Political Weekly,* April 2, 2005, Vol. XL, No.14, p. 1459.
8. Abhijit Banerjee *et al.,* "Strategy for Economic Reform in West Bengal ", *Economic and Political Weekly,* Vol.XXXVII, No.41, October 12-18, 2002 p. 4218.
9. Romesh Diwan, "Economic Reforms as Ideology", *Economic and Political Weekly,* Vol. XXX, No.30, July 29, 1995, p. 73.
10. J. Mohan Rao, "Economic Reforms and Ecological Refurbishment – A Strategy for India", *Economic and Political Weekly,* Vol. XXX, No.28, July - 15, 1995, pp.1759-1760.
11. Vijay Joshi, I.M.D Little, *India Economic Reforms 1991-2001,* Oxford University Press, Delhi, 1997, pp :1991-2001.
12. Pankaj Ghemawat, Murali Patibandla, "India's Expose since the Reforms" *Economic and Political Weekly,* Vol. XXXIII, No.20 May 16-22, 1998 pp. 1198.
13. C. Rangarajan, "Economic Reforms: Some Issues and Concerns", *The Indian Economic Journal,* Vol.49, No.2, October-December 2001-02, pp. 1-3.
14. Neela Mukherjee, "World Trade Organization and Small and Medium Enterprises from a Developing Country's Perspective: A Study of Indian Small Scale Industries" *The Indian Economic Journal,* Vol.48, Oct-Dec 2000-01, No.2, pp. 18-27.
15. N.Mahalingam, "Need for Modernization of Small Scale Industries", *Kisan World,* vol.29, 2004, pp 13-14.
16. Danish A. Hashim, "Post MFA: Making the Textile and Garment Industry Competitive", *Economic and Political Weekly,* Vol.XL, No.2, January 8, 2005, p. 117.
17. Anuradha Seth, "Cost Efficiency of Small Manufacturing Enterprises – Implications for Employment Policy", *Economic and Political Weekly,* November 25, 1995, pp.130-131.
18. K.Sundar *et al.* "The Role of Small Industries Development Bank of India in Financing SSI", *Southern Economist,* May 2002, Vol.41, pp.27-29.

19. B. Krishnamūthy and C.S.Yatanali, Small Scale Sector, Protection to Competition, *Southern Economist*, 41st year of publication volume 41 Number 5, July, 2002 paper page 17 to 20.
20. G.K.Chadha and P.P Sahu, Small Scale Agro - Industry in India: Low Productivity is its Achilles Head", *Indian Journal of Agricultural Economics*, Vol.58, No.3, July-September 2003, pp.540-41.
21. Rajshri Jayaraman and Peter F.Lanjou "Small-Scale Industry, Environmental Regulation, and Poverty: The Case of Brazil, *The World Bank Economic Review*, Vol.18, No.3, 2004, p 443.
22. Rana Bijoy Deb, "Employment Generation in Small Units: A case Study", *Yojana*, Vol.48, May 2004, pp. 42.
23. Neelam Jain, "Small Scale Industries in the New Millennium", *Southern Economist*, Vol.43, No.10, September 15, 2004, p.19.
24. P.Chinnaiyan and R.Nandagopal, "Accessibility of Bank Finance by SSI: A Case Study", *Southern Economist*, Vol.43, No.21 March 1, 2005, p.26.
25. Pardip Singh Shehrawat, S.N.Labaria, "Strategies for shaping future of Small Scale Agro-processing Industries", *Indian Economic Panorama*, Vol.10, July 2000, pp.18-19.
26. N.Rasul "Food Processing Industry – An Overview," *Third Concept*, January 2002, 1994 p.47.
27. M.Soundarapandian, "Liberalisation in Small Scale Industries—Needs and Issues", *Third Concept*, January 2002, p.47.
28. Valasamma Antony, "Rahabilitation of Sick SSI Units – A few Guidelines", *Southern Economist*, Vol. 42, November – May 2003.
29. Dinesh Awasthi, "Labour Process and Production in Micro and Small Enterprises: The Indian Experience", *The Indian Journal of Labour Economics*, Vol.47, No.4 2004, p. 871.
30. T.S. Papola, "Small and Micro Enterprises is a Globalising Economy: Some Perspectives on Policy Framework for their Integration", *The Indian Journal of Labour Economics*, Vol.47, No.4, 2004, p.891.
31. Rajarshi Majumder, "Productivity Growth in Small Enterprises, Role of Inputs, Technologial Progress and Learning by doing", *The Indian Journal of Labour Economics*, Vol.47, No.4, 2004, p. 901.
32. Vandana Parashar, "Micro and Small Enterprises in India: Status, Growth and Policy", *The Indian Journal of Labour Economics*, Vol.41, No.4, 2004, p.929.
33. Sambit Kumar Mishra, "Productivity in Small Textile Business Sector in Orrisa", *The Indian Journal of Labour Economics*, Vol.47, No. 4, 2004, p. 1128.

34. K. Nageshwara Rao, "Labour Process and Productivity in Mining Industry", *The Indian Journal of Labour Economics*, Vol.47, No.4, 2004, pp.1122.
35. Hrudanand Mishra, "Labour Productivity in Micro and Small Enterprises in Indian Economy: An Overview", *The Indian Journal of Labour Economics*, Vol.47, No.4, 2004, p.1119.
36. Sarthi Acharya, Niru Acharya, "Structural Adjustment and Small Producers, Reflections from Case Studies", *Economic and Political Weekly*, Vol.XXX, No.1, January 7, 1995, pp.45-46.
37. A.Raghurama and N. Hala Naik, "Marketing Problems of Small Scale Units in Dakshina Kannada", *Southern Economist,* Vol. 42, November 21, pp.7-11.
38. D.Sree Ramulu, "Growth and overall Performance of Indian Small Scale Enterprises", *Indian Economic Panorama*, January 2004, Vol.13, No.4, pp. 20-21.
39. T.Rajendra Prasad, "Corporate Policy and Small Enterprises in Karnataka", *Southern Economist,* Vol.42, Number 22, pp. 15-19.
40. K.G. Karmakar and G.D.Banerjee, "Agro-Processing Industries– A Link between Agriculture and Industry", *IASSI Quartely* Vol.22, No.3, 2004, pp.92-101.
41. Raj Kishore Barik, "Importance and Potentiality of Small Scale Industries in Nagaland", *Southern Economist*, Vol.49, No.12, November 2005, p.20.
42. Rashid R. Pansare,"Trends in Financing SSI Sector in India", *Southern Economist*, November 15, 2005, p.5.
43. Krishnamuthy and C.S.Yatanali, Small Scale Sector, Protection to Competition, *Southern Economist*, 41st year of publication volume 41 Number 5, July, 2002, pp. 17-20.
44. V.Padmanand and V.G Patel, *Managing India's Small Industrial Economy– The Catalytic Role of Industrial Counsellors and Policy-makers*, Sage Publications India Pvt. Ltd., 2004, New Delhi, p.14.
45. Rakesh Basant, "Corporate Response to Economic Reforms ", *Economic and Political Weekly*, Vol.XXX No.10, March 4-10, 2000, p. 813.
46. A. Raghurama, "Globalisation and Challenges for Small Scale Sector in India", *Southern Economist*, Vol. 43, No.19, February, 2005, p.13.
47. T.A. Bhavani, "Small-Scale Units in the Era of Globalisation – Problems and Prospects", *Economic and Political Weekly*, July 20th 2002, Vol.XXX VII, No.29 pp.3041-3042.
48. V.Anbumani *et al.* " An Econometric Estimation of Policy Shift on the Production, Function in Small Scale basis Metal and Alloys Industries", *Organizational Management*, Vol.XXI, No.1, April-June, 2005, pp. 62-63.

49. Sudip Chaudhuri, "Economic Reforms and Industrial Structure in India", *Economic and Political Weekly,* Vol.XXXVII, No.2, Jan. 12-18, 2002. pp. 160-162.
50. S.Nanjundan, "Economic Reforms and Small Scale Industries", *Economic and Political Weekly,* Vol.XXX, No.4, Jan. 27, 1996, p.191.
51. Goldar, R.N. and V.S. Ranganathan, "Economic Reforms and R and D Expenditure in Industrial Firms in India", *The Indian Economic Journal* Vol.46, No.2, 1998, pp. 60-75.
52. R.Thamarajakshi, "Agricultural and Economic Reforms", *Economic and Political Weekly,* Vol.XXXIV, No.33, August 14, 1999 , pp. 2293-95.
53. *Indian Economic Survey,* 1999, Government of India, New Delhi, 2000.
54. S.P. Gupta, "Economic Reform and its Impact on Poor", *Economic and Political Weekly,* Vol.XXX, No.22, June 3, 1999, pp.1295-1312.
55. Neela Mukerjee, "World Trade Organization in India", *The Indian Economic Journal,*Vol.48, October-Devember, 2000-01, No.2, pp.27-28.
56. Ravindra, H. Dholakia, Deepak Kapur, "Economic Reforms and Trade Performance Private Corporate Sector in India", *Economic and Political Weekly,* Vol. XXXVI, No.49, December 8-14, 2001.
57. G.K.Chadha, "Impact of Economic Reforms on Rural Employment", *Indian Journal of Agricultural Economics,* Vol.56, No.3, July-Sept. 2001, pp. 524.
58. Ritu Dewan, "Captive Workers in Captive Small-Scale Factories Impact of Globalisation on the Gendered Urban Labour in Greater Mumbai", *The Indian Journal of Labour Economics,* Vol.47, No.4, 2005.
59. S.N.Rajesh Raj and Malathy Duraisamy, "Unorganised Manufacturing Sector in the Pre and Post Reform Period: An analysis of Indian States", *The Indian Journal of Labour Economics,* Vol.47, No. 4, 2004, p.1124.
60. G.G.Somayajalu and V.Venkararamana, "Impact of EXIM Policy 2001-WTO on Small and Medium Enterprises", *Southern Economist,* Volume 40, Number 23 & 24 April 2002.
61. S.Vaidehi, S.Nirmala Mary and K.Raja Mohan Rao, "WTO and Small Scale Industries", *Kurushetra,* Vol.52, No.2, December 2003.
62. Vilasini G.Patkar, Sanjay S.Kaptan, "Village Industries: Problems and Prospects in the post-Liberalisation Era", *Jagriti,* Vol.49 No.12, Nobermber 2005, p. 15.
63. Nilanjan Banik, "An Analysis of India's Export during the 1990s", *Economic and Political Weekly,* November 3, 2001, Vol.XXXVI, No.44, pp.4222-4223.

64. E.Mubarak Ali and A.M.Mohamed Sindhasha, "IT based Services to Agriculture and a Agro-based Industries", *Kisan World*, December 2004, Vol. 31, No.12, p.35.
65. P.K.Vasudeva, "Is Small Industry ready for a QR-Free Regime?", *Economic and Political Weekly*, January 6-12, 2001 pp. 22 to 24.
66. V.Balu, "Smart Strategies for Small Enterprises", *Indian Economic Panorama,* October 2001, Vol.11, No.3, p.7.
67. http://www.imf.org/external/pubs/ft/gfsr/2007/01/pdf/ summary.pdf
68. httt://www.imf.org/external/pubs/ft/scr/2007/cr07175.pdf
69. Mick Silver, *Do unit value Export, Import and Terms of Trade Indices represent of misrepresent price Indices?* "International Monetary Fund 2007", May 2007.
70. htttp://www.imf.org/external/pubs/ft/wp/2007/wp07115.pdf
71. Muranda Xafa, *Global Imbalances and Financial Stability*, "International Monetary Fund 2007", May 2007.
72. Rufus Yerxa and Bruce Wilson, "Key issues in WTO Disputes Settlement", *World Trade Organisation* October 2005.
73. Katerine A.Hagen, *The International Labour Organization: Can it Deliver the Social Dimension of Globalisation*? "Dialogue on Globalization", October 2003.
74. Stephanie Seguino and Maria Sagrario, "Does Gender have and Effect on Aggregate Saving? An emprirical analysis", *International Review of Applied Economic* Vol. 17, No.2, 2003.
75. Thiam Hee Ng, "Foreign Direct Investment and Productivity evidence from the East Asian Economics", United National Industrial Development Organisation 2006.
76. Peter Raynard and Maya Forstater *Corporate Social Responsibility – Implications for Small and Medium Enterprises in Developing Countries*, United Nations Industial Development Organisation, Vienna, 2002.
77. UNDP, Essentials, "Evaluation Office", No.1, Nov.1999, p. 9.
78. M.H Balasubramanya, "Small-Scale Industries in India in the Globalisation Era : Performance and Prospects", *International Journal of Management and Enterprises Development* 2005, Vol. 2, No.1, pp. 122-139.
79. Fabio Russo, *UNIDO Strengthening Indian SME Clusters: UNDIO Experience* July 1999, p.15.

3. New Economic Policy Relating to SSI Sector

1. SSI Policy before Liberalisation

It has been often said, even by dispassionate observers, that our economic policies built on ideological considerations and economic assumptions are far removed from the realities of the Indian situation. Whatever may have been the indeological elements influencing the thinking on economic policies in the formative period of the pre-independence days, in the actual formulation of economic policies since independence, the effort has been not to be too closely identified with any ideology, but to work out a policy that will draw upon all these ideological positions. The eagerness to balance conflicting ideologies is also seen in the pronouncements on the "socialistic" or "socialist" pattern of society in the Second Five Year Plan, which the Third Plan also reproduced with approval.

Indian policy-makers and Indian economists have not felt it necessary, to undertake an independent examination of India's economic problems and to design an appropriate economic policy to deal with them the pattern has been to usually accept theories and formulations prevalent in other parts of the world, particularly in Britain and the USA. Hence, it is not surprising that at various levels Indian economic policy has come under the strong influence of what in the late forties and the early fifties was that latest theoretical formulation in economics, viz., Keynesian economics. What made Keynesian economics appealing was not only its novelty, but its direct concern with practical problems and policy matters. The Keynesian influence has entered into Indian economic policy not only directly, but also through its indirect impact on that branch of economics which is styled as "economics of underdeveloped countries".

Much of the criticism directed at the economic policies of the Government relates to the "basic strategy" followed by it, in terms of its efforts to build upon industrial base, the resulting emphasis on investiment and foreign aid, and its choice of the industry-mix. To some extent, there has been a strong pressure on the Government to reverse its strategy, to stress the consumer goods output, more resources to agriculture, to go easy on heavy industries and the expansion of the public sector.

One of the basic issues of a development strategy that recongnizes a conflict between short-term and long-term gains is the decision on how the limited short-term gains for the process are to be distributed. In a mixed economy, these gains can be distributed either by the creation of substantial volmes of new employment among the poorer classes at socially desired rates of real wages, or through a radical reallocation of existing wealth and incomes. The latter course was deliberately eschewed by the Indian planners. At the same time, the employment problem has been often regarded by them as subsidiary to the basic strategy. The need to create more jobs has been considered to impose a conflict between more jobs and more goods. And, there is considerable perplexity that the problem of poverty is getting more and more acute. "In some quarters, this leads to the view that concern with 'welfare' objectives has slowed down the 'growth' of the economy. It is time to soft-pedal on 'welfare' and to press on with 'growth' of the economy. Such are fruits of acute perception that score common sense".

This strange paradox would make a little more sense if the amount of resources that could be devoted to the production of consumer goods without jeopardizing the future growth of the economy was itself a bottleneck. However, there is not clear evidence that this is so in the country. Rather, there is plentry of evidence of resources used in the production of non-essentials and of serious maldistribution of the available supply of basic consumer goods, such as food stuff. There are clear indications to show that this is not the result of a failure of the Government to intervene or its unwillingness to do so. It is more a question of perhaps the political will and of the lack of any clear recognition of where intervention is essential and where it would most bear fruit.

The industrialization of rural areas was taken up long before Independence. It received added emphasis from the beginning of the plan era. This emphasis is reflected in the two Industrial Policy Resolutions of 1948 and 1956 and also finds place in the Directive Principles of State Policy in the Constitution of India.

The aim of the State Policy will be to ensure that the decentralized sector acquires sufficient vitality to be self-supporting and its development is integrated with that of the large-scale industry. The State will, therefore, concentrate on measures designed to improve the competitive strength of the small-scale producer. For this, it is essential that the technique of production should be constantly improved and modernized.

The policy was further reiterated in the successive five year plans. From these a gradual evolution of policy of the Government of India towards integrated industrialization of the rural and less developed areas can be seen. The main highlights of the policy are (a) development of advanced small-scale industries sector, (b) dispersion of industries, (c) promotion of industries in selected industrially backward areas, and (d) development of village and household industries.

The Industrial Policy Resolution of 1956, emphasizing that only by securing a balanced and coordinated development on industrial and agricultural economy in each region can the entire economy attain higher standards of living, laid stress on measures for improving the competitive strength of small-scale producers and development of small-scale industries as ancillaries to large-scale industries. By the end of 1954, on the organizational side, six All India Boards were set up or reconstituted in the place of the erstwhile Cottage Industries Board. The All India Handloom Board and the All India Handicrafts Board wee constituted in October 1952 and November 1952 respectively.

The All India Khadi and Village Industries Board was set up in February 1953 for preparing and organizing programmes of production and development of khadi and village industries. This Board was later converted into a statutory commission in April 1957. The Small Scale Industries Board was constituted in November 1954 to co-ordinate all activities regarding small-scale industries. The Central Silk Board was established as early as 1949 and was reconstituted in April 1952. A statutory Coir Board was set up in July 1954 to promote the development for coir industry under the control of the Central Government. The activities of these six Boards, taken together, cover the entire field of village and small-scale industries. During the First Plan, village and small industries and small-scale industries were supported both by specific measures of assistance and by an appropriate State policy–promotional and positive measures.

In the Second Plan, an independent position was carved out for the development of the small sector. For instance, on the eve of Second Five year Plan, the Village and Small Scale Industries Committee (known as Karve Committee) was constituted. The committee observed that even in the traditional village industries, to the extent immediately possible, technical improvements should be adopted and for the future, there should be a regular programme of gradual transition to better techniques. At the same time, where new capital investment had to be made, it should be, as far as possible, on improved equipment, the improvement being in some cases in the nature of additions to or adaptations of existing equipment.

With a view to extending work opportunities, raising progressively the standard of living of other artisan, and bringing about a more balanced and integrated rural economy, the Third Plan laid emphasis on the need for encouraging further growth of industries in rural areas and small towns as well as in less development areas with market industrial growth potential. Positive forms of assistance, such as improved skills, supply of technical guidance, better equipment, and liberalized credit were provided.

Emphasis was laid on integrated development of khadi and village industries.

The Fourth Plan provided for systematic indentification of under developed regions and initiating concrete action programmes for widespread diffusion of industries. Special emphasis was also laid on the development of agro-based industries. The plan aimed at removing the various constraints on the adoption of improved technology on a wider scale to ensure the benefits of economic and social objectives.

The Fifth Plan emphasis on "minimum needs programme" lends added significance to the issue of minimizing differences in the levels of living in different areas through intensifying growth of industries in larger regions and backward areas. The broad strategy of Fifth Plan covers the following:

(i) develop and promote entrepreneurship and provide a "package of consultancy services" so as to generate maximum opportunities for employment particularly self-employment;

(ii) facilitate fuller utilization of the skills and equipment of the persons already engaged in different small industries;

(iii) progressively improve the production techniques of these industries so as to bring them to a viable level; and

(iv) promote these industries in selected "growth centers" in semi-urban and rural areas including backward areas.

An innovative feature in the budget for 1975-76 was the presentation by the Finance Minister of a paper outlining a strategy for integrated rural development. In pursuance of this programme, work on the preparatory phase has already begun and a technical group under the chairmanship of Director-General, Indian Council of Agricultural Research, has been constituted. An ad hoc provision of Rs.15 crores has been made in 1967-77 budget for initiating programme whose basic objective will be the scientific use of all the natural resources in the village. This will not only help in enlarging the rural employment opportunities but also lead to diversification of rural occupations.

Special programmes such as small, marginal farmers and agricultural labourers development programmes, drought-prone areas programmes, tribal and hill areas project, agricultural credit, etc., have all been brought within the ambit of activities under integrated rural development. An important differences in the approach towards the development of village and small industries as envisaged in the Fourth Plan and the Fifth Plan is that steps are being taken to facilitate flow of institutional credit in a much larger measure that in the past, particularly for the traditional industries' sector, so as to promote development of viable industries.

The commercial banks and other financial institutions are being geared up to serve the needs of the rural population. Even at the non-government level organized action, such as the Habitat Indian movement, has been initiated with the "total development of the village" as their objective. There is, thus, at different levels, a greater awareness of the urgency of the need for promoting rural development.

In November 1977, the Working Committee of the Janata Party adopted a statement on economic policy. According to this, the new thrust of the Janata economic policy would be growth for social justice rather than growth with social justice. The party called upon the Government to evolve a national plan for the development of village and cottage industries taking into account the evolving pattern of demand. The statement on industrial policy of the Government (December 1997) emphasizes the effective promotion of cottage and small industries widely dispersed in rural areas and small towns. To quote, the statement observes:

It is the policy of the Government that whatever can be produced by small and cottage industries must only be so produced. For this purpose, an exhaustive analysis of industrial products has been made to indentify those items which are capable of being established or expanded in the small-scale sector. The list of industries which would be exclusively reserved for the small-scale sector has been significantly expanded and will now include more than 500 items compared to about 180 items earlier.

An annual review of reserved industries will be undertaken in order to ensure that reservation accorded to the small scale sector is efficient and is also continually expanded as new products and new process capable of being manufactured in the small-scale sector are identified.

Government will consider introducing special legislation for protecting the interest of cottage and household industries with a view to ensuring that these activities which provide self-employment in large numbers get due recognition in our industrial development.

The focal point of development for small-scale and cottage industries will be taken away from the big cities and State capitals to the district headquarters. In each district, there will be one agency to deal with all requirements of small and village industries. This will be called the District Industries Centre. Under the single roof of the District Industries Centre, all the services and support required by small and village entrepreneurs will be provided.

In order to provide effective financial support for promotion of small village and cottage industries, the Industrial Development Bank of India has taken steps to set up a separate wing to deal exclusively with the credit requirements of this sector. It will coordinate, guide and monitor the entire range of credit facilities offered by other institutions for the small and cottage sector, for whom separate wings will be set up in these institutions particularly nationalized banks. Banks will also be expected to earmark a specified propotion of their total advances for promotion of small, village and cottage industries. It is the policy of the Government to see that no worthwhile scheme of small or village industry is given up for want of credit.

In the light of experience, the Government proceeded step by step to liberalize the industrial licensing system. Several industries were freed from licensing and investment projects up to specified limits were delicensed. In the context of the Government's approach to the Fourth Plan, a "Core Sector" emerged: industries of importance to the national economy, industries having direct linkage with such core industries, and industries with long-term prospects for exports were all considered as basic, critical, and strategic for the growth of the economy. Larger houses were made eligible to participate in any of these listed industries provided the said industry was not reserved for the public sector or for the small-scale sector. Foreign branches and subsidiaries became eligible to participate in industries not included in the list. Industries other than those in the large category of house were allowed free expansion. They could also set up new industries with investment up to Rs.1 crore without licences. The impact of the new wind of liberalism was diluted somewhat by the Monopolies and Restrictive Trade Practices Act.

In recent years the Monopolies Commission has adopted a more pragmatic approach to matters referred to it. But this again reveals the fact that the Commission does not have a proper framework for decision does not also have research orientation. The enquiries and procedures, therefore, tend to be dilatory, irksome, and frustrating. Every industrial house has to categorize itself as a monopoly or dominant undertaking and to prove the requisite function to the Commission for purposes of registration. The Commission does not consider seeking and obtaining such data or relying on its own analysis and probes as a normal part of its function. The weak internal organization of the Commission and the conceptual confusion have prevented the Commission from setting out clearly the positive aspects of monopoly control for purposes of orderly industrial expansion.

The limitation of foreign investment to a minority of the equity in new projects is the declared policy of the Government. Exceptions are invoked here also. Two wholly foreign owned and two foreign majority-owned ventures were licensed in 1956-57. In 1957-58, three foreign majorities were sanctioned, one with 83 per cent holding. Over the two years, 1958-60, no less than 18 ventures with foreign majorities were sanctioned, in some cases ranging up to 90 per cent and, atleast in one case, 100 per cent,

Multinationals are usually under fire in public debates and atleast one report – the Hathi Committee Report (1974-75) has advocated strong action, including the takeover of drug companies. But administrative decisions are still guided by expediency, and foreign collaborations still find favour albeit for one reason or another. Foreign companies and multinationals make hay while the sun shines. They are operating not only in sophisticated areas of manufacture but also in such areas as soft drinks, biscuits, toothpaste, cosmetics, and a range of consumer products in which India has know-how to sell.

An illustrative list of foreign companies operating in India with data on equity holding. The capital holding of foreign companies in Indian subsidiaries today probably averages about 68.8per cent. Looking at the structure of equity holdings of foreign companies in 217 Indian subsidiaries operating in India, about 43 per cent 93 companies seemed to have 100 per cent holdings, 14 companies has equity capital participation ranging between 80 per cent and 100 per cent. Another 25 companies has 70 per cent to 80 per cent participation, and an equal number had equity participation ranging between 60 per cent and 70 per cent. There were four companies with equity participation of less than 50 per cent. In recent years some of the companies have gone in for dilution of foreign capital holding.

The guidelines issued in 1973 explicitly declared the Government's objective of ensuring dilution of equity capital held by foreign companies. They were required to raise for all expansion equity capital from Indian investors through the open market. Yet there was no reference in the policy guidelines to any reduction in the holding of shares by foreign investors. This meant that dilution could take place only in relation to the enlarged capital base and that too in terms of percentage and not in absolute terms. Whatever the contribution of foreign companies, India has had to pay dearly for it. Many Indian companies in simpler areas of manufacture are driven to the wall or forced to fall back upon Government subsidies and other forms of protection undesirable on a large-term basis.

New Indian enterprise is often stifled and the development of indigenous know-how discouraged.

2. LPG Policy

India's reform programme began in the middle of a macro economic crisis that erupted in early 1991. The crisis was brought to a head by a steep fall in foreign exchange reserves to about 1 billion (equal to two weeks' imports), a sharp downgrading of India's credit rating, and a cut-off of foreign private lending. Its basic underlying features were high inflation (12% and rising), large public and current account deficits (approximately 10% and 3% of GDP respectively), and a heavy and growing burden of domestic and foreign debt.

External shocks played only a minor role in the crisis. Oil prices increased following the Iraqi invasion of Kuwait in August 1990, but only for a few months. This mini-shock would normally have been weathered without undue difficulty, but it impinged on an economy which was in a highly vulnerable state due to unsustainable macro-economic policies over a prolonged period. The cut-off of foreign lending was not an exogenous shock but a reaction to the unsound macroeconomic position.

The roots of the crisis can be traced back to India's reaction to the earlier crisis of 1979-81 when world oil prices doubled. This exogenous shock changed India's current account position from near balance in 1978 to a deficit of 2 per cent of GDP (30% of exports) in 1981. Remarkably, there was hardly any current account adjustment for the rest of the decade despite favourable developments such as a softening of oil prices and rising domestic oil production. The current account deficit averaged 25 per cent of exports from 1982 to 1984: from 1985 to 1990 it averaged not less than 40 per cent of exports. These deficits were covered by heavy borrowing from the IMF and from commercial sources.

From 1982 to 1985 the persistence of current account deficits was the result of the almost complete stagnation of exports which was in turn largely the real exchange rate was allowed to appreciate by 15 per cent from 1979 to 1981 and remained at that level for the next four years. From 1986 exchange rate policy became more flexible and the real exchange rate depreciated substantially. Exports revived strongly in response and grew in real terms at 10 per cent per annum between 1986 and 1990. But by then the export boom was insufficient to outweigh the combination of rising interest payments on external debt and the rapid growth of imports induced by fiscal deterioration.

While exchange rate policy must take part of the blame for the lack of current account adjustment and the heavy accumulation of foreign debt, the heart of the problem lay in the reversal of India's erstwhile fiscal prudence. The fiscal deficit of the Central Government which had averaged about 4.5 per cent of GDP in the second half of the 1970 *crept* up to 8.5 per cent of GDP by 1985/86 and stayed at that level thereafter. Similar increases occurred in the deficits of the consolidated Government and of the public finances was responsible both for the persistence of the current account deficit and the inflationary upsurge at the end of the decade.

The economy grew rapidly during the 1980s. GDP growth rose from the long standing rate of 3.6 per cent per annum (1965-80) to 5.5 per cent (1980-90). Some of the growth was unsustainable, being the direct result of the fiscal deficits; but part of it was the product of desirable policy changes, in particular the deregulation of controls on industry and investment. These reforms, half-hearted and piecemeal though they were, proving to be effective, but foundered in the macro-economic crisis at the end of the decade. More comprehensive reforms were needed but in a stable fiscal setting.

The New Economic Policy is a set of policies and administrative procedures introduced in July 1991 to bring about changes in the economic direction of the country. It has got two major components: stabilisation and structural reforms. These two policies–stabilization and structural adjustment policies are introduced as New Economic Policy with the three broad categories, namely Liberalisation, Privatisation and Globalisation (LPG).

Privatisation

Privatisation is, in fact, a recent phenomenon. The very word "Privatisation" causes a lot of misunderstanding, premature polarization and arguments that are beside the point. Some believe that market. Others interpret the word as a check on the Government or rolling back its activities. Generally speaking privatisation refers to the transfer of activities from the public sector to the private sector. It can take a variety of forms. It can mean the sale of wholly owned Government enterprises either fully or in part. Privatisation can also be a partnership between the Government and business through the transfer of responsibilities from the Government to private sector.

The privatization is an important device in the hands of policy makers to reform the Public Sector Undertakings (PSUs). Some of the important objectives of privatization may be :

(a) Fiscal objectives (reducing revenue deficits).
(b) Economic objectives (efficiency through competition).
(c) Socio-political objectives (emphasizing consumer in preference to workers).
(d) Administrative objectives (reducing cost of bureaucracy).
(e) Ideological objectives (strengthening and deepening individualism, property rights, etc.).

Just as the main concerns of policy-makers, their objectives and the reasons behind privatisation have differed from country to country, the modes of privatisation have also varied from country to country. Majority of the countries have preferred public offering of PSU shares. The following Table 3.1 gives a synoptic view of privatisation in different countries of the world.

It will be clear from Table 3.1 that leaders of different countries, at different times have taken resort to different forms of privatisation of the State-Owned Enterprises (SOEs) in their countries in accordance with the circumstances prevailing in their countries.

Table 3.1 : Privatisation at a Glance

Country	*Year/ Pioneer*	*Reasons for Privatisation*	*Objectives of Privatisation*	*Modalities*	*Special Features*	*Concern for Policy-makers Privatisation*
SOUTH KOREA	1969 Roh	- Excessive Government Control	- Equitable income distribution which will benefit the low income group	Non-divest-ture options	- PE Reforms - Government acts	- People's percaption of their Ownership Rights
CHILE	1974 Augusto Pinochet	- Inefficiency	- To finance financial deficit - To increase economic efficiency	Public offering	- Propetty ownership was distributed. - Efficiency was improved - Dependence on public sector was reduced.	- Lack of trans-parency in divestitute
U.K.	1979 Margaret Thatcher	- Financial deficits	- Promote wide share ownership - Reduce the power of trade union	Public offering of shares	- Denationalisation - Introduction of Golden Share' - Key legislations passed - Importance of marketing techniques realized	- Trade unions opposition. - Social cost of restructuring

Table 3.1 *(Contd.)*

U.S.A.	1980 Ronald Reagan	- Economic inefficiencies	- Two break bureaucratic strangleholds - Reduced cost - Efficient use of resources	Contracting with the private firms	- New Concept Regonomics' introduced	- Increase competition
MEXICO	1983 Miguel dela Madrid	- Severe economic lapses	- To increase efficiency and productivity - Maximisation of revenue	Public offering of Private shares	- Persistent courageous and difficult process of adjustment of large enterprises - Revenues put in stabilization fund.	- Strong Labour Unions - Started with Privatisation
MALAYSIA	1983 Mahatir Mohammad	- Increase in Government expenditure budgetary deficits - Deteriorating terms of trade and deficits in the external account	- To reduce financial and administrative burden of the Government - To promote competition, improve efficiency and productivity	Public offering	- Built-in-safety clauses to protect the interest of sons of the soil	- Equity concerns - Unemployment

Table 3.1 *(Contd.)*

ZAMBIA	1984 Kaunda	- Fiscal deficits slow monetary expansion	- Restructured the overall investment holding company Privatisation all commercially oriented parastatals and public utilities	Management Contracts	- Strengthened safety net - Strengthened Central Coordination	- Political commitment - Inadequate incentives
JAPAN	1985 Doko Toshio	- Financial crisis - Negative economic growth - Reduction in tax revenue	- Overcome fiscal crunch - Increase efficiency and competition - Eliminate redundant work-force	Fragmentation Public offering of shares	- Deregulation - Special fund for financial support - Cautious opening of the market	- Massive redundant labour force -Confrontational labour management relation
RUSSIA	1987 Gorbachov	- Inefficiency	- Two transform non-competitive and inefficient monopolies into market oriented enterprise	Vouchers to every Russian citizen born. before January 1, 1991	- Role of foreigners in divestiture	- Political opposition - Enterprise valuation
ARGENTINA	1989 Carlos Menem	- Inefficiency - Losses/deficits	- End to the state corporate hegemony - Reducing foreign debt	Private sale Join-Venture	- Strong Trade Unions - Political instability - Government administration reforms	- Economic Problems - Enterprise valuation problems

Table 3.1 *(Contd.)*

CHINA	Mid 1980s Deng Xisoping	- Poor management - Inefficiency - Financial losses - Resources wastage	- Revitalise enterprises - Improve motivation and productivity	Non-divestiture options	Economic reforms - Focus on control Property rights	Role of political parties
INDIA	1991 Narasimha Rao	- Severe fiscal and balance of payments deficits	- Improve Governments financial position - Improve the performance of PEs by increaseing efficiency, managerial autonomy.	Disinvestment	- Preference for Greenfield cold Privatisation - Improvement of performance through MOU	Trade Unions with political support. - Large size of many PEs - Employee owenership

Source: Monthly Public Opinion Surveys, Vol.LI No.2, November 2005, pp.30-31.

One factor which has been common with respect to the PSUs in all the countries, irrespective of the philosophy of development followed by them, is that they, except for some initial years, started breeding inefficiencies. Labour-friendly legislations, overstaffing, under utilization of installed capacities, strikes resulting in millions of man-hours lost involvement of political parties etc. made thing so complicated that almost all the SOEs, except for a few for reasons explained elsewhere, become white elephants for their respective governments. The Governments, in the ultimate analysis, were left with no choice except to put them into private hands.

The process of privatisation has already set in though its speed in some of the countries is very slow. In India, though the Government initiated structural reforms fifteen years ago, there is hardly any change in bureaucratic attitude. The need of the hour is to bring about a sea change not only in our policy measures but in the attitude of all those who are at the helm of affairs if the process of privatisation is to yield result for the benefit of the common men.

There are three stages of privatisation at macro-level:

(i) No expansion of public sector, or
(ii) Expansion of public sector at a lower rate, or
(iii) Reduction of public sector so that private sector expands. There may be three specific measures for the privatisation at micro-level, i.e., ownership, organizational and operational measures.
(iv) *Ownership Measures :* This mainly refers to denationalization of public enterprises, which may be legal or partial. Legal denationalization means transfer of majority ownership rights and benefits alongwith management to private enterprise. Partial denationalization implies transfer of ownership upto 40 per cent to the private entrepreneurs so that State holds majority ownership.

(v) *Organisational Measures :* One of the organizational services for the privatisation is the creation of a holding company, which will be under direct Government control with subsidiaries working under market discipline within the general supervision of the holding company. Another organizational device for privatisation is leasing the assets of a public enterprise, without disturbing ownership structure, to the best bidder and the ownership of the public enterprise is retained by the State and only the operations are given to the private parties. The lease agreement may consists of necessary terms and conditions guaranteeing to preserve publicness in the operations. This device of privatisation ensures the Government to assess the comparative benefits that the enterprise has in the public and private sectors.

(vi) *Operational Measures :* The elements of privatisation can be introduced by encouraging the public enterprise management to acquire certain inputs across the market than produce them internally. This may yield two benefits. The input costs are likely to be low reflecting economies of scale of their supply. Secondly, it may promote ancillaries outside the enterprise. Another operational measures, suggested for privatisation, in 'contracting out' certain ancillary services such as canteen maintenance and cleaning of buildings, maintenance of parks, watch and ward etc., to private parties.

Another operational measure bringing in elements of privatisation is to force a public enterprise as if it were a private enterprise in the sense of being bound by market discipline in investments, cost-minimization, pricing and production functions. The criteria for these aspects can be laid down under market disciplines.

Vuylsteke has categorized privatisation into the following techniques:

1. Public offering of shares.
2. Private sale of shares.
3. New private investment in a State-Owned Enterprise (SOEs).
4. Sale of Government or State Enterprises assets.
5. Reorganisation of fragmentation into small units.
6. Management/Employment buy out.
7. Lease and management contract.

In India, it was the late Mrs. Indira Gandhi's Government, which had initiated actions regarding the privatisation. However, the first clear pronouncement on the public sector outlining the change in policy was made by the late Prime Minister, Mr. Rajiv Gandhi in his first broadcast to the nation in 1984 when he said "the public sector has spread into too many areas where it should not be. We will be developing our public sector to undertake jobs that the private sector cannot do. But we will be opening up more to the private sector so that it can expand and the economy can grow more freely. In India changes for farreaching consequences were taking place.

In nutshell, the Government believes that privatisation should increased competition, not decrease it. It will not support the emergence of any monopoly that only restrict competition. It also believes that there must be a direct link between privatisation and social needs.[1]

Globalization

Globalization is a process of breaking (erasing) the political, economic, social, cultural, ecological, geographical and educational barriers and integrating the whole world into a 'Global Village'. The product of globalization process should realize the çoncepts like "Whole Earth is one Family" and "All people shall be prosperous".

International Monetary Fund (IMF) defines Globalization as, "the growing economic interdependence of countries world-wide through increasing volume and variety of cross border transactions in goods and services and of international capital flows and also through the more rapid and widespread diffusion of technology".

Charles U. L. Hill defines Globalization as, "the shift towards a more integrated and interdependent world economy. Globalization has two main components – the Globalization of markets and the Globalization of production."

In general, Globalization refers to a constellation of forces: economic, technological, ecological and cultural structures that are emerging on a global scale. Globalization is increasing the independency and integration of the individual countries of the world".

In the Globalizing world, the economy has changed dramatically to transform into a global economy characterized not only by free trade in goods and services but even more, by free movement of labour, capital, skill and entrepreneurship.

Globalization encompasses the following features:

(i) Operating and planning to expand business throughout the world,
(ii) Erasing the differences between domestic market and foreign market,
(iii) Buying and selling goods and services from/to any country in the world,
(iv) Establishing manufacturing and distribution facilities in any part of the world based on the feasibility and viability rather than national consideration.
(v) Product planning and development are based on market consideration of the entire world,
(vi) Sourcing of factors of production and inputs like raw materials, machinery, finance, technology, human resources, (labours/workers) managerial skills from the entire globe,

(vii) Global orientation in strategies, organizational structure, organizational culture and managerial expertise, and

(viii) Setting the mind and attitude to view the entire globe as a single market.

Global Companies/Institutions plan or venture not only on national markets, but also venture globally and view themselves as a global company/institute. Executives and employees of such companies/institutes are trained and tuned in world-wide operations. As essential conditions for Globalization, the Governments of various countries should provide the following conditions for smoothening the process.

(i) Liberalizing the rules and regulation of control,

(ii) Removal of Quotas and Tariffs,

(iii) Providing freedom to the business and industry,

(iv) Providing infrastructural facilities,

(v) Removal of bureaucratic hurdles,

(vi) Encouraging research and development,

(vii) Encouraging the competitiveness based on quality, price, delivery, customer service etc.,

(viii) Providing autonomy to the public sector to compete with private sector companies,

(ix) Providing administrative and Governmental support,

(x) Developing money and capital markets.

Globalization does not take place in a single instance. It take place gradually through an evolutionary approach. According to Ohamae, Globalization has five stages. They are:

(i) Domestic company/institute exports to foreign countries through the dealers or distributors or branches of the home country.

(ii) In the second stage, the domestic company/institute exports to foreign countries directly on its own.

(iii) In the third stage, the domestic company/institute becomes an International Company/institute by establishing production and marketing operations in various key foreign countries.

(iv) In the fourth stage, the company/institute replicates a foreign company/institute in the foreign country by having all the facilities including R&D, full-fledged human resources etc.

(v) In the fifth stage, the company/institute become a true foreign company/institute by serving the needs of foreign customers just like the host country's company serves.

Thus, Globalization means globalizing the marketing, production, investment, technology and other activities.

Companies globalize their operation through the following means:

(i) Exporting directly,
(ii) Exporting indirectly,
(iii) Licensing/Franchising,
(iv) Contract Manufacturing,
(v) Establishing Full Marketing Facilities,
(vi) Establishing Manufacturing Facilities,
(vii) Joint Venture,
(viii) Mergers, and
(ix) Strategies Alliance.[2]

Liberalization

In the name of liberalization we are opening up of our SSIs to large and most competitive multi-nationals and domestic large-scale industries.

This liberalization approach has created a highway to foreign companies to enter into common consumption market like food items, chilled cucumbers, coconut products, exercise books, maize floor, rice floor, wheat floor, potato chips, biscuits, chocolates, talcum powder, toothpaste, condensed milk, instant tea and coffee, poultry preparations, meat products including common salt.[3]

The support of liberalization approach, reveals that the impact of QRs removal will not have a disastrous effect on domestic industries and not led to flood of imports. But it create competitiveness among the Indian entrepreneurs and availability of goods and services will be increased to Indian consumers.

The fundamental feature of the new economic policy is that– it provides freedom to the entrepreneurs to establish any industry/ trade/business venture. The entrepreneurs are not required to get prior approval for any new venture. What they are needed is that they have to fulfil certain conditions to get into a line of one's choice. The procedure involving a case by case examination of the proposals for new ventures has been wiped off. Apart from this, the entrepreneurs are no longer needed licenses to come into business. The capital markets have also been freed and opened to the private enterprises. A new company can now be floated with new issue of shares, debentures etc. In case the entrepreneurs require imported equipment, they are no longer required to approach the Central authority for foreign exchange.

Liberalization means a clear subordination of the domestic to global and international, indicating a containment of space available to domestically defined and democratically shaped polities. Clear property rights and widespread private owenership are considered essential for markets to perform efficiently and equitably. And the State is expected to provide for these. Quest for liberalization has seen the re-emergence of complex framework of trade negotiations – GATT, WTO, MIGA, TRIMS, TRIPS and so on. And States have been instrumental in binding economies and markets of specific regions to these not so freely negotiated terms of trade. State is expected to take active interst in creating conditions through intervention for the growth of markets.

Basic tenets of liberalization carry a reform agenda which includes flexibility in the hiring and firing of workers, the freedom of entry of capital, the ready availabilility of land for new business activites and adequate infrastructure. The ending of State monopolies in banking, insurance and telecoms, the transfer of ownership of State-owned enterprises to private owners and the closure of loss-making State firms come in addition to unshackling the private sector. Trade liberalization, foreign direct investment, private financing of infrastructure, tax reforms, financial enterprises, labour law reforms, land law refoms and a reorientation of Government social policy are major aspects of the process of liberalization.[4] Its ultimate aim is of integration with the global economy.

The opening up India's economy in the Nineties brought about substantial changes in domestic as well as import tariffs. Industrial licensing was virtually deregulated. Global players were encouraged to set up shop in India in many fields, such as automobiles, electronics, computers and telecommunication.

As a sequel to this liberalization, the medium scale sector has also come into prominence. The medium scale sector focuses mainly on supplies to large projects, heavy engineering industries, the automobile sector and hi-tech areas like white goods, horticulture, fisheries, etc. Thus, there are strong signals to the industry to come up to global standards of technology and productivity to compete in the opened up economy.[5]

After the Independence in 1947, import controls were relaxed through the expansion of the OGL list in a stop-go fashion, with the First Five-Year Plan (1951-56) representing a period of 'progressive liberalization' [Bhagwati and Desai 1970:282]. But a foreign exchange crisis in 1956-57 put an end to this phase of liberalization and comprehensive import controls were restored and maintained until 1966. In June that year, under pressure from the World Bank. India devalued the rupee from Rs. 4.7 to Rs. 7.5 per dollar. The 57.5 per cent devaluation was accompanied by some liberalization of import licensing and cuts in import tariffs and export subsidies for approximately a year. But by 1968, intense domestic reaction to the devaluation led India to turn inward with vengeance. Almost all liberalizing initiatives were reversed and import controls tightened. This regime was consolidated and strengthened in the subsequent years and remained more or less intact until beginning of a period of phased liberalization in the late 1970s.

By about 1976, however, the resulting obsolescence of the capital stock and technology of many industries was becoming apparent, and a steady liberalization of imports of capital equipment and of technology started soon after.[6]

Liberalisation has unfolded the emergence of a new stronger contractual relationship which can be incorporated under the concept of NIE, in the form of agreements and responsibilities between external agencies and the indigenous state [Toye, 1993]. In the Indian case, this has taken the form of contracts between the State and the IMF. Thus, India's changing relationship with the IMF, underpinned by the conditionalities laid down by the latter, is expected to have a major influence in shaping 'free market' policies. For instance, India's loan of $ 1.8 billion from the IMF led to uncertainty about the implications of such a transaction, India's attempts to adopting domestic policies. These have included deregulation of industry, more encouragement to foreign investment, liberalization of foreign trade regimes, major reform of public sector enterprises (including privatisation) and sweeping reforms of the financial sector [Roy, 1995]. The extent to which such policies will be accommodated is closely linked to the interests of the different industrial groups.

The thinking behind liberalization, the support and opposition it has given rise to among diverse interest groups, and its impact on growth and development, pose critical questions on some of the major concerns related to NIE. In essence, the shift to liberalization has led to a re-assessment of development goals and strategies. This provides the context within which collective action, through pressure groups, to challenge any adverse effects of liberalization, such as aggravation of poverty, can be assessed.[7]

The Congress Government led by Mr. Narasimma Rao anounced the New Industrial Policy in July 1991. The main aim of the New Industrial Policy was :

(a) to unshackle the Indian industrial economy from the cobwebs of unnecessary burcaucratic control,
(b) to introuduce liberalization with a view to integrate the Indian economy with the world economy,
(c) to remove restrictions on direct foreign investment as also to free the domestic entrepreneur from the restrictions of MRTP Act, and
(d) the policy aimed to shed the load of the public enterprises which have shown a very low rate of return or were incurring losses over the years.

All these reforms of industrial policy led the Government to take a series of initiatives in respect of policies in the following areas: (a) Industrial licensing; (b) Foreign investment, (c) Foreign technology policy; (d) Public sector policy; and (e) MRTP Act.

Industrial licensing to be abolished for all projects except for a short list of industries related to security and strategic concents social reasons, hazardous chemicals and over riding environmental reasons and items of elitist consumption industries reserved for the small scale sector will continue to be so reserved.

In order to invite foreign investment in high priority industries requiring large investments and advanced technology, it was decided to provide approval for direct foreign investment upto 51 per cent foreign equity in such industries.

To provide access to international markets, majority foreign equity holding upto 51per cent equity would be allowed for trading companies primarily engaged in export activities.

With a view to injecting the desired level of technological dynamism in Indian industry, Government would provide automatic approval for technology agreements related to high priority industries within specified parameters. No permission will be necessary for hiring of foreign technicians, foreign testing of indigenously developed technologies.

The original concept of the public sector has also undergone considerable dilution. The most striking example is the take-over of sick units from the private sector. This category of public sector units accounts for almost one-third of the total losses of Central Public Enterprises. Another category of public enterprises which does not fit into the original idea of the public sector being at the commanding heights of the economy is the plethora of public enterprises which are in the consumer goods and services sectors.

With the growing complexity of industrial structure and the need for achieving economies of scale for ensuring higher productivity and competitive advantage in the international market, the interference of the Government through the MRTP Act has to be resticted. Towards this end:

(i) The pre-entry scrutiny of investment decisions by so-called MRTP companies will no longer be required. Instead, emphasis will be on controlling and regulating monopolistic, restrictive and unfair trade practices rather than making it necessary for the monopoly houses to obtain prior approval of Central Government for expansion, establishment of new undertakings, merger, amalgamation and take-over and appointment of certain directors.

(ii) The thrust of policy will be more on controlling unfair or restrictive business practices.[8]

The New Industrial Policy comprised the elimination of all entry barriers, to most industries as well as the associated constraints on scale and technology. Industrial liberalisation was complemented by trade liberalisation on scale and technology. Industrial liberalisation was complemented by trade liberalization in the form of drastic reduction in custom duties and removal of restrictions on imports of raw materials, intermediates and capital goods.

3. New Industrial Policy and Small Scale Industry

The New Industrial Policy for small scale industry was announced by the Government of India on August 6, 1991. Keeping in view the sectors potential for output, employment and export, the new policy has conferred greater focus on the promotion and nurturing of tiny enterprises within the small scale sector. The major elements of the new policy with respect to tiny enterprises are:

(i) enhancement of investment limits in plant and machinery from Rs. 2 lakhs to Rs. 5 lakhs irrespective of their location;
(ii) inclusion of industry-related service and business enterprises as small scale industries;
(iii) easier access to institutional finance;
(iv) priority in Government Purchase Programme;
(v) relaxation of certain provisions of labour laws;
(vi) widening the scope of the National Equity Fund to cover projects upto Rs. 10 lakhs for equity support; and
(vii) enlargement of single window loan scheme to cover projects upto Rs. 20 lakhs with working capital margin upto Rs. 10 lakhs and channelising composite loan through commercial banks.

To mitigate the problem of inadequate access of small scale industries to credit, the new policy envisages a shift of emphasis from "Subsidised/Cheap Credit" to "the adequate flow of credit". It is proposed to set up a special monitoring agency to oversee that the genuine credit needs of the small scale sector fully met.

To provide access to the capital market and to encourage modernization and technical upgradation, the new policy proposes equity participation in the small scale industries by other industrial undertakings upto 24 per cent of their total shareholdings.

To enhance the supply of risk to the small scale sector, a Limited Partnership Act is proposed to be introduced shortly.

To encourage and facilitate location of industries in rural backward areas a new scheme of Integrated Infrastructure Development of small scale industries is proposed with active participation from State Governments and financial institutions.

Further to improve productivity and competitiveness of small scale industrial units a Technology Development Cell (TDC) is proposed to be set up in SIDO.

Marketing of products is another problem faced by the small scale industries in total export, an Export Development Centre is proposed to be set up in SIDO to further augment export activities of small scale sector. It was also proposed to introduce a suitable legislation to ensure prompt payment of bills to the industrial units.

The main objective of the Industrial Policy, 1999 was to create congenial environment for the SSIs to cope up the emerging challenges of globalization. To focus fully on the promotion and development of small scale industries a separate Ministry of Small Scale Industries and Agro and Rural Industries was created. The policy initiative include the following:

(i) The annual turnover limit for the calculation of working capital limit for SSI units was raised to Rs. 5 crores from Rs. 4 crores;

(ii) The maximum ceiling limit for Composite Loan Scheme was increased to Rs. 5 lakhs;

(iii) To increase flow of credit to SSI sector, a new credit insurance schemes was launched;

(iv) Small scale industries were allowed to pay excise duty on a monthly basis;

(v) The small scale industrial units producing goods in rural areas are allowed excise exemption on third party branded goods;

(vi) The definition of small scale and ancillary industrial units was revised by reducing investment limit in plant and machinery to Rs. 1 crore from Rs. 3 crores;

(vii) Special package for the development of small and village industries in North Eastern regions are announced. The industrial units in the North Eastern Region were given exemption from excise duty for 10 years from the date of commencement of production; and

(viii) Special emphasis was given for the units which have high export potential.[9]

The key elements of India's policy for the support of small scale industries have been small scale industry reservations, fiscal concessions by way of lower excise duties, preferential allocation of and subsidization of bank credit, extension of business services by the Government and preferential procurement by the Government. Thus small scale industry has been sought to be protected from the competition of large companies both through reservations as well as fiscal concession. Extension of business services by the Government was considered necessary in the absence of equivalent services being available in the private sector.

4. New Small Enterprise Policy, 1991

India's Small Industry Policy, has been a widely known phenomena. The relative merits of less capital intensity and more labour absorption capacity among others have endeared the sector to the policy-makers as an instrument to achieve a variety of economic objectives such as employment generation, production of mass consumption goods, balanced regional development and equitable distribution of income.

In the pre-reforms era (1947-48 to 1990-91) when Indian economy was subject to controls and regulations, SSIs emphasized protected growth of the sector with a two-prolonged strategy, developing institutional network and offering protective benefits. As a consequence, quantitative performance its policy towards the Small Sector, necessitated a change in the direction for small industry policy.

Apparently the policy does not signify any major deviation from the past. But a minute perusal does indicate that the policy intends to promote competitiveness of the sector, more than anything else. Unlike in the past, the policy does not contain, mere intentions of the Government, it has proposed clear for the Sector–(1) Finance, (2) Marketing, (3) Technology, as indicated by Table 3.2.

The primary objective of this policy is to impart more vitally and growth impetus to this sector. The packages are: (1) Ceiling of investment raised to Rs.5 lakhs from Rs.2 lakhs, (2) Locational restrictions on setting up of these industries removed, (3) Equity participation by other industrial units in SSI not exceeding 24 per cent of the total share holding, (4) Introduction of new legal form of organization of business, namely restricted or limited partnership, (5) Setting up of a monitoring agency to ensure that the genuine credit needs of this sector are fully met; review all regulations, procedures and modifications to ensure their operations, encouraging industry associations, expansion of Entrepreneurship Development Programmes and further liberalisation of schemes of National Equity Fund and Single Window Loans.

Table 3.2: Essential Features of the SSI Policy: 1991

Sl. No.	*Objectives*	*Major Features*
1.	To meet the emerging credits to demand for	Emphasis to shift from cheap credit, adequate credit equity participation by other undertakings, domestic, foreign upto 24 per cent
2.	To strengthen small industry marketing	Introduction of factoring services through Banks Marketing of mass consumption goods. Under common brand name setting up sub-contracting exchanges
3.	To upgrade technology and promote modernization	Technology development cell in SIDO Quality Counselling and Testing Technology Information Centres Technology Upgradation Programmes

Source : SIDO Report on Functions and Activities, (1992-93) "Policy Measures for promoting and strengthening Small, Tiny and Village Industries", Department of Small Industry, Government of India, pp. 4-16.

From Table 3.3, it appears that the Government is evolving a focused approach for SSI development in the 90s which has 3 dimensions.

The SSI policy measures are analysed in six categories . They are:

Table 3.3 : New Policy Initiatives for SSIs in 1990:Major Areas

Sl. No.	*Technology*	*Finance*	*Marketing*
1.	Technology Bureau to be set up by SIDBI	Factoring services by SIDBI and PSBs	Setting up of sub-contracting exchanges
2.	Quality counselling centres to be set up	SIDBI branches in SSI clusters	Access to inter-nationalexhibitions by SIDBI, NSIC
3.	Exhibitions for technology purchase	Exclusive bank branches in SSIs	Credit rating arrangements districts
4.	Technology development and modernization fund to be set up	National equity fund for SSIs	SIDO to support export promotion
5.	Collaborative technology upgradation programmes	Financial support acquire ISO-9000 Certificate	ED Programmes to be arranged by SBI

Source : Balasubramanya, M.H. (2000), "India's Small Industry Policy in the 90s – Waning Protectionism", *The Indian Economic Journal,* Vol.47, No.2, pp.76-79.

1. Policy of Reservation,
2. Licensing Policy,
3. Imports and Export Policy,
4. Price and Purchase Preference Policy,
5. Labour Policies and
6. Rehabilitation of Sick Units.

Policy of Reservation

Reservation of products for exclusive manufacture in the SSI sector has been one of the important policy measures for promoting this sector. This policy was initiated in 1967 with 47 items. At present 812 items are reserved in the sector. Abide Hussain Committee has recommended for total abolition of the reservation for SSIs. But the Government felt that the complete dereservation is not desirable and it should be done in a phased manner.

As per reservation policy no medium/large scale enterprises

are allowed to manufacture reserved items except under 50° export obligation. Those who had been producing reserved items prior to the date of reservation can continue to do so after obtaining a Carry On Business (COB) Licence from the Government, any violation of the policy of reservation is punishable.

The reserved items fall under the following broad categories :

(i) Food and allied industries;
(ii) Textile products including hosiery;
(iii) Wood and wood products;
(iv) Paper products;
(v) Leather and leather products including footwear;
(vi) Rubber products;
(vii) Plastic products;
(viii) Chemical and chemical products;
(ix) Glass and ceramics;
(x) Mechanical engineering;
(xi) Electronic equipments and components;
(xii) Transport equipment, auto parts, bicycle parts; and
(xiii) Miscellaneous (Sport goods, stationery items etc.).

Licencing Policy

The reserved manufacturing items in small scale sector do not require any prior licence. In the new industrial policy, the Government has prepared a list of industries (Schedule II) for which industrial licensing is compulsory. In the case of Small Scale Sector, if an item is listed in Schedule II and is also listed in the list of reserved items for small scale sector, the small scale unit does not require an industrial licence. Similarly those units which have received Secretariat for Industrial Approvals (SIA) or DGTD registration for the manufacture of these items, are also not required to apply for an industrial licence for the manufacture of these items. The locational restrictions have been minimized.

Import and Export Policy

Export policy of the Government has remained liberal to promote exports from small scale sector. The export strategy for small scale sector includes simplification of export procedures and to provide incentives to small scale sector for higher production and to minimum export earnings. With a view to promote exports, the Government has formulated Export-Import Policy after consulting various trade bodies. To improve exports, Government has taken the following measures:–

(i) To encourage the exports from small scale sector, Government provides required assistance and support to exhibit the products in the International Exhibitions so as to give an opportunity to SSI units to display their products in the world market;

(ii) To acquaint SSI Exports of the latest packaging standards, techniques etc., the Government organized training programmes on packaging of exports in various parts of the country;

(iii) To encourage SSI units to produce quality of goods 'National Awards for Quality Products' are given to the outstanding small scale units, who have made significant contribution for improving quality of their products. Further "National Export Awards" will be given to those entrepreneurs who have made outstanding exports performance.

To meet the challenge of international competition and to promote exports of SSI products, the following promotional schemes are also being implemented:

1. Technology Development and Modernization Fund Scheme for the development and modernization of SSI Units.
2. Quality Awareness Scheme to give awareness about the quality of goods to SSI units.

3. Subsidy for obtaining ISO-9000 quality certification by way of reimbursing 75 per cent of their expenditure to obtain ISO-9000 certification.
4. Other schemes for technology improvement are: Tool Rooms, Process-*cum*-Product Development Centres, UPTECH etc.

Price and Purchase Preference Policy

The Stores Purchase Policy of the Government prior to 1989 was in the form of categorization of items in six major groups. However, after July, 1989, the categorization of items was reduced to the following two major groups:

(i) Items reserved for exclusive purchase from SSI, and
(ii) Others which are out of reserved list.

Assistance under Government Store Purchase Programme in the form of reservation of products for exclusive purchase from SSI and price performance is one of the major instruments for providing marketing support to SSIs. Under this programme, the Government provide a number of facilities to SSIs. These include reservation of certain products for exclusive purchase from SSI and price preference upto 15° in case of selected items which are produced in both large scale as well as small scale units. The Price Preference of 15° is available to SSI units to compensate scout of non-availability of economies of scale, poor resource base, poor access to raw material etc. as compared to large scale sector.

Rehabilitation of Sick Units

Sickness in SSI Sector is attributed to a number of factors. Non availability of credit is one of the major factors responsible for rendering SSI Sick Units. Government has taken various measures from time-to-time to detect sickness at the incipient stage and rehabilitation of sick units in small scale sector. The Nayak

Committee set up by RBI had gone into sickness of SSIs in detail and recommended various measures.

Labour Policies

Labour Act has been simplified to assist the small establishments. 'Labour Laws Act 1988' covers labour related acts such as:

(i) Establishments employing 10-19 persons require to maintain only 3 registers and to submit only core returns only.
(ii) Establishments employing less than 10 persons to maintain only 1 register and submit only one annual core return.
(iii) Inspections are being conducted on annual basis however in default cases establishments are liable to random inspections.
(iv) In view of liberalization small scale establishment employing upto 20 persons are inspected once in 2 years, and establishments employing more than 20 persons are inspected annually.

Simplification of labour legislation, procedures and inspections is under process with a view to bring SSI units closer to Labour Market.

5. World Trade Organization and Small Scale Industries

With the emergence of WTO and its conditionality, many of the existing support systems for protection and promotion of Small Scale Sector will have to be dismantled. Small Scale Industries will have to compete on their own and find a place for themselves in domestic as well as international marketing. Therefore, it is necessary to understand and examine the objectives and conditionalities of WTO and its implications on Small Scale Sector.

The Uruguay Round of Negotiations under the aegis of GATT, World Trade Organisation (WTO), came into being on 1st January,

1995, as the only body dealing with the rules of trade between the nations. WTO, is located in Geneva, Switzerland. It has 136 countries as members, including India. China is expected to join WTO soon. The objective of WTO is to ensure freer, more transparent and more predictable trading regime in the world. It is based on sound legal system and its agreements are ratified by the Parliaments of member countries. No country controls WTO. The decision-makers are the designated Ministers of member countries. WTO is responsible for overseeing implementation of all agreements-multilateral (signed by all WTO members) and plurilateral (signed by a group of members for specific issues), that have been negotiated under Uruguay Round or will be negotiated in future. It provides a forum for further negotiations on matters covered by the agreements as well as on new issues. It is responsible for settlement of disputes among member nations and periodic reviews of the Trade Policies of the members nations. The WTO agreements cover the following:

General Agreement of Tariffs and Trades (GATT)

It deals with issues of Trade in merchandise and goods of all member countries, e.g., all industrial goods, consumer durables etc. There are large number of Agreements relating to trade and goods which are as follows:

1. Agreement on valuation of Goods,
2. Agreement on Pre-shipment Inspection,
3. Agreement on Technical Barriers to Trade (TBT),
4. Agreement on Sanitary and Phytosanitary Measures (SPS),
5. Agreement on Import Licensing Procedure,
6. Rules applicable to exports,
7. Agreement on Subsidies and Countervailing Measures,
8. Agreement on Safeguard Measures,
9. Agreement on Anti-Dumping Measures,
10. Trade-Related Investment Measures (TRIMs),

11. Market Access Negotiations,
12. Agreement on Textiles and Clothing (ATC),
13. Agreement on Agriculture,
14. Agreement on Government Procurement, and
15. Agreement on State Trading Enterprises.

Main Provisions of Agreements

(i) Tariffs and Trade

GATT functions on five basic principles:

1. Protection to domestic industry through tariffs only,
2. Non-tariff barriers (like import licensing, quotas etc.) are to be eliminated,
3. Reduction in tariff and other trade barriers are to be done through negotiations,
4. No discrimination among WTO member countries (MFN), and
5. Equal treatment to imported goods and domestic goods.

(ii) Phasing out of Quantitative Restrictions

Quantitative restrictions are to be phased out in a specific time frame.

1. Developing countries like India were given more time to adjust.
2. Countries suffering from Balance of Payments were allowed delayed removal of quantitative restrictions to restrict imports.
3. Developing countries have to adopt price based measures (i.e., import surcharge) instead of quantitative restrictions (i.e., restrictive import licensing).
4. Quantitative restrictions were abolished by WTO

members. In its place tariffs were applied. Quotas levied for import of textile products from developing countries may be phased out completely by 1st January, 2005.

(iii) Subsidies

There are three types of subsidies: (1) Prohibited Subsidies, (2) Permissible Actionable Subsidies, and (3) Permissible Non-Actionable Subsidies.

1. *Prohibited Subsidies*: These subsidies are prohibited because they affect trade and likely to have adversely effect the interests of other Members. Export promotion policies like tax exemptions etc. are targeted under this category.
2. *Permissible Actionable Subsidies*: These subsidies are permissible as long as they do not hurt the interests of other Members. They are essentially production subsidies which are not prohibited but actionable subject to challenge by other Member country.
3. *Permissible Non-actionable Subsidies*: These subsidies are also called green subsidies. These subsidies are not specific and are granted on the basis of objective criteria that are economic in nature and horizontal in application and do not favour certain enterprise over others and are not specific. They are non-actionable. There are three subsidies in this category: basic research and pre-competitive development subsidies, assistance to disadvantaged regions and assistance to adopt existing facilities to new environment requirement. Importing countries cannot levy countervailing measures given by Government to SMEs which are identified on the basis of their size or number of employees would non actionable.

(iv) Anti-dumping Measures

GATT rules deal with two types of unfair practices which distort conditions of competition. These are: (1) If the goods benefit from the subsidies (2) If goods are dumped in the foreign market. The agreement on Anti-dumping practices (ACP) and Agreement on Subsidies and Countervailing Measures (SCM) authorize countries to levy compensatory dues on import of products that are benefiting from 'unfair trade practices'. The criteria and procedures employed by both the agreements for determining injury is similar.

(v) Trade-Related Investment Measures (TRIMs)

Government often impose conditions on foreign investment to direct flow of investment in accordance with certain national priorities. Conditions that can affect trade are known as trade-related investment measures. There are twenty four such TRIMs that countries chiefly use.

The Agreement prohibits use of five TRIMS viz:

(i) *Local Content Requirements (LCRs)* – imposing use of certain amount of local inputs in production.
(ii) *Trade Balancing Requirement* – limiting use of import content in proportion to the export of investing company.
(iii) *Trade Balancing Requirement* – restrictions on import to an amount or value of the product exported.
(iv) *Exchange Restrictions* – restrictions on access to foreign exchange to an amount of foreign exchange earnings attributable to the enterprise.
(v) *Domestic Sales Requirement* – requiring to sell certain proportion locally.

The first two are inconsistent with GATT's National Treatment principle and rest were prohibited as they are termed as Quantitative Restrictions.

(vi) Government Procurement

Government and its agencies are significant buyers of goods and services to the tune of 10 per cent to 15 per cent of GNP. The rules of GATT exempt them to purchase their requirements from the domestic manufacturer even at higher price for its own use or consumption. The agreement requires the signatories to accord MFN and National treatment to Government purchases as well as agreed purchases listed in the annexes by each country.

(vii) Agreement on Textiles and Clothing (ATC) and Agreements on Agriculture

WTO Agreements on Textiles and Clothing and Agreement on Agriculture specifically are for two distinct sectors. Under the ATC, the restrictions maintained by developed countries on import of Textiles and Garments from developing countries are to be phased out by 2005 progressively. Under the agreement on Agriculture, the high subsidies maintained by countries, have been converted into 'tariffs'. Tariff represents commitment not to increase tariffs beyond listed rates. These are called bound rates which serve as a ceiling. Further tariffs have been reduced and closed markets are obliged to open progressively. Bound rates in India have been fixed by and large at 40 per cent for finished goods and 25 per cent for intermediaries. For agricultural, goods, the bound rates are 100 per cent for processed food 150 per cent and edible oils 300 per cent. The maximum bound rate in India on manufacturing goods will be 38.5 per cent.

(viii) World Trade and Environment

The Agreement on Technical Barriers to Trade (TBT) provides that mandatory standards should be adopted by Governments to protect health and safety of the people and environment. The agreement also covers process and production methods of certain products. The Agreement on thc Application of Sanitary (for human and animal) and Phytosanitory (for plants) Measures (SPS Agreement) allows discrimination due to differences in climate, incidence of pests or disease in different countries, but the emphasis is on adoption of international standards.

(ix) State Trading Enterprises (STEs)

In many countries State Trading Enterprises are engaged in import and export of certain goods particularly food and food products and commodities traded in bulk. The STEs are broadly defined as "Governmental and non-governmental enterprises, including marketing boards, which have been granted exclusive or special rights or privileges, including statutory or constitutional powers, in exercise of which they influence, through purchases or sales, the level or direction of imports or exports." The GATT rules impose two main obligations on STEs. Firstly, these enterprises should conduct their business on the basis of considerations and secondly, it is required that WTO be notified of relevant information on the activities of STEs. The GATT rules apply on STEs. For example in India, some of the STEs are MMTC, STC, PSUs in petroleum sector etc.

1. General Agreement on Trade in Services (GATS)

It deals with the services such as banking, insurance, consultancy etc., and GATS operates on three levels viz., general principles, annexes on specific sectors and member countries' commitments for the market access. It also provides for transparency in regulations, mutual recognition of qualifications of service providers etc. besides Most Favoured Nation (MFN) principle. Annexes deal with specific service sectors like Financial Services, Tele-communications, Maritime Transport etc.

2. Trade-Related Intellectual Property Rights (TRIPR)

It covers with intellectual property e.g. Patents, Copy rights, Trade marks, Industrial designs, Layout designs for integrated circuits, Geographical indications and undisclosed information or trade secrets. The object of intellectual property is creation of human intellect. The Agreement is built on the existing international conventions dealing with Intellectual Property Rights. The objectives are: application of basic principles, protection to IPRs, enforcement, dispute settlement and provisions for transitional arrangements. To get protection under IPRs most of the developing countries are required to make or amend the existing laws.

TRIPR Agreement covers seven categories of intellectual property :

- (i) Industrial Design,
- (ii) Trade Mark,
- (iii) Copy Right and related rights,
- (iv) Geographical indications,
- (v) Layout Design of integrated circuits, and
- (vi) Protection of undisclosed information – Trade secrets.

Today's business world is extremely competitive and technology is changing at a very fast rate than ever before. The award of exclusive rights/monopoly to the original inventor and penalty/ punishment to the infringer of such rights are the basis for creation of IPR related laws. Safeguarding the IPRs ensures better returns on inputs of the R&D efforts. If the invention is safeguarded by securing the IPR then the risk due to disclosure is totally eliminated. The exclusive rights/monopoly are granted by the Government only if the invention meets the criteria of award of such rights.

GATT and GATS follow three part structure viz., general principles, associate agreements/annexes on specific sectors/issues and commitments of member countries. The TRIPS agreement contains general principles only that are followed by members.

Impact of WTO on Small Scale Sector

1. WTO agreements do not discriminate on the basis of size of increased welfare at a global level. Market access through

enhanced efficiency is the central theme of WTO agreements. Reduction in tariffs, elimination of tariffs escalation and dismantling of non-tariff barriers including quantitative restrictions will make SSIs to face competition both from Multi-National Companies (MNCs) and Indian large companies.

2. The WTO Agreement on Technical Barriers lays an emphasis on standards of international recognition in products. As such developing countries have to face tough competition against quality standards from developed markets. The inability of the small scale units to upgrade their technologies, to achieve product standardization as per International Standards/Bureau of Indian Standards Certification and to secure foreign collaborations both financial and technical may put them in a disadvantageous position. SSIs have technical and financial limitation to obtain ISO Standards and adhering to requisite designs, packaging, patents/brands. Price competitions etc., and therefore lose opportunities in the global market. Due tc financial constraints, SSIs are not in a position, to set up their own R&D facilities.
3. The policy to attract foreign investment in India has a direct impact on SSIs as some of the MNCs have introduced their superior quality and technology products in the Indian market so that local industrial units tend to loose major market share enjoyed by them previously. Such products include soft drinks, electronic music goods, computer hardware, cosmetics, electronic equipment etc. The marketing strategy adopted by the MNCs has been to price their products low as compared to Indian product prices, offer goods on replacement or exchange basis etc., to capture the market.
4. GATT provides for imposition of quantitative restrictions on imports for balance of payments reasons. India has built up large foreign exchange reserves in relation to imports and is under pressure to remove all Quantitative

Restrictions at the earliest. Removal of Quantitative Restrictions means dismantling the reservation policy on SSI products. Due to removal of QRs, many SMEs specially in the consumer goods sector will find it difficult to survive as more imported products will find easy access to Indian Market. There may be stiffer competition coming from low cost producers from the neighbouring countries (LDCs) such as Nepal, Bangladesh, Sri Lanka and China. Items reserved for the SSIs will not face competition from similar products being imported from all over the world and produced by large scale global manufactures. With the removal of QRs, the restrictions on the export of raw hides and shines and semi-processed leather, etc., which is a dominant export industry in the small scale sector in India are also to be removed. Indian SSI Sector will be adversely affected due to poor competitive strength, slow technological upgradation and flow of costly credit to SSIs as compared to non-SSI units, poor infrastructure facilities, absence of VAT, obsolete laws, rules, regulations, ignorance of WTO provisions among small scale entrepreneurs, most of the units do not work in groups or clusters therefore, are not able to have the advantage of common facilities and lack of international exposure.

5. As Quantitative Restrictions have to be removed, the protection level by way of tariff has also come down. The substantial reduction of tariff levels over the years will make SMEs to suffer from high cost of inefficiency and low support facilities which results in reduced competitive strength of SSI units. The reduced tariff rates will affect the Indian SMEs depending upon the level of import intensity of exportable items and demand for importable products.
6. As the domestic market is going to be exposed to external competition, SMEs may have to be cautious against possible dumping by their competitors from abroad. Anti-

dumping charges by the importing countries may do serious damage to the export prospects. SSIs in India are unable to defend or take counteractive measures due to their ignorance, lack of necessary data and problem of accessibility to information.

7. The SMEs are likely to be deprived of market access not only in the case of technology intensive items but even for many labour intensive items because most of the countries define their SMEs in terms of employment or turnover and therefore, when any dispute arises they will not treat an Indian SSI as a small enterprise. Since most of the countries use employment or turnover criterion for defining SSI, there is need to examine the SSI definition in the light of employment as is prevalent in most of the countries.
8. In the event of Agreement on Trade and Investment, the SMEs may have to struggle hard for its survival in an unprotected environment in the domestic market because the SMEs of other countries would be given same treatment in India as are given to our SMEs. For SMEs, Government is substantially large buyer in India. There are reservation policies and price support mechanism for the purchase of products from small sector. These are non-statutory and having no legal binding. If it is challenged by member countries, Government may have to be opened up to foreign competition as a result SMEs will be adversely affected.
9. Import of goods will increase competition in all category of products including reserved items for SSIs. Due to low technology of Indian industry, Indian products find it difficult to compete with advanced countries.
10. The impact of TRIPS will be on all business. The main source of technology for SMEs-reverse engineering will be difficult with the stricter IPR regime and ignorance of law will be no excuse because the burden of proof is on infringer.

11. The New Patent Act would have its effect mainly on drugs, pharmaceuticals, agro-products, agro-chemicals and Information Technology because patented products cannot be produced without licence. The new patent regime might encourage the Indian SMEs' to go for new inventions. India has great advantage in IT industry but the absence of venture capital will affect the industry adversely.
12. Agreement on Sanitary and Phyto sanitary measures would mainly affect agro-based and dairy products because it requires heavy investment to be complied with the developed countries. Environment issues affect the SMEs as most of the products are produced with obsolete technology.
13. The issues relating to labour standards also would hamper the growth of export market of garments, carpets, brassware, handicrafts etc., as these units employ a large number of child labour in our country.
14. With the removal of quantitative restrictions, the enterprises in the reserved list have to face competition from imports of large scale and most of the organizations including Government Departments purchase their consumables in bulk quantity. Due to their small size, SSIs could not be able to meet the demand as in the case of Multinational Companies.

General Implications

The general implications on account of WTO can be summarized as follows:

1. The impact of WTO and its agreements are on every economic activity of agriculture, trading, service or manufacturing.
2. World markets are opening up due to lowering of tariffs

and dismantling of other restrictions in developed and developing countries. Enlightened and awakened entrepreneurs have greater opportunities to benefit from their comparative advantages.

3. Domestic markets will be increasingly threatened because of lowering of tariffs leading to freer entry of foreign goods and because of foreign companies establishing manufacturing bases locally.
4. Whereas the developing countries will have greater opportunities in sectors in which they have cost-based comparative advantages e.g., Textiles, Agriculture etc., the developed countries will benefit by opening of service sector and tightening of Intellectual Property Rights. However, without corresponding reforms in their domestic economic policies developing countries may fail to benefit from WTO regime.
5. Export Markets will become tougher because of competition among developing countries having similar comparative advantages.
6. There is a wave of standardization blowing across the globe, products from developing countries are to face tougher quality standards in developed markets, particularly in the areas where they have comparative cost advantage.
7. Every company whether serving domestic or international market, will have to undertake internal exercise to identify factors affecting its international competitiveness in terms of cost as well as quality. It will importable or tariffs are further lowered or both.
8. The WTO regime will benefit those countries more which show with and skills in the on-going dialogue. The Governments that are in constant touch with their industries and affected groups will be able to determine with the best of their advantage.
9. The international trade is increasingly becoming knowledge based. The entrepreneurial ability will come to force in the new environment.

All the above issues are a matter of serious concern for the small scale sector. Government should take a wise decision on Reservation Policy and provide proper package of assistance to products effected by dereservation so that their competitive power is enhanced. Effective steps are also needed towards upgradation of technology and availability of credit at reasonable rate of interest. A general programme of Interest Subsidy for Technology Upgradation be launched. To strengthen the marketing of SSI products, a separate market and export promotion center of Small Scale Entrepreneurs be created. To overcome these hindrances it is proposed to have a world-wide data base system which will provide information on cost structure of products in various countries. It should also be made mandatory for each member country to provide free and unrestricted cost information as may be desired by another member.

The Small Scale Industries should determine themselves to survive without availing of the benefit of high tariff barriers or non tariff barriers like import licensing. It cannot hope to get subsidies from Government indefinitely. The industry has to face competition both from domestic and abroad markets by raising their level of efficiency and competitiveness. The industry has to face competition from the neighbouring developing countries and also non-tariff barriers like environmental conditions, health, safety and technical standards from developed countries. Therefore, it is necessary to upgrade its technology and modernise, adopt modern marketing, management practices and improve the quality of its products and be efficient and competitive. Indian industry will also have to pay special attention to quality, environmental health, safety and technical standards. The Government has also to think over its existing policies and programmes after having an in depth study and to carry out necessary changes immediately. They have to take steps to make the sector aware of the implications and to safeguard itself and to avail optimum benefits. Awareness and timely adherence to the changing scenario has to be a prime key of success otherwise high competitive due to openness of economy, redundancy of reservation policy, application of bound rates etc., may affect the growth and survival of the Small Scale Industries.

REFERENCES

1. IIPo: Analytical Study Report on Privatisation of Public Sector Undertakings (PSUs) – Changing Indian Scenario, *Monthly Public Opinion Survey*, Vol.LI No.2, November 2005, pp.28-33.
2. Shriped S. Bolashetty, "Trade in Indian Higher Education Service Sector: Implications of WTO's GATS", *University News,* Vol.43, No.36, September 5-11, 2005, pp.1-2.
3. C. Srinivasalu, "Rural Industrialisation Developmental Approach *versus* Liberalisation", *Southern Economist,* Vol. 40, March, 2002, pp. 9-10.
4. A.K. Ojha "Globalization and Liberalization: Prospects of Now", *Third Concept,* August 2002, Vol. 16, No. 186, pp. 13-15.
5. R.N. Sengupta, "Preparing SMEs in India to meet New Challenges", *SBI Monthly Review*, November 1998, pp. 578-589.
6. Arvind Panagariya, "Growth and Reforms during 1980s and 1990s", *Economic and Political Weekly*, June 19-25, Vol. XXXIX, No. 25, pp. 2581-2593.
7. Sumit Roy, "New Institutional Economics, State and Development", *Economic and Political Weekly,* July 29, 1995, Vol. XXX, No. 30, pp. 65-72.
8. Ruddar Datt, K.P.M. Sundharam, "Industrial Policy on Indian Planning", *Indian Economy,* S. Chand and Company Ltd., New Delhi, 2004, pp. 175-186.
9. Syed Vazith Husain, *Small Scale Industries in the New Millennium*, Sarup and Sons, New Delhi, 2003, pp. 30-37.

4. SSI After Economic Reforms

The present chapter has been divided into two parts. The first part analyses the origin and growth performance of SSI in India. The functioning of Small Scale Industry in Tamil Nadu is explained in the second part of the chapter. The growth and performance analysis deals with Number of Units, Investment, Employment and Production etc.

Secondary data have been used for analysing the performance of SSI. Tamil Nadu, the most popular State, in the country was selected for the field study. Madurai and Dindigul districts having traditional Industries of Small Scale Sector particularly, Textile based industry, had been purposively selected.

1. Performance of SSI in India

The phenomenal growth of industries in the small scale sector has been striking feature in the economic development of the country since Independence. It has contributed to the overall growth of the Gross Domestic Product as well as in terms of employment generation and export. The performance of small scale sector in terms of critical parameters like number of units (both registered and unregistered). Investment, production, employment and exports are explained in this section.

Number of Units

The number of units, both registered and unregistered SSI units, after implementation of New Economic Policy is presented in Table 4.1.

Table 4.1 : The Performance of SSI Sector from 1990-91 to 2000-01 in India

Year	*No. of Units (No. in lakhs)*		
	Registerved	*Unregisteved*	*Total*
1990-91	13.78	5.70	19.48
1991-92	14.98 (8.71)	5.84 (2.46)	20.82(6.88)
1992-93	16.48 (10.01)	5.98 (2.40)	22.46(7.88)
1993-94	17.76 (7.77)	6.12 (2.34)	23.88(6.14)
1994-95	19.44 (9.46)	6.27 (2.45)	25.71(7.66)
1995-96	20.18(3.81)	6.40(2.07)	26.58(3.88)
1996-97	21.53(6.69)	6.50(1.56)	28.03(5.46)
1997-98	22.82(5.99)	6.62(1.85)	29.44(5.03)
1998-99	24.06(5.43)	6.74(1.81)	30.80(4.62)
1999-2000	25.26(5.43)	6.86(1.78)	32.12(4.29)
2000-01	26.72(5.78)	6.98(1.75)	33.70(4.94)
2001-02	27.31 (2.21)	7.11 (1.86)	34.42(4.92)
2002-03	28.49 (4.32)	7.23 (1.69)	35.72 (3.8)

Source: Annual Report, Ministry of SSI, 1990-91 to 2002-03.
Note : Figures within parenthesis denotes growth rate of SSI units.

Regarding the total number of units, registered SSI units were 28.49 lakhs, unregistered units were 7.23 lakhs of the total number of units (35.72 lakhs) in 2002-03. From Table 4.1, it is clear that the growth rate of the SSI units had declined from 6.14 per cent in 1993-94 to 4.92 per cent in 2000-01 but the number of SSI units increased from 19.4 lakh units in 1990-91 to 35.72 lakh units in 2002-03. It is inferred that despite there is a growth of number of SSI units in India, after liberalization, the percentage of growth rate has declined due to the policy changes in the SSI sector.

The State-wise registered SSI units in India during the period from 1987-88 to 2005-06 is given in Table 4.2. Table 4.2 indicates that the registered SSI were at higher level (more than 50,000 units) in the States of Punjab, U.P., M.P., Pondicherry in the year1987-88. But at the time of implementation of NEP (1990), more than 2 lakhs were registered SSI units in Tamil Nadu. At present, the registered SSI units in Tamil Nadu was higher among the various States.

Table 4.2 : State-wise and Year-wise Number of Registered SSI Units in India

Sl. No.	States/UTs	1987-88 (1)	1995-96 (2)	1996-97 (3)	1997-98 (4)	1998-99 (5)	1999-00 (6)	2000-01 (7)	2001-02 (8)	2002-03 (9)	2003-04 (10)	2004-05 (11)	2005-06 (12)
1.	Jammu and Kashmir	9080	25165	26363	28471	29387	30667(P)	32040	39680	32462	32051	16753	17131
2	Himachal Pradesh	6983	14015	14593	15232	15941	16602	17562	17432	18029	18493	12475	12801
3.	Punjab	51507	145471	147563	149405	151180	152768	161598	154686	155507	156001	66608	66997
4.	Chandigrah	1310	2880	2952	2965	3007	3042	3218	2704	3106	3138	1376	1370
5.	Uttaranchal	NA	NA	NA	NA	NA	NA	NA	27415	35870	36136	17911	19433
6.	Haryana	23481	94462	98455	63623	53321	54375	88271	67413	55552	55681	40305	40454
7.	Delhi	10188	25174	25284	25303	25306	25342	26807	15740	19808	19802	7477	7518
8.	Rajasthan	29477	71479	74450	77047	80229	83651	88486	84256	91881	93427	51033	53248
9.	Uttar Pradesh	53370	302557	323475	341788	361033	382027(P)	402606	289569	393894	397010	192140	212367
10.	Bihar	35366	101221	108148	114296	119107	123933(P)	130903	74491	92928	95299	57589	59077
11.	Sikkim	66	275	296	305	312	130(P)	349	338	339	353	213	218
12.	Arunachal Pradesh	326	766	926	945	959	971	1027	579	643	724	355	376
13.	Nagaland	183	741	757	782	813	1059	1120	698	1761	2037	1645	1874
14.	Manipur	2078	4928	5157	5314	5439	5588	5911	5778	5876	5840	4832	4872
15.	Mizoram	917	3018	3515	3702	4028	4413	4668	4217	4951	5078	3361	3483
16.	Tripura	800	5833	5901	5946	6001	6058	6406	2039	2133	2163	1033	1038
17.	Meghalaya	588	2005	2166	2323	2514	2711	2868	3768	3098	4312	2800	2813
18.	Assam	4430	19242	20721	21954	23196	24109	25503	24947	26945	28103	17834	19032
19.	West Bengal	46795	145713	147462	149148	150327	151340	160087	69269	154125	155076	44374	44768
20.	Jharkhand	NA	NA	NA	NA	NA	NA	NA	33021	41448	41760	20017	20616
21.	Orissa	8328	16623	17173	17931	18732	19513	20641	22324	23590	23757	14327	14835
22.	Chhattisgarh	NA	NA	NA	NA	NA	NA	NA	62979	40157	67800	36396	36870
23.	Madhya Pradesh	76218	233225	243481	256849	268741	277804	289042	171376	216194	217175	119425	126876
24.	Gujarat	35000	129455	141951	153497	164785	174899	185008	178261	193758	200245	157385	162654

Table 4.2 : (*Contd.*)

25. Daman and Diu	147	693	920	1135	1455	1507	1594	1505	1910	2081	1402	1319
26. Dadra and Nagar Haveli	152	409	454	618	870	978	1035	1135	1374	1623	1089	1120
27. Maharashtra	39210	112916	117132	121039	124950	128321	135738	102761	132176	133127	66210	66989
28. Andhra Pradesh	40525	115353	124504	143073	150675	159944	169189	165341	182215	186329	127007	130418
29. Karnataka	2772	5118	5278	5488	5761	5921	6263	4842	6476	6628	2544	2611
30. Goa	NA	47	51	58	63	72	76	84	86	93	92	98
31. Lakshadweep	25717	133114	148275	166484	184166	202325	214019	224524	243401	249551	165191	167478
32. Kerala	57213	202210	228936	257079	284943	313861	332002	309162	384336	404783	240130	258493
33. Tamil Nadu	2159	4209	4255	4484	4722	4873	5155	4362	5188	5393	2201	2268
34. Pondichery Islands	NA	NA	NA	NA	NA	NA	NA	NA	1295	NA	NA	NA
35. Nicobar	323	1038	1071	1116	1151	1180	1248	1210	NA	1399	870	941
INDIA	593769	2017499	2152794	2261256	2378070	2503641	2672188	2305725	2735652	2808149	1587281	1657096

Source : Ministry of SSI, New Delhi, 2006.

Table 4.3 shows that there was no change in the location of the SSI units during the periods 1987-88 and 1994-95. The employment generation of SSI units in rural areas had increased from 33.3 per cent in 1987-88 to 34.4 per cent in 1994.95. But the production level of the rural SSI units in India had increased from 26.8 per cent to 34.9 per cent during the same period. The results of the *urban SSI* units in terms of number of units, production and employment is presented in Table 4.4. It is clear that the employment generation by urban SSI units had declined from 66.7 per cent in 1987-88 to 65.6 per cent in 1994-95.

Investment Level of SSI in India

The fixed investment level of SSI sector in India is given in Table 4.5. Table 4.5. clearly indicates the year-wise and category-wise performance of SSI during the period of 11 years (1990-91 to 2002-03). The highest level of investment was increased in every year during the period from 1996-97 to 2000-01.

The Government (Central and States) have taken a number of measures to solve the problems of these industries, such as lack of credit facilities, modern technology, new innovations, organized marketing, unsatisfactory arrangements for the supply of raw materials and competition from large-scale units. In 1996-97, the fixed investments level at current price is Rs.64,839 and it increased to Rs.89,276 lakhs in 2001-02 .

Through an extensive nation-wide survey of small-scale industries, which stood registered as on March 31,1988, extremely useful insights came up on their operation, separately for rural and urban areas. A similar survey of small-scale industries, although based on a much smaller sample-size, was undertaken during 1994-95 also. In this section, we bring out some important insights emanating out of these two surveys; for fixed investment at the two-digit level of industrial grouping, the rural-urban break-up is not available for the 1994-95 survey. The small-scale industrial sector consists of a highly desparate group of units, varying markedly in terms of capital employed the range of market

Table 4.3 : Percent Share of Rural Areas in Production Units, Employment, Production and Fixed Investment in Small Scale Industrial Sector by Major Industry Group: 1987-88 and 1994-95

Broad Industry Group		*Percentage share of Rural Areas*							
		No. of Units		*Employment*		*Production*		*Fixed Investment*	
		1987-88	*1994-95*	*1987-88*	*1994-95*	*1987-88*	*1994-95*	*1987-88*	*1994-95*
	(1)	*(2)*	*(3)*	*(4)*	*(5)*	*(6)*	*(7)*	*(8)*	*(9)*
Food Products	(20+21)	63.2	61.9	53.5	50.8	42.9	36.4	48.5	—
Beverages	(22)	484	45.6	19.9	30.6	14.0	20.4	32.1	—
Cotton Textiles	(23)	27.3	36.7	22.2	32.2	19.9	4.1	25.2	—
Wool Synthetic	(24)	38.4	35.3	20.4	28.5	8.1	37.4	18.3	—
Jute, Mesta	(25)	25.6	37.9	29.8	27.6	11.3	7.0	36.1	—
Textile Products	(26)	54.1	51.0	23.4	21.8	7.0	37.5	15.3	—
Wood Products	(27)	55.6	54.8	46.9	49.0	35.5	11.9	42.7	—
Paper Products	(28)	16.4	21.4	15.2	20.9	12.8	19.5	16.8	—
Leather Products	(29)	58.0	47.8	31.0	30.3	33.4	84.9	29.2	—
Chemical Products	(30)	25.8	34.3	26.0	37.6	23.1	41.3	29.0	—
Rubber Plastic Coal Products	(31)	29.3	37.2	34.0	40.0	28.0	29.6	30.4	—
Non-met. Min Products	(32)	55.3	57.8	62.1	58.6	56.1	12.5	54.4	—
Basic Metal	(33)	14.0	22.4	19.8	34.8	21.3	47.3	22.4	—
Metal Products	(34)	34.2	33.9	23.7	26.6	23.8	9.3	20.5	—
Non-Electrical Machinery	(35)	17.9	24.2	13.0	21.0	10.3	12.5	14.3	—
Electrical Machinery	(36)	12.0	21.2	11.5	20.9	11.8	24.6	14.7	—
Transport Equp.	(37)	26.0	30.6	16.0	22.8	12.9	83.7	17.9	—
Other Manufacturing umits	(38)	22.6	23.6	17.1	22.2	11.2	7.7	16.3	—
All Manufacturing		42.2	42.2	33.3	34.4	26.8	34.9	29.4	—

Source: Ministry of SSI, Nirman Bhavan, New Delhi.

Table 4.4 : Percent Share of Urban Areas in Production Units, Employment, Production and Fixed Investment in Small Scale Industrial Sector by Major Industry Group: 1987-88 and 1994-95.

Broad Industry Group		*Percentage Share of Urban Areas*							
		No. of Units		*Employment*		*Production*		*Fixed Investment*	
		1987-88	*1994-95*	*1987-88*	*1994-95*	*1987-88*	*1994-95*	*1987-88*	*1994-95*
	(1)	*(2)*	*(3)*	*(4)*	*(5)*	*(6)*	*(7)*	*(8)*	*(9)*
Food Products	(20+21)	36.8	38.1	46.5	49.2	57.1	63.6	51.9	—
Beverages	(22)	51.6	54.4	80.1	69.4	86.0	79.6	67.9	—
Cotton Textiles	(23)	72.7	63.3	77.8	67.8	80.1	95.9	74.8	—
Wool Synthetic	(24)	61.6	64.7	79.6	71.5	91.9	62.6	81.7	—
Jute, Mesta	(25)	74.4	62.1	70.2	72.4	88.7	93.0	63.9	—
Textile Products	(26)	45.9	49.0	76.6	78.2	93.0	62.5	84.7	—
Wood Products	(27)	44.4	45.2	53.1	51.0	64.5	88.1	57.3	—
Paper Products	(28)	83.6	78.6	84.8	79.1	87.2	80.5	83.2	—
Leather Products	(29)	42.0	52.2	69.0	69.7	66.6	15.1	70.8	—
Chemical Products	(30)	74.2	65.7	74.0	62.4	76.9	58.7	71.0	—
Rubber Plastic Coal Products	(31)	70.7	62.8	66.0	60.0	72.0	70.4	69.6	—
Non-met. Min Products	(32)	44.7	42.2	37.9	41.4	43.9	87.5	45.6	—
Basic Metal	(33)	86.0	77.6	80.2	65.2	78.7	52.7	77.6	—
Metal Products	(34)	65.8	66.1	76.3	73.4	76.2	90.7	79.5	—
Non -Electrical Machinery	(35)	82.1	75.8	87.0	79.0	89.7	87.5	85.7	—
Electrical Machinery	(36)	88.0	78.8	88.5	79.1	88.2	75.4	85.3	—
Transport Equp.	(37)	74.0	69.4	84.0	77.2	87.1	16.3	82.1	—
Other Manufacturing Units	(38)	77.4	76.4	82.9	77.8	88.8	92.3	83.7	—
All Manufacturing		57.8	57.8	66.7	65.6	73.2	65.1	70.6	—

Source: Ministry of SSI, Nirman Bhavan, New Delhi.

Table 4.5 : Fixed Investment in SSI Sector in India

Year	*Fixed Investment at Current Prices (Rs. in lakhs)*
1996-97	64839 (13.57)
1997-98	70891 (9.33)
1998-99	77531 (9.37)
1999-2000	82411 (6.29)
2000-01	89276 (8.33)

Source : Ministry of SSI, Nirman Bhavan, New Delhi, 2002.
Note : Figures within parenthesis denotes the growth rate.

operation, linkages with higher echelons of industrial enterprises, and so on. All these details are not available separately for units in rural and urban areas. All the same, rural-urban contrasts can be captured in a variety of ways.

Tables 4.6 and 4.7 set out rural-urban and backward, non-backward area differences in respect of a few important indicators. For rural areas, the share of each of the total fixed investment, and investment in plant and machinery, and employment is much lower than their share in the number of units while the reverse is true for metropolitan cities; for urban areas, all the shares generally move in tandem. Consequently, per unit levels are the lowest for rural areas, next higher for urban areas, and much higher for metropolitan cities, practically for all indicators.

Table 4.6 : Investment Level of Small Scale Industries in India by Rural-Urban Location 1987-88 and 1994-95

Area of Location	*Percent share in*				*Working Capital*	
	Fixed Investment		*Investment P&M*			
	1987-88	*1994-95*	*1987-88*	*1994-95*	*1987-88*	*1994-95*
Rural	29.4	14.4	28.6	35.2	22.4	29.1
Urban	52.0	49.1	51.0	48.9	50.7	54.2
Metropolitan	18.6	36.5	20.4	15.9	26.9	16.6
All	100.0	100.0	100.0	100.0	100.0	100.0
Backward	46.6	39.8	45.3	38.7	36.4	36.5
Non-Backward	53.4	60.2	54.7	61.3	63.6	63.5

Sources : (1) Government of India, Report of the Second All-India Small Scale Industrial Units 1987-88, Ministry of Industry, August, 1992.
(2) Government of India, Report on Sample Survey of Small Scale Industrial Units 1994-95,Ministry of SSI and ARI,2000.
P & M – Plant & Machinery.

Table 4.7 : Some Structural Parameters in Small Scale Industrial Sector by Rural-Urban Location: 1987-88 and 1994-95

Area of Location	*Fixed Investment*		*Per Unit Level (000'Rs.)*			
			Investment in P&M		*Working Capital*	
	1987-88	*1994-95*	*1987-88*	*1994-95*	*1987-88*	*1994-95*
Rural	111	267	65	167	65	481.31
Urban	173	313	101	202	130	781.74
Metropolitan	302	478	197	342	334	1249.27
All	160	309	95	200	123	698.29
Backward	120	255	69	160	72	527.7
Non-Backward	225	360	138	238	206	857.8

Sources :(1) Government of India, Report of the Second All-India Small Scale Industrial Units 1987-88, Ministry of Industry, August, 1992.

(2) Government of India, Report on Sample Survey of Small Scale Industrial Units 1994-95,Ministry of SSI and ARI,2000.

P & M – Plant & Machinery.

On an average, during 1987-88, for a small-scale unit in urban areas, investment in fixed assets or in plant and machinery was 50-60 per cent higher while the number of persons employed was only about 25-30 per cent more than with its rural counterpart. The rural-urban gaps have tended to widen, most markedly in respect of employment per unit, during 1987-88 and 1994-95. It implies that the employment content of every unit of capital invested is relatively higher with rural units compared with urban units, and still higher compared with metropolitan units. In recent years, the employment content of capital invested in rural units has gone up still further.

Production of SSI in India

The category-wise production level of small scale enterprise for the period from 1990-91 to 2000-01 is given in Table 4.8. The Table 4.8 reveals that the production value of SSI during the study period (1990-91 to 2002-03) was increased from Rs. 1,55,340 crores to Rs. 7,42,021 crores. The growth rate of production was only 7.1 per cent in 1993-94 and 8.23 per cent in 2001-02.

Table 4.8 : The Production Performance of SSI Sector in India

(*Rs. in crores*)

Year	*Production (at current prices)*	*Growth Rate*	*Production*	*Growth Rate*
1991-92	1,78,699	(15.0)	1,60.156	(3.10)
1992-93	2,09300	(17.1)	2,25,626	(40.87)
1993-94	2,41,648	(15.4)	2,41,648	(7.1)
1994-95	2,98,886	(23.69)	2,66,054	(10.10)
1995-96	3,62,656	(21.34)	2,96,385	(11.40)
1996-97	4,11,858	(13.5)	3,29,935	(11.3)
1997-98	4,62,641	(12.3)	3,57,749	(8.43)
1998-99	5,20,650	(12.54)	38,52,296	(6.8)
1999-2000	5,72,887	(10.03)	4,16,736	(10.8)
2000-01	6,45,496	(12.67)	4,50,450	(8.09)
2001-02	6,70,316	(8.03)	4,51,033	(8.23)
2002-03	7,42,021	(7.5)	5,14,292	(7.5)
1,55,340	-	1,55,340	-	*Note*

Figures within parenthesis denotes growth rate.

Source: Ministry of SSI, Nirman Bhavan, New Delhi.

Employment Level of SSI in India

The major aim of development policy in India is to provide employment to its million of unemployed. India's economy is agricultural oriented, but the rapid rise in its population with consequent pressure on land has led the planners to lay greater emphasis on decentralised industrial development. The core of the problem in countries like India is surplus agricultural labour and obsolescence of traditional small scale industries, giving rise to a large number of unemployment labour. The employment provided by the small scale industries is depicted in Table. 4.9.

Small Scale Industries has generated employment to 185.64 lakhs (4.03% growth rate) in the year 2000-01 as against 129.80 lakhs (3.59% growth rate) in the year 1991-92. The performance of employment generation has been continuously increasing over the period of ten years. All types of small scale industries had generated large amount of employment opportunities to rural people. It has contributed 178.5 lakhs (4.03% of growth) which is increased to 185.64 lakhs (4.0% of growth) in the year 2002-03.

Table 4.9 : Employment Level in SSI Sector in India

Year	*Employment (No. in Lakhs)*
1990-91	125.30
1991-92	129.80 (3.59)
1992-93	134.06 (3.3)
1993-94	139.38 (4.0)
1994-95	146.56 (5.15)
1995-96	152.61 (4.13)
1996-97	160.00 (4.8)
1997-98	167.20 (4.5)
1998-99	171.58 (2.62)
1999-2000	178.5 (4.03)
2000-01	185.64 (4.0)
2001-02	192.23 (3.5)
2002-03	199.65 (3.9)

Note : Figures within parenthesis denotes percentage.
Source: Ministry of SSI, Nirman Bhavan, New Delhi.

Table 4.10 : Investment Level of Small Scale Industries, in India by Rural-Urban Location 1987-88 and 1994-95

Area of Location	*Employment*		*Employment per Unit*	
	1987-88	*1994-95*	*1987-88*	*1994-95*
Rural	33.3	15.1	4.97	3.0
Urban	50.4	49.0	6.61	8.5
Metropolitan	16.3	36.0	10.4	32.7
All	100.0	100.0	-	8.5
Backward	-	38.5	-	6.7
Non-backward	-	61.5	-	10.1

Source : Government of India, Report of the Second All India Small Scale Industry Units 1987-88, Ministry of Industry, August, 1997.

Export Performance of Small Scale Sector

The erratic availability of raw materials and their rising prices present formidable difficulties in adhering to the schedules of production and maintaining the production cost ultimately they create serious problem at the sales stage. Small units, which fare-well in normal times, hardly to anything to cultivate and develop the sales systematically. As a result of it, they suffer and shiver even with the slighted depression. The attitude of the small scale entrepreneurs towards selling the products is a crucial factor in the success and growth of his enterprise.

On the expórts front, there has been an increase with Rs. 9,664 crores worth exports in 1990-91 which has over the years increased to Rs. 43,946 crores in 1997-98. The figures of exports for the years 1998-99 and 1999-2000 are Rs. 48,979 crores and Rs. 54,200.47 crores respectively, with the increase over the previous years in percentage terms being 11.45 per cent and 10.66 per cent respectively. The provisional/estimated figure for export for the year 2000-01 is 59,978 crore showing an increase of 10.66 per cent over 2000-01.

Table 4.11: Export Performance of SSI Sector in India

Year	*Export (Rs. in crores)*
1990-91	9,664 (26.74)
1991-92	13,883 (43.65)
1992-93	17,784 (28.11)
1993-94	25,307 (42.29)
1994-95	29,068 (14.86)
1995-96	36,470 (25.50)
1996-97	39,249 (7.61)
1997-98	44,442 (11.97)
1998-99	48,979 (11.45)
1999-00	54,200 (10.66)
2000-01	69,796 (10.66)
2001-02	71,243 (2.07)
2002-03	86,012 (20.72)

Note : Figures within parenthesis denote growth rate.
Source: Ministry of SSI, Nirman Bhavan, New Delhi, 2004.

The level of export of SSI products had increased from Rs. 17,784 crores (28.11) in 1992-93 to Rs. 59,978 crores (10.66) in 2000-01. Even though, there is a growth of 5 times in export of SSI products, the growth rate of the export had fallen year by year.

Export from the small scale sector over a period of time has acquired great significance in India's foreign trade. The SSI sector today constitutes a very important segment of India's economy and it accounts for nearly 40 per cent of the gross value of output in the manufacturing sector and about 50 per cent of the total exports from the country.

The small industries due to their inherent strength of low capital investment, high employment generation, maximum utilization of capacity, flexibility in operation, etc. are highly conducive for rapid industrialization and generation of export surpluses.Direct export from the SSI sector accounts for 35 per cent of the total exports and non-traditional products account for more than 95 per cent of the SSI exports.

There is three-fold increases in exports of SSI products. The sports goods, readymade garments, woolen garments and knitwear, plastic products, processed food and leather products dominate in exports of SSI sector. Export promotion from the small scale sector has been awarded a high priority in India's export promotion strategy.

Performance of SSI under DIC in India

The District Industries Centers programmes was initiated in May, 1978, as a centrally sponsored scheme. With the objective of developing the small tiny and cottage sector industries in the country and to generate greater employment opportunities especially among rural and backward areas. The establishment of DICs at the district level aimed at providing support facilities/ concessions/services in dispensed rural areas and other small towns. There were 430 centrally approved DICs which covered almost all parts of the country except metropolitan cities at the time of the withdrawal of the central sponsorship in 1993-94.

At present, there were 520 DICs have been set up almost one for each district throughout the country and DICs are being operated by respective States. Under DIC programme, the

Table 4.12 : Export in India

(Rupees in crores)

Year	*Food Based*	*Forest Based*	*Animal Husbandry Based*	*Textile Based*	*Chemical Based*	*Engineering Based*	*Miscellaneous Based*	*Total*
1991-92	603.9	187.4	3066.8	5868.6	2166.2	1390.0	600.7	13883.4
1992-93	840.5	240.1	3460.8	8274.1	2287.2	1950.0	732.2	17784.9
1993-94	1716.0	193.7	3921.1	1331.7	2874.2	2065.0	1170.2	13271.9
1994-95	1761.7	111.8	5065.0	1515.7	3270.0	2325.0	1377.8	15427.1
1995-96	5155.8	237.6	5534.8	17596.3	3517.5	3025.0	1403.2	36470.2
1996-97	4868.6	520.3	4153.0	19423.4	5399.2	3390.0	1493.9	39248.4
1997-98	4620.2	358.4	5954.7	19509.8	7967.0	4400.0	1632.0	44442.1
1998-99	6253.1	543.5	4643.1	24766.9	4869.0	4818.0	3088.8	48982.4
1999-00	4392.06	734.46	5853.0	24705.72	7644.8	5420.0	4152.32	52902.36

Source : Ministry of SSI, Nirman Bhavan, New Delhi, 2002.

entrepreneurs will get all the facilities and assistance under one roof at the district and sub-district level.

The extension services provided by the DICs include:

1. Dissemination of information,
2. Supply of machinery and equipment,
3. Provision of raw materials and quality inputs,
4. Arrangement for credit facilities,
5. Marketing and consultancy.

DIC programme has emerged as the focal point for all industrial activities at district level.

The performance and growth of Small Scale Industries are analysed by four important indicators, namely number of units, Employment, Investment, and Production. The overall performance of Small Scale Industry Enterprises in India is exhibited in Tables 4.13 and 4.14.

Tables 4.13 and 4.14 reveals that the numbers of small scale units under DIC were increased from 1376 units in 1987-88 to 9348 units in 1998-99. After the implementation of New Economic Policy, there is a tremendous growth in the number of units under DIC in India. The growth rate is 579.6 per cent.

The small scale sector plays a vital role for the growth of the country. It contribute 579.6 per cent Growth Rate in number of Units, 511.1 per cent Growth Rate in Employment, 650.3 per cent Growth Rate in Fixed Investment and 213.3 per cent Growth Rate in Production. The Fixed Investment level had the highest growth rate.

It has been estimated that a lakh rupee of investment in fixed assets in SSI sector produces 4.62 lakh worth of goods and services. The small scale sector has grown rapidly over the years.

The output of SSI sector rose from Rs. 7200 crores in 1973-74 to Rs. 155340 crores in 1990-91 and is estimated to Rs. 645496 crores during 2000-01.

Table 4.13 : State-wise Performance of India

Sl. No.	Name of the States Union Territory	No. of Units under DIC 1987-88	No. of Units under DIC 1998-99	Employment generated Per DIC (Number) 1987-88	Employment generated Per DIC (Number) 1998-99
1.	Andaman and Nicobar	162	527	836	2256
2.	Andhra Pradesh	1705	5774	12006	36400
3.	Arunachal Pradesh	NA	NA	NA	NA
4.	Assam	277	1864	2155	9139
5.	Bihar	916	7662	4784	12464
6.	Chandigarh	NA	2960	NA	28300
7.	Dadra and Nagar Haveli	244	873	4200	11651
8.	Daman and Diu	79	732	617	12192
9.	Delhi	10038	130218	121972	1171962
10.	Goa	1636	2883	11329	19716
11.	Gujarat	1813	8249	14577	45417
12.	Haryana	1946	7458	8805	42012
13.	Himachal Pradesh	582	2271	2128	9541
14.	Jammu and Kashmir	649	1864	2904	8087
15.	Karnataka	2133	10978	12844	53537
16.	Kerala	1837	12670	12094	58520
17.	Lakshadweep	NA	122	NA	515
18.	Madhya Pradesh	1642	6365	3529	15019
19.	Maharashtra	995	7832	11863	52087
20.	Manipur	260	761	1277	3785
21.	Meghalaya	117	654	956	3719
22.	Mizoram	306	1300	1408	7819
23.	Nagaland	NA	NA	NA	NA
24.	Orissa	553	2162	4620	14272
25.	Pondicherry	305	1071	2180	8686
26.	Punjab	3778	16445	17184	71167
27.	Rajasthan	1076	3491	4539	14921
28.	Sikkim	22	99	344	965
29.	Tamil Nadu	3011	17086	28231	100746
30.	Tripura	NA	NA	NA	NA
31.	Uttar Pradesh	935	6280	612	25775
32.	West Bengal	2872	10446	19490	38415
	All India	1376	9348	10603	64796
	Growth Rate (%)		579.6		511.1

Source: Handbook of Statistics, 1989, DIC(SSI) New Delhi and compiled from SIDBI Report on SSI.

Note : Indicates for the year 1996-97,

N.A : Not available.

Table.4.14 : State-wise Performance of SSI in India

Sl. No	Name of the States/ Union Territory	Fixed Investment Per (DIC) (Rs. Million) 1987-88	1998-99	Production per (DIC) Rs. Million 1987-88	1998-99
1.	Andaman and Nicbar	21.0	39.5	45.0	230.0
2.	Andhra Pradush	272.1	736.3	NA	NA
3.	Arunachal Pradesh	NA	NA	NA	NA
4.	Assam	58.6	926.3	189.0	372.8
5.	Bihar	87.7	213.3	231.0	479.9
6.	Chandigrah	NA	8247	NA	7900
7.	Dadra and Nagar Haveli	160.0	1530	1100	21000
8.	Daman and Diu	NA	NA	NA	NA
9.	Delhi	4012.0	26040*	25306*	65100*
10.	Goa	254.0	1095.5	NA	NA
11.	Gujarat	467.1	2901.0	NA	NA
12.	Haryana	296.6	1265.2	1469.9	3130.4
13.	Himachal Pradesh	67.3	470.3	204.3	NA
14.	Jammu and Kashmir	80.9	954.5	216.5	919.9
15.	Karnataka	347.8	2026.9	1329.9	NA
16.	Kerala	276.8	1878.8	812.1	5724.6
17.	Ladshadweep	NA	9.0	NA	69.0
18.	Madhya Pradesh	57.8	300.2	437.2	NA
19.	Maharashtra	420.1	7533.9	3503.9	NA
20.	Manipur	26.0	46.9	37.4	NA
21.	Meghalaya	17.8	49.4	54.0	NA
22.	Mizoram	46.3	193.3	49.0	426.7
23.	Nagaland	NA	NA	NA	NA
24.	Orissa	104.3	580.1	438.2	NA
25.	Pondicherry	90.5	564.3	450.0	5697.8
26.	Punjab	472.8	2837.5	2313.7	12500.0
27.	Rajasthan	134.9	903.3	541.0	NA
28.	Sikkim	26.0	53.7	38.7	120.3
29.	Tamil Nadu	572.0	4100.5	2375.3	0422.2
30.	Tripura	NA	NA	NA	NA
31.	Uttar Pradesh	172.1	611.9	653.9	1808.7
32	West Bengal	268.3	NA	1581.3	NA
	All India	303.8	2279.6	1495.8	4686.3
	Growth Rate (%)		650.3		213.3

Source: Handbook of Statistics, 1989, DIC(SSI) New Delhi and compiled from SIDBI Report on SSI.

Note : Indicates for the year 1996-97,

* Indicates for the year 1997-98, N.A : Not available.

The SSI sector in India creates largest employment opportunities for Indian population next to agriculture. It has been estimated that a lakh rupees of investment in fixed assets in the small scale sector generates employment for four persons. The employment in the SSI sector increased from 39.70 lakhs in 1973-74 to 125.30 lakh in 1990-91 and it increased to 185.64 lakhs in 2000-01. It is clear that a lakh rupee of investment in fixed assets in the small scale sector generates employments for four persons.

Table 4.15 : Distribution of Number of Units and Output in Major Branches of Small Scale Industrial Sector by Location 1987-88

Area of Location		*Percentage Share within Production Location*					
		Mfg/ Assmbling only	*Processing*	*Job Work*	*Repairing Services*	*Combined*	*Overall*
Rural	A	37.00	58.60	38.60	45.90	40.20	42.20
	B	24.80	43.00	30.50	27.50	18.00	26.80
Urban	A	50.40	36.00	51.30	50.80	45.30	48.00
	B	52.30	44.30	45.00	56.20	48.60	50.90
Metropolitan	A	12.60	5.40	10.10	3.30	12.50	9.80
	B	22.90	12.70	24.50	16.30	33.40	22.30
All	A	100.00	100.00	100.00	100.00	100.00	100.00
	B	100.00	100.00	100.00	100.00	100.00	100.00
Backward	A	57.10	71.00	61.60	70.50	63.00	62.20
	B	40.70	56.90	32.50	60.00	32.40	42.20
Non-Backward	A	42.90	29.00	38.40	29.50	36.70	37.80
	B	59.30	43.10	67.50	40.00	67.60	57.80

Sources :(1) Government of India, Report of the Second All-India Small Scale Industrial Units 1987-88, Ministry of Industry, August, 1992.

(2) Government of India, Report on Sample Survey of Small Scale Industrial Units 1994-95, Ministry of SSI and ARI, 2000.

P & M – Plant & Machinery.

From Table 4.15, it is evident that the performance of DIC programme was commendable and the number of SSI units (10.5) per DIC had increased from 1376 in 1987-88 to 9348 units in 1998-99. The employment generated per DIC in 1987-88 was 10603 and it was increased to 64796 in 1998-99. The ratio of investment to production was 1:4.9 in 1987-88 and it was declined to 1:2.1 in 1998-99. The rate of growth in production and investment is not responding to the growth rate of the SSI units.

According to the SSI sector survey conducted by Ministry and National Informatics Centre, food products industry ranked first in generating employment (13.1%) As per the survey, the per unit employment was the highest (20) in units engaged in beverages, tobacco products and next ranks textile products (17). The exports of SSI sector constitutes Rs. 393 crores in 1973-74 and it rose to Rs. 9664 crores in 1990-91 and is expected to a target level of Rs. 59978 crores in 2000-2001.

Table 4.16 looks at the share of rural areas as also of the backward areas, for the same set of industrial activities as in Table 4.15. The small size and inferior position of the rural units is evident from the fact that under each type of industrial activity, their share of production is smaller than their share in the number of units. In metropolitan cities, it is reverse while in respect of urban units, there is a nodding balance between the two shares. The backward area units share the fate of rural units.

Table 4.16 : Distribution of Number of Units and Output in Major Branches of Small Scale Industrial Sector by Location 1994-95

Area of Location		*Percentage Share within Production Location*					
		Mfg/ Assmbling only	*Processing*	*Job Work*	*Repairing Services*	*Combined*	*Overall*
Rural	A	38.40	57.10	44.00	43.50	38.40	42.20
	B	33.40	54.20	3.50	33.70	66.30	34.90
Urban	A	50.10	38.00	46.30	52.30	51.80	48.50
	B	47.00	35.40	92.10	51.40	26.50	48.10
Metropolitan	A	11.50	5.00	9.70	4.20	9.80	9.30
	B	19.50	10.40	4.30	14.90	7.20	17.00
All	A	100.00	100.00	100.00	100.00	100.00	100.00
	B	100.00	100.00	100.00	100.00	100.00	100.00
Backward	A	43.60	61.60	47.10	56.10	49.4	48.30
	B	37.20	62.60	5.90	34.70	67.10	38.70
Non-Backward	A	56.40	38.40	52.90	43.90	50.60	51.70
	B	62.80	37.40	94.10	65.30	32.90	61.30

Note: A share in Units B share in output.
Source : The same as in Table 4.15.

Tables 4.15 and 4.16 give a more detailed picture, for 1987-

88 and 1994-95, on rural areas share in the number of small-scale units, employment, fixed investment (for 1987-88 only) and production, for 18 two-digit level major industry groups. In particular, industrial activities based on raw materials originating in rural areas (e.g. food processing, beverages and tobacco products, cotton textiles, wool and silk textiles, wood, paper and leather products, etc.) would have an entirely different competitive complexion compared with those which draw upon materials, skills, markets, etc. from the urban areas.

Although the relative placement of the four types of shares differ from one industry group to the other, in rural and in urban (inclusive of metropolitan) areas, yet, on a broad plane, it is fairly obvious that for most of the agro-processing industries in the rural areas, the employment, investment and production shares do not deviate much from one another. It is equally noticeable, however, that the share of rural units in all these categories is much higher than the other three shares. It follows that rural units in all these branches are of relatively smaller size, most notably in terms of per unit level of output. Such rural-urban differentials were discernible earlier also when we looked at the employment and production structure of the unorganized manufacturing sector.

Many among the other set of industries portray a sharp contrast. For example, for rural units engaged in the manufacture of rubber and plastic products, chemicals and chemical products, non-metallic mineral products, basic metal products, electrical machinery, etc., there is a remarkable balance among the four types of shares. These are the modern small-scale industries located in rural areas perhaps under the special development programmes and possibly due to the well-measured economic calculus of urban entrepreneurs, and so on. The tendency of proliferation, discernible on a subdued scale, under the agro-based group of industries, is ruled out in their case; their location and operation are selective and hopefully governed by a pre-calculated economic rationale of the entrepreneurs engaged in such enterprises. The outcome is thus reassuring; the case of rural industrialization need not necessarily be prompted by employment consideration alone; in the matter of fixed investment and production shares too, such industries in rural areas compare well with their urban counterparts.

2. Performance of SSI in Tamil Nadu

The share of Tamil Nadu in all India production of small scale industries has been significant. The main problem of these industries is that of low productivity and they could sustain only when the demand is generated by projecting the projects as socially desirable. As the Narasima Committee has point out, these industries have to face stiff and unfair competition from large scale organized units. The Committee recommended establishment of Marketing Corporation to look into the problems of marketing.

The volume of production in small scale industries in Tamil Nadu is given in Table 4.17. Table reveals that the number of small scale industries was 138404 units in 1991-92 and it increased to 387597 units in 2000-01. The growth of number of SSI units are at 3 times after the NEP implementation. Similarly, the investment level also increased from Rs. 3210.20 crores in 1991-92 to Rs. 11567.22 crores in 2000-01 after Economic Reforms. The production level had contributed to the extent of Rs. 16747 crores in 1991-92 and Rs. 78261.66 in 2000-01.

The employment level had generated 1176700 persons in 1991-92 and 2902122 persons in 2000-01 in the SSI sector. It has increased at double level to total employment in Small Seale Industries.

Table 4.17 : Performance of SSI in Tamil Nadu from 1991-92 to 2000-01

Year	*No. of Units*	*Investment (Rs. in Crores)*	*Production (Rs. in Crores)*	*Employment (No.)*
1991-92	138404	3210.20	16747.00	1176700
1992-93	157892	3757.50	20219.00	1310500
1993-94	178114	4332.00	24048.00	1425300
1994-95	207357	5184.00	29436.00	1638200
1995-96	234409	5977.00	35161.00	1828600
1996-97	263845	6912.00	41687.00	2033000
1997-98	295004	7966.00	48675.00	2250900
1998-99	324627	9350.00	58432.00	2451000
1999-00	354939	10623.00	70987.00	2667200
2000-01	387597	11567.22	78261.66	2902122

Source: Directorate of Industries and Commerce, Chennai, 2002.

Table 4.18 : Number of SSI units in Tamil Nadu after Liberalization

SL No	*District*	*1990*	*1991*	*1992*	*1993*	*1994*	*1995*
1.	North Arcot	7145	7910	8849	10160	NA	NA
2.	South Arcot	5358	6066	6523	7184	NA	NA
3.	Annal (Q.M)	2032	NA	NA	NA	NA	NA
4.	Chengal Pattu	11060	12660	14460	16272	NA	NA
5.	Coimbatore	15089	16826	17252	19524	NA	24792
6.	Dharmapuri	3300	3767	4251	4883	NA	6240
7.	Kanya Kumari	6369	2618	2955	3784	NA	4971
8.	Kamarajar	2392	7213	8033	3858	NA	NA
9.	Chennai	14797	16326	16354	17978	NA	21285
10.	Madurai	6498	7166	7958	8860	NA	11728
11.	Dindigul	NA	2273	2724	3418	NA	5001
12.	Nilgiri	930	971	1154	1549	NA	2139
13.	Pasumpon Thevar	8818	1385	1617	2087	237	NA
14.	Periyar	1220	6215	6968	8180	10456	NA
15.	Pudukkotai	5687	3168	3382	3524	4047	4758
16.	Ramnad	814	964	1151	1553	1710	2184
17.	Salem	11634	13082	14503	16511	18246	22606
18.	Nagapattinnam	NA	NA	5587	2714	3303	3463
19.	Tiruchy	5831	6611	7301	8040	3989	10368
20.	Tirunelveli	6198	3650	3520	4589	5299	6078
21.	V.O. Chidambaranar	NA	3377	3862	4448	5271	NA
22.	Thanjavur	4486	4954	NA	3776	4469	5343
23.	Vellore	NA	NA	NA	NA	NA	11198
24.	Cuddalore	NA	NA	NA	NA	NA	8511
25.	Kanchipuram	NA	NA	NA	NA	NA	21086
26.	Virdhunagar	NA	NA	NA	NA	NA	10838
27.	Sivagangai	NA	NA	NA	NA	NA	2935
28.	Erode	NA	NA	NA	NA	NA	12880
29.	Thothtukudi	NA	NA	NA	NA	NA	6241
30.	Thiruvanamalai	NA	NA	NA	NA	NA	1960
31.	Villupuram	NA	NA	NA	NA	NA	751
32.	Karur	NA	NA	NA	NA	NA	NA
33.	Perambalur	NA	NA	NA	NA	NA	NA
34.	Theni	NA	NA	NA	NA	NA	NA
35.	Namakkal	NA	NA	NA	NA	NA	NA
36.	Thivuvallur	NA	NA	NA	NA	NA	NA
37.	Thiruvarur	NA	NA	NA	NA	NA	NA
	Total	119658	127202	138404	152792	62027	207356

Source: Directorate of Industries and Commerce, Government of Tamil Nadu.

Table 4.18 (*Contel.*)

SL No.	*District*	*1996*	*1997*	*1998*	*1999*	*2000*	*2001*
1.	North Arcot	NA	NA	NA	NA	NA	NA
2.	South Arcot	NA	NA	NA	NA	NA	NA
3.	Annal (Q.M)	NA	NA	NA	NA	NA	NA
4.	Chengal Pattu	NA	NA	NA	NA	NA	NA
5.	Coimbatore	27635	30409	33510	36579	39595	42956
6.	Dharmapuri	7090	8058	9035	10019	10907	11994
7.	Kanya Kumari	5858	6676	7554	8429	9318	10308
8.	Kamarajar	NA	NA	NA	NA	NA	NA
9.	Chennai	24583	27697	30818	33560	36682	40094
10.	Madurai	13447	15827	17351	18539	19616	20813
11.	Dindigul	60707	7033	7938	8892	9835	10697
12.	Nilgiri	2367	2617	2867	3123	NA	3666
13.	Pasumpon Thevar	NA	NA	NA	NA	NA	NA
14.	Periyar	NA	NA	NA	NA	NA	NA
15.	Pudukkotai	5502	NA	7022	7772	NA	9359
16.	Ramnad	2700	NA	3708	4115	NA	5207
17.	Salem	25829	NA	30358	32041	NA	35646
18.	Nagapattinnam	3831	NA	4614	5102	5480	5950
19.	Tiruchy	11848	NA	13474	14197	NA	15727
20.	Tirunelveli	6969	NA	8749	9719	NA	11594
21.	Chidambaraner	NA	NA	NA	NA	NA	NA
22.	Thanjavur	6229	NA	7553	8022	NA	9078
23.	Vellore	12418	13643	14927	16111	17470	18854
24.	Cuddalore	9157	9928	10792	11668	12445	13415
25.	Kanchipuram	21529	24613	26030	27265	28502	29858
26.	Virdhunagar	12464	14104	15602	17236	18860	20257
27.	Sivagangai	9533	NA	4731	5334	NA	6619
28.	Erode	14516	NA	17756	19351	NA	22772
29.	Thothtukudi	7058	NA	8671	9341	NA	11538
30.	Thiruvanamalai	2496	NA	3592	4120	4651	5242
31.	Villupuram	1271	NA	2480	3059	3605	4190
32.	Karur	NA	NA	1408	2420	2949	3542
33.	Perambalur	NA	NA	357	624	988	1270
34.	Theni	NA	NA	908	1510	2204	3067
35.	Namakkal	NA	NA	1153	2192	3068	4098
36.	Thiruvallur	NA	NA	1599	3592	6196	8293
37.	Thiruvarur	NA	NA	347	695	1076	1493
	Total	2,89,037	1,60,605	4,10,599	3,24,627	2,33,347	3,87,597

Source: Directorate of Industries and Commerce, Government of Tamil Nadu, 2002.

Table 4.18 shows that the SSI units had dominated in the districts of Coimbatore (42,956), Chennai (40,094) and Cuddalore (29,858). Many districts were having the SSI units around 5000, especially in Theni (4098), Perambalur (3067), Thiruvanamalai (4190), Thothukudi (5242), Salem (5950), Nilgiri (3666) districts. Most of districts having the vast potentials could not be properly utilized by the SSI sectors in Tamil Nadu. The deliciencing policy helps the SSI entrepreneur to start the new units. So, there is a good responsibility in the starting of new units and the performance in terms of SSI units in Tamil Nadu. The industry wise classification of SSI in Tamil Nadu is given in Table 4.19.

Table 4.19 : Industry Classification of Small Scale Industries in Tamil Nadu

Sl. No.	*Details of Classifaction Industry Group*	*Dindigul*	*Madurai*	*Total*	*%*
1.	Food Products	1308	1931	35002	9.8
2.	Beverages, Tobacco & Tobacco Products	67	92	2680	0.7
3.	Cotton Textile	239	506	23653	6.6
4.	Wool, Silk & Synthetic Fibre Textile	53	185	2670	0.7
	Jute, Hemp and Mesta Products				
5.	Hosiery and Readymade	3	27	319	0.08
6.	Garments	3274	4652	78964	22.2
7.	Wood and Wooden Products	270	670	16421	4.6
8.	Paper and Paper Products	320	1370	20519	5.7
9.	Leather and Leather Products	551	300	10022	5.7
10.	Rubber and Plastic Product	301	937	13173	2.8
11.	Chemical and Chemical Products	176	827	16853	3.7
12.	Non-metalic Mineral Products	343	489	11576	4.7
13.	Basic Metal Products	56	270	5067	3.2
14.	Metal Products and Parts	547	1559	20640	1.4
15.	Machinery Parts except Electrical	505	1314	26054	5.8
16.	Electrical Machinery & Apparatus	126	560	10975	7.3
17.	Transport Equipments	78	425	10094	3.09
18.	Other Manufacturing Industry	1618	3502	50257	2.8
	Total	9835 (2.7)	1961 (0.5)	354939	14.1

Soure: Industries Commissioner and Director of Industries and Commerce, Chennai.

Table 4.19 reveals that the share of Tamil Nadu in number of units of SSI has been significant. It hold the first place of SSI Jute,

Hemp and Mesta products (22.2%)-(78,964), Manufacturing Industry (14.1%)-(50.257), Food and Food Products (9.8%)-(35,002), Machinery Parts and except Electrical (7.3%)-(26054) and Cotton Textiles (6.6%) Cotton Textiles industry group are dominated in Tamil Nadu.

It is clear that during the period from 1991-92 - 2000-01, the SSI units concentrated on the industrially backward groups of Wool, Silk and Synthetic Fibre Textiles, Jute, Hemp and Mesta Products, Beverages, Tabacco and Tobacco Products, Basic Metal Products, Transport Equipments, etc.

3. Performance of SSI in Study Districts (Madurai and Dindigul Districts)

Secondary data regarding the number of units, Investment, Employment were collected from the various reports and annual reports of the Department of SSI. The SSI sector had been sub-divided into 8 categories , such as, Food and Agro-based, Forest based, Animal Husbandry based, Textile based, Chemical based, Mineral based, Engineering based and other Miscellaneous industries. The performance of SSI in the study districts – Dindigul, Madurai are analysed in this section.

From Table 4.20, it is clear that a total of 22241 SSI units were functioning in Madurai district in 2002-02. At the time of implementation of NEP (1991-92), the functioning SSI units were 7958 in Madurai district. The Investment level was Rs.669.9 lakh in the year 2001-02 as against on 172.8 lakh in the year 1991-92. The Employment level of SSI was 63271 persons in 1991-92 and it increased to 166121 persons in the year 2001-02. The production level of SSI was Rs. 4571.46 lakh in 2001-02 as against Rs.899.12 lakh in 1991-92 in Madurai district.

Table 4.21 reveals that the number of registered small scale industry had increased from 7958 in 1991-92 units to 22241 units in 2001-02. During the ten years period, the growth of the small scale industries was high level. The Textile based industry (6235 units) agro-based industries (4038 units), Mineral based industries

(5100 units), Miscelleaneous based industries (2309 units) are dominated in the development performance in Madurai district for the ten years. Due to the Government policy and other unfavourable business condition, the Animal Husbandry based industry (1155 units), Engineering based industry (1006 units) and Chemical based industry (619 units) had the slow growth during the study period.

Table 4.20 : Year-wise performance of SSI in the Madurai District

Year	*No. of Units*	*Investment (Rs.)*	*Employment (No.)*	*Production (Rs.)*
1991-92	7958	172.8	63271	899.12
1992-93	9386	222.5	73556	1266.35
1993-94	10814	272.2	83841	1633.58
1994-95	12243	321.9	94126	2000.82
1995-96	13671	371.6	104411	2368.05
1996-97	15099	421.3	114696	2735.29
1997-98	16528	471.0	124981	3102.52
1998-99	17956	520.7	135266	3469.76
1999-00	19384	570.5	145551	3836.99
2000-01	20813	620.2	155836	4204.23
2001-02	22241	669.9	166121	4571.46

Source: District Industries Centre Record, Madurai, 2002.

Table 4.22 reveals that the maximum limit of the investment was Rs. 121.5 lakhs in Agro based Industry. It is high level performance compared with other industries. The total investment level had increased from Rs. 172.8 lakhs in 1991-92 to 669.9 lakhs in 2001-2002. This district has given more importance to all industry. The Textile based industry Rs.186.8 lakhs and Mineral based industry Rs.152.6 lakhs dominated in the investment performance in Madurai district during the ten years.

Due to the Government policy and other unfavourable business conditions, Animal Husbandary based industry (Rs.33.8 lakhs), the Engineering based industry (Rs.29.3 lakhs) and Chemical based industry (Rs.17.6 lakhs) had the slow growth in the investment level during the study period.

Table 4.21 : Category-wise Classification of Number of Units of SSI in Madurai District (1991-92 to 2001-02)

Year	*Agro & Food Based*	*Forest Based*	*Animal Husbandry Based*	*Textile Based*	*Chemical Based*	*Mineral Based*	*Engineer-ing Based*	*Miscellaneous Based*	*Total*
1991-92	1444	636	413	2231	221	1824	359	830	7958
1992-93	1703	750	487	2631	261	2152	424	978	9386
1993-94	1962	864	562	3031	301	2479	489	1126	10814
1994-95	2222	979	636	3432	340	2807	535	1292	12243
1995-96	2481	1093	710	3832	380	3134	618	1423	13671
1996-97	2740	1207	784	4232	420	3461	683	1572	15099
1997-98	2999	1321	858	4632	459	3789	747	1723	16528
1998-99	3258	1435	932	5033	499	4116	812	1871	17956
1999-00	3518	1549	1007	5433	539	4444	876	2018	19384
2000-01	3777	1664	1081	5834	579	4772	941	2165	20813
2001-02	4038	1779	1155	6235	619	5100	1006	2309	22241

Source: District Industries Centre Record, Madurai, 2002.

Table 4.22 : Category-wise Classification of Investment level of SSI in Madurai District (1991-92 to 2001-02) (Rupees in lakhs)

Year	*Agro & Food Based*	*Forest Based*	*Animal Husbandry Based*	*Textile Based*	*Chemical Based*	*Mineral Based*	*Engineering Based*	*Miscellaneous Based*	*Total*
1991-92	31.4	14.8	9.9	48.4	5.7	40.6	8.8	18.7	172.8
1992-93	40.3	18.7	11.5	62.3	6.2	51.0	10.0	23.1	222.5
1993-94	49.3	22.7	14.1	76.2	7.5	62.4	12.2	28.3	272.2
1994-95	58.4	26.7	16.7	90.2	9.2	73.8	14.5	33.4	321.9
1995-96	67.4	29.7	19.3	104.1	10.3	85.2	16.7	39.5	371.6
1996-97	76.4	34.6	22.8	118.1	12.6	96.5	19.1	44.7	421.3
1997-98	85.4	38.6	24.4	132.9	13.1	108.9	21.3	49.0	471.0
1998-99	94.5	42.6	27.0	146.9	14.4	119.4	23.5	54.0	520.7
1999-00	103.5	46.6	30.6	160.8	16.8	131.8	26.7	59.2	570.5
2000-01	112.5	49.6	32.2	173.8	17.2	142.2	28.0	64.4	620.2
2001-02	121.5	52.6	33.8	186.8	17.6	152.6	29.3	69.6	669.9

Source: District Industries Centre, Madurai, 2002.

The employment generated by the SSI sectors in Madurai district during the study period is exhibited in Table 4.23. It is clear from the table that the SSI had generated employment for 166121 persons in 2001-02. But at the time of implementation of NEP, the employment generation by SSI sector was only 63271 persons in 1992-93. There was a growth of (166121) employment generation in the study period.

Table 4.24 shows that of the total production Rs.4571.46 lakhs the textile units has produced (1281.6 lakhs) in Madurai district in 2001-02. But it was only Rs.899.12 lakhs at the time of implementation of NEP. Following the textile based units (Rs.1281.6 lakhs), Mineral based units (Rs.1048.8 lakhs) and Food based units (Rs.829.5 lakhs) were dominated in the Madurai district of Tamil Nadu.

The block-wise classifications of SSI units in Madurai district is given in Table 4.25. The study found that nearly 50 per cent (48.2%) of the SSI units are located in the Madurai Corporation Limited. The remaining 51.8 per cent of the SSI units are located in the rural areas. The localization of the industries in rural and urban are equal in Madurai district. In Madurai district, Agro-based industry (21.8%) and Engineering based industry (17.0%) are dominated.

Small scale industries are capital light and is suitable to the country like India where capital is deficient. It helps in mobilizing capital. An essentially agrarian economy, people have a tendency to keep there money savings is early. These industries are run with local labour and locally available materials. Thus they help in the proper utilization of local resources.

It is clear from Table 4.26 that 47.8 per cent of SSI units are clear located in Madurai Corporation areas (urban centres) and the order of preference of the SSI entreprenurs in Madurai district are : Textile based (28%), Building based (22.9%), Food based (18.1%) and electric based (10.4%).

Table 4.27 reveals that the maximum level of the investment was Rs. 173.8 in (28%) Textile based industry and Rs.142.2 (22.9%) in Mineral based industry. The minimum level of

Table 4.23 : Category-wise Classification of Employment Level of SSI in Madurai District (1991-92 to 2001-02) (Number of Persons)

Block-wise in Madurai District	*Agro Based*	*Forest Based*	*Animal Husbandry Based*	*Textile Based*	*Chemical Based*	*Mineral Based*	*Engineer-ing Based*	*Miscellaneous Based*	*Total*
1991-92	11482	5059	3287	17737	1762	14508	2861	6571	63271
1992-93	13348	5882	3821	20620	2049	16866	3326	7639	73556
1993-94	15215	6704	4356	23504	2335	19225	3791	8707	83841
1994-95	17081	7526	4890	26387	2622	21583	4256	9776	94126
1995-96	18948	8349	5424	29269	2908	23941	4721	10844	104411
1996-97	20814	9171	5957	32153	3195	26299	5187	11912	114696
1997-98	22681	9994	6493	35036	3481	28658	5652	12980	124981
1998-99	24547	10816	7027	37919	3768	31016	6117	14049	135266
1999-00	26414	11639	7562	40803	4055	33375	6582	15117	145551
2000-01	28280	12461	8096	43686	4341	35733	7047	16185	155836
2001-02	30146	13283	8630	46569	4627	38091	7512	17253	166121

Source: District Industries Centre Record, Madurai.

Table 4.24 : Category-wise Classification of Production Level of SSI in Madurai District (1991-92 to 2001-02)

Block	*Agro Based*	*Forest Based*	*Animal Husbandry Based*	*Textile Based*	*Chemical Based*	*Mineral Based*	*Engineer-ing Based*	*Miscellaneous Based*	*Total*
1991-92	163.1	71.9	47.7	252.0	25.0	206.1	40.6	93.4	899.12
1992-93	229.7	101.2	66.7	355.0	35.3	290.4	57.3	131.5	1266.35
1993-94	296.4	131.6	85.8	458.9	45.4	374.5	74.8	169.6	1633.58
1994-95	363.0	160.1	104.9	561.9	56.2	458.7	90.4	207.7	2000.82
1995-96	429.7	189.3	123.0	663.8	66.9	543.9	107.1	246.9	2368.05
1996-97	496.3	218.7	142.0	766.8	76.2	627.2	123.6	246.9	2735.29
1997-98	563.9	248.1	161.2	869.7	86.4	711.3	140.3	284.1	3102.52
1998-99	629.6	277.5	180.2	972.7	96.7	795.6	156.9	322.2	3469.52
1999-00	696.3	306.8	199.3	1075.6	106.8	879.7	173.5	360.6	3836.99
2000-01	762.9	336.2	218.4	1281.6	117.1	964.0	190.1	398.5	4204.23
2001-02	829.5	365.6	237.5	1325.5	127.4	1048.3	206.7	436.6	4571.46

Source: District Industries Centre Record, Madurai.

Table 4.25 : Block-wise Performance of SSI in Madurai Disrict (2000-01)

Block	*No. of Units*	*Investment Rs.*	*Employment (Persons)*	*Production Rs.*
Alanganallur	613	18.3	4589	123.8
Chellampatti	252	7.5	1887	50.9
Kallikudi	311	9.3	2328	62.8
Kottampatti	514	15.3	3848	103.8
Madurai-East	2131	63.5	15956	430.5
Madurai-West	1749	52.1	13095	353.3
Melur	814	24.3	6095	164.4
Sedapadi	502	14.9	3759	101.4
Thirumangalam	1101	32.8	8244	222.4
Thirupparankundram	902	26.8	6754	182.2
T. Kallupatti	371	11.0	2778	74.9
Usilampatti	814	24.2	6095	164.4
Vadipatti	794	23.6	5945	160.3
Madurai Corporation	9945	296.3	74462	2008.9
Total	20813	620.2	155836	4204.23

Source: District Industries centre Record, Madurai.

investment was Rs.112.5 (18.1%) in Agro-based industry and Rs.64.4 (10.3%) Miscellaneous. The textile industry required the highest percentage 28 per cent of investment for fixed capital. The Madurai Corporation (47.7%) and Madurai East (10.2%) has good performance in SSI investment in 2000-01.

Small scale industries are quick yielding in nature. In other words their gestation period is very much low when compared to their large scale counterparts. These industries are labour intensive and provide innumerable employment opportunities explained in Table 4.28. A given investment SSI industries can provide 10 to 15 times more employment than the industries have special significance in rural areas of India which face the inverse problem of seasonal unemployment and low wages. Indian economy is characterized by the migration of labour resource from rural areas to urban areas. There is no need for sophisticated technology and any person with some basic training would be able to run small scale industries. Table 4.29 explained the production level in block-wise and industry-wise details of SSI in Madurai district.

Table 4.26 :Block-wise SSI Units in Madurai District (2000-01)

(*No. of Units*)

Block	*Food Based*	*Forest Based*	*Animal Husbandry Based*	*Textile Based*	*Chemical Based*	*Building Based*	*Engineer-ing Based*	*Electric Based*	*Miscellaneous Based*
Alanganallur	Total	(18.1)	(7.9)	(5.2)	(28)	(2.8)	(22.9)	(4.5)	(10.4)
Chellampatti	112	49	32	172	17	141	28	62	613(2.9)
Kallikudi	46	21	13	71	7	58	12	24	252(1.2)
Kottampatti	56	25	16	87	9	72	14	32	311(1.5)
Madurai-East	93	41	27	144	15	118	23	53	514(2.5)
Madurai-West	387	170	111	597	59	488	96	223	2131(10.2)
Melur	317	140	91	490	49	401	79	182	1749(8.4)
Sedapadi	148	65	42	228	23	187	37	84	814(2.0)
Thirumangalam	91	40	26	141	14	115	23	52	502 (5.02)
Thirupparankundram	200	88	57	309	31	252	50	114	1101(5.3)
T. Kallupatti	163	72	47	253	25	207	41	94	902 (4.3)
Usilampatti	67	30	19	104	10	85	17	39	371(1.8)
Vadipatti	148	65	42	228	23	187	36	85	814 (3.9)
Madurai Corporation	144	64	42	222	22	182	36	82	794 (3.8)
	1805	795	516	2788	278	2280	450	1033	9945(47.8)
	3777	1664	1081	5834	579	4772	94	2161	20813

Source : District Industries Centre, Madurai, 2002.

Table 4.27 : Block-wise Lnvestment level of SSI Units in Madurai District

(*Rs. in lakhs*)

Block-wise in Madurai District	*Food Based*	*Forest Based*	*Animal Husbandry Based*	*Textile Based*	*Chemical Based*	*Engineer-ing Based*	*Electric Based*	*Miscellaneous Based*	*Total (%)*
Alanganallur	Total	(18.1)	(7.9)	(5.1)	(28)	(2.7)	(22.9)	(4.5)	(10.3)
Chellampatti	3.3	1.5	0.9	5.1	0.5	4.2	0.8	1.9	18.3 (2.9)
Kallikudi	1.4	0.6	0.4	2.1	0.2	1.7	0.3	0.7	7.5 (1.2)
Kottampatti	1.7	0.7	0.5	2.6	0.2	2.1	0.4	0.9	9.3 (1.5)
Madurai-East	2.7	1.2	0.8	4.3	0.4	3.5	0.7	1.6	15.3 (2.4)
Madurai-West	0.2	5.1	3.3	17.8	1.8	14.5	2.9	6.6	63.5(10.2)
Melur	9.4	4.2	2.7	14.6	1.4	1.2	2.3	5.4	52.1 (8.4)
Sedapadi	4.4	1.9	1.3	6.8	0.7	5.7	1.1	2.5	24.3 (3.9)
Thirumangalam	2.7	1.9	0.8	4.2	0.4	3.4	0.7	1.5	14.9 (2.4)
Thirupparankundram	5.9	2.6	1.7	9.2	0.9	7.5	1.5	3.4	32.8 (5.2)
T. Kallupatti	4.8	2.1	1.4	7.5	0.7	6.1	1.2	2.8	26.8 (4.3)
Usilampatti	1.9	0.9	0.6	3.1	0.3	2.5	1.1	1.1	11.0 (1.7)
Vadipatti	4.4	1.9	1.2	6.8	0.7	5.5	1.1	2.5	24.2 (3.9)
Madurai Corporation	0.2	1.9	1.2	6.6	0.6	5.4	13.4	2.4	23.6 (3.8)
	54.7	23.6	15.3	83.1	8.2	68.9	13.4	31.7	296.3 (47.7)
	112.5	49.6	32.2	173.8	17.2	142.2	28.0	64.4	(100)

Source : District Industries Centre Record, Madurai, 2002.

Table 4.28 : Block-wise Employmet Level of SSI in Madurai District

(Number of persons)

Block-wise in Madurai District	*Food Based*	*Forest Based*	*Animal Husbandry Based*	*Textile Based*	*Chemical Based*	*Engineer-ing Based*	*Electric Based*	*Miscellaneous Based*	*Total (%)*
Alanganallur	Total		12461			4341	35733	7047	16185
Chellampatti	833	367	238	1286	128	1052	207	477	4589 (2.9)
Kallikudi	343	151	98	529	53	433	85	196	1887 (1.2)
Kottampatti	422	186	121	653	65	534	105	242	2328 (1.5)
Madurai-East	698	308	200	1079	107	882	174	400	3848 (2.5)
Madurai-West	2895	1276	829	4473	444	3659	721	1657	15956 (10.2)
Melur	2376	1047	680	3671	365	3003	592	1360	13095 (8.4)
Sedapadi	1106	487	317	1709	170	1397	276	633	6095 (3.9)
Thirumangalam	682	300	195	105	105	862	170	390	3759 (2.4)
Thirupparankundram	1496	659	428	2311	229	1890	373	856	8244 (5.3)
T. Kallupatti	1226	540	351	1893	188	1549	305	701	6754 (4.3)
Usilampatti	504	222	144	779	77	637	126	288	2778 (1.8)
Vadipatti	1106	487	317	1709	170	1398	276	633	6095 (3.9)
Madurai Corporation	1079	475	309	1666	166	1363	269	617	5945 (3.8)
	13513	5954	3868	20874	2074	17074	3367	7733	74462 (47.8)
	28280		8096	43686					155836 (100)

Source : District Industries Centre Record, Madurai, 2002.

Table 4.29 : Block-wise Production Level of SSI in Madurai District

(*Rs. In lakhs*)

Block-wise in Madurai District	*Food Based*	*Forest Based*	*Animal Husbandry Based*	*Textile Based*	*Chemical Based*	*Engineering Based*	*Electric Based*	*Miscellaneous Based*	*Total (%)*
Alanganallur	Total		336.2	218.4	1178.6	117.1	964	190.1	436.6
Chellampatti	23.4	9.9	6.4	34.7	3.4	28.3	5.6	12.8	123.8(2.9)
Kallikudi	9.2	4.1	2.6	14.2	1.4	0.3	2.3	5.3	50.9 (1.2)
Kottampatti	11.4	5.1	3.3	17.6	1.7	14.3	2.8	6.5	62.8 (1.5)
Madurai-East	19.1	8.3	54.1	29.1	2.9	23.8	4.7	10.7	103.8 (2.5)
Madurai-West	78.1	336.2	22.3	120.7	11.9	98.7	19.5	44.7	430.5 (10.2)
Melur	0.18	28.2	18.3	99.1	9.8	81.0	15.9	36.6	353.3 (8.4)
Sedapadi	29.8	13.1	8.5	46.0	4.5	37.6	7.4	17.0	164.4 (2.0)
Thirumangalam	18.4	8.1	5.3	28.4	2.8	23.2	4.6	10.5	101.4 (5.02)
Thirupparankundram	40.3	17.8	11.5	62.3	0.3	50.1	10.0	23.1	222.4 (5.3)
T. Kallupatti	33.1	14.5	9.4	51.0	5.07	41.7	8.2	18.9	182.2(4.3)
Usilampatti	13.6	5.9	3.8	20.9	2.08	17.1	3.3	7.7	74.9 (1.8)
Vadipatti	29.8	13.1	8.5	46.1	4.6	37.6	7.4	17.1	164.4(3.9)
Madurai Corporation	29.1	12.8	8.3	44.9	4.5	36.7	7.2	16.6	160.3(3.8)
	364.5	76.7	104.3	563.1	55.9	460	90.8	208.6	2008.9(47.8)
	762.9								4204.23 (100)

Source: District Industries Centre Record, Madurai, 2002.

A high level of production was provided by the Mineral-based industry and Textile-based industry in Madurai district of Tamil Nadu. The Madurai corporation area SSI units had produced (47.8%) of total production in Madurai district. Following the Madurai Corporation, the Madurai East block has generated the production for 430.5 lakhs (10.2%) through the SSI in 2000-01.

Table 4.30 : Number of Units of SSI after Liberalisation

Year	*Total No. of Units*	
	Tamil Nadu	*Madurai*
1991-92	138404	7958
2000-01	387597	20813

Source: Directorate of Industries and Commerce, Chennai 2002.

The number of units of SSI enterprise for the pericd from 1990-01 to 2000-01 is given in Table 4.30. It reveals that the number of units of SSI during the study period (1991-92 to 2000-01) was increased from 138404 to 387597 in Tamil Nadu. In Madurai district, two times increase was incurred in registered SSI units from 7958 in 1991-92 to 20813 in 2000-01.

Table 4.31: Investment of SSI after Liberalisation (*Rs. in lakhs*)

Year	*Investment Level*	
	Tamil Nadu	*Madurai*
1991-92	3210.20	172.8
2000-01	11567.22	620.2

Source : Directorate of Industries and Commerce, Chennai 2002.

Table 4.31 indicates the investment level of SSI after liberalization. Table reveals that the investment level of SSI during the study period (1991-92 to 2000-01) was increased from Rs.172.8 lakhs in 1991-92 to Rs.620.2 lakhs in 2000-01 in Madurai district.

Table 4.32 : Production Level of SSI after Liberalisation

(Rs. in lakhs)

Year	*Production Level*	
	Tamil Nadu	*Madurai*
1991-92	16747.00	899.12
2000-01	78261.66	4204.23

Source: Directorate of Industries and Commerce, Chennai 2002.

Table 4.32 reveals that the production value of SSI sectors Tamil Nadu and Madurai are doubled. Table 4.33 reveals that the employment level of SSI during the study period (1991-92 to 2000-01) was increased from 11,76,700 persons to 29,02,212 person in Tamil Nadu. And the employment level of SSI was increased from 63,271 persons to 1,55,836 persons in Madurai district.

Table 4.33 : Employment Level of SSI after Liberalisation

(Number of persons)

Year	*Employment Level*	
	Tamil Nadu	*Madurai*
1991-92	11,76,700	63271
2000-01	29,02,212	155836

Source: Directorate of Industries and Commerce, Chennai 2002.

Table 4.34 : Industry-wise Number of Units of SSI in Tamil Nadu 2000-01

Sl.No.	*Industries*	*Tamil Nadu*	*Madurai*
1.	Food based	70340	3777
2.	Forest based	30995	1664
3.	Animal Husbandry based	20140	1081
4.	Textile based	108659	5834
5.	Chemical based	10800	579
6.	Mineral based	88876	4772
7.	Enginnering based	17530	941
8.	Miscellaneous	40257	2161
	Total	387597	20813

Source: Directorate of Industries and Commerce, Chennai, 2002.

Table 4.34 reveals that the share of Tamil Nadu in number of units of SSI has been significant. It holds the first place of SSI in Textile based industries (28%). Mineral based industries (22.9%) and Food based industry (18.1%) are also dominated in Tamil Nadu.

Table 4.35 : Industry-wise Investment of SSI in Tamil Nadu (2000-01)

Sl.No.	*Industries*	*Tamil Nadu (Rs. in crores)*	*Madurai (Rs. in lakhs)*
1.	Food based	2199	112.5
2.	Forest based	1002.4	49.6
3.	Animal Husbandry based	492.2	32.2
4.	Textile based	3351.6	173.8
5.	Chemical based	402.9	17.2
6.	Mineral based	2273.5	142.2
7.	Enginnering based	745.5	28.0
8.	Miscellaneous	1099.8	64.4
	Total	11567.22	64.4

Source: Directorate of Industries and Commerce, Chennai, 2002.

Table 4.35 reveals that the Chemical based industry (2.7%) and Animal Husbandry based industry (7.9%) had the very low investment level in Madurai district. Table 4.36 reveals that Textile based industry secured the first place in employment generation in Madurai district.

Table 4.36 : Industry-wise Employment Level of SSI in Tamil Nadu (2000-01)

Sl.No.	*Industries*	*Tamil Nadu (Rs. in crores)*	*Madurai (Rs. in lakhs)*
1.	Food based	5,26,668	28280
2.	Forest based	2,32,074	12461
3.	Animal Husbandry based	1,50,79	8096
4.	Textile based	8,13,581	43686
5.	Chemical based	80,864	4341
6.	Mineral based	6,65,456	35733
7.	Enginnering based	1.31.255	7047
8.	Miscellaneous	3,01,423	16185
	Total	29,02,122,8	1,55,836

Source: Directorate of Industries and Commerce, Chennai, 2002.

Table 4.37: Industry-wise Production Level of SSI in Tamil Nadu (2000-01)

Sl.No.	*Industries*	*Tamil Nadu (Rs. in crores)*	*Madurai (Rs. in lakhs)*
1.	Food based	14,202.7	762.9
2.	Forest based	6258.3	336.2
3.	Animal Husbandry based	4066.5	218.4
4.	Textile based	21939.8	1178.6
5.	Chemical based	2180.6	117.1
6.	Mineral based	17945.4	964.0
7.	Enginnering based	3539.5	190.1
8.	Miscellaneous	8128.5	436.6
	Total	78261.66	4204.23

Source: Directorate of Industries and Commerce, Chennai 2002.

The production level of SSI shows that the Textile based industry (28%) and Mineral based industry (22.9%) are dominated in Madurai district explained in Table 4.37.

The performance of Small Scale Industry (SSI) in Dindigul district is assessed by the number of units during the study period 1991-92 to 2001-02. The year-wise and industry-wise SSI units is given in Table 4.38.

Table 4.38 : Year-wise Performance of SSI in Dindigul District

Year	*No. of Units*	*Investment Rs.*	*Employment (persons)*	*Production Rs.*
1991-92	2724	88.8	32518	462.11
1992-93	3610	114.3	37804	650.8
1993-94	4496	140.1	43090	839.5
1994-95	5382	165.6	48376	1028.3
1995-96	6268	191.1	53662	1217.0
1996-97	7154	216.6	58948	1405.8
1997-98	8040	242.1	6223	1594.5
1998-99	8926	267.6	69520	1783.3
1999-00	9812	293.1	74806	1972.0
2000-01	10697	318.7	80093	2160.79
2001-02	11584	344.1	85379	2349.5

Source: District Industries Centre Record, Dindigul, 2002.

From Table 4.39, it is clear that of the total 11584 SSI units, 2724 SSI textiles units are functioning in Dindigul district in

Table 4.39 : SSI in Dindigul District

(No. of Units)

Year	Food Based	Forest Based	Animal Husbandry Based	Textile Based	Chemical Based	Engineering Based	Electric Based	Miscellaneous	Total (%)
1991-92	494	259	163	742	118	511	81	352	2724
1992-93	605	348	216	983	157	678	107	516	3610
1993-94	316	428	269	1225	195	844	134	585	4496
1994-95	976	513	322	1466	234	1011	160	700	5382
1995-96	1137	597	375	1707	272	1177	187	816	6268
1996-97	1298	685	428	1949	311	1343	213	931	7154
1997-98	1458	766	481	2190	349	1509	240	1047	8040
1998-99	1619	850	534	2431	388	1676	266	1162	8926
1999-00	1780	935	587	2673	426	1843	293	1275	9812
2000-01	1941	1019	640	2914	465	2009	319	1390	10697
2001-02	2102	1103	693	3155	504	2175	345	1507	11584

Source: District Industries Centre, Dindigul, 2002.

2001-02. But it was only 29 units at the time of implementation of NEP. Following the Textile based industries (3155 units), Mineral-based Industry (2175 units), Food-based Industry 2102 units) were dominated in the Dindigul district of Tamil Nadu.

The investment pattern of the small scale entrepreneurs in Dindigul District is presented in Table 4.40. The textile industries required the highest percentage (30.9%) of investment for fixed capital. The Engineering based industry required the lowest level of investment (1.3%). The Textile-based industry had required the investment of Rs.93.8 lakhs in the year 2001-02 as against Rs.24.1 lakhs in the year 1991-92. The investment level of Textile industry was 30.9 per cent to the total investment level of small scale industries. Mineral based industry had invested only 14.3 per cent in the study period.

Table 4.41 reveals that Textile-based industries had generated more employment during the study period. It had generated 85379 persons employment opportunities during the period 2001-02 it was only 32518 persons in 1992-93. Of the total employment generation of 23623 persons in 2001-02, textile based had provided the employment for 8859 persons. Following the Textile based, (445 persons) had generated the highest level of employment in the SSI sector of Dindigul district.

Table 4.42 the study found that the total production of Rs.2349.5 lakhs the textile units had produced Rs.641.69 lakhs in Dindigul district in 2001-02. But it was only Rs.123.62 lakhs at the time of implementation of NEP. Following the Textile-based units (Rs.641.69 lakhs) Mineral based units (Rs.442.54 lakhs) and Food-based units (Rs.427.39 lakhs) were dominated in the Dindigul district.

Table 4.40 : Investment Level of SSI in Dindigul District *(Rupees in lakhs)*

Year	*Food Based*	*Forest Based Based*	*Animal Husbandry*	*Textile Based*	*Chemical Based*	*Engineer -ing Based*	*Electric Based*	*Miscellaneous*	*Total*
1991-92	16.1	8.4	5.3	24.1	3.8	16.7	2.6	11.9	88.8
1992-93	20.7	10.8	6.8	31.1	4.9	21.4	3.4	15.2	114.3
1993-94	25.4	13.3	8.3	38.2	6.0	26.3	4.1	18.5	140.1
1994-95	30.0	15.7	9.9	45.1	7.1	31.1	4.9	21.8	165.6
1995-96	34.6	18.2	11.4	51.7	8.3	35.9	5.7	25.3	191.1
1996-97	39.3	20.6	12.9	59.0	9.4	40.6	6.4	28.4	216.6
1997-98	43.9	23.0	14.4	65.9	10.5	45.4	7.2	31.8	242.1
1998-99	48.5	25.5	16.0	72.9	11.6	50.2	7.9	35.0	267..6
1999-00	53.1	27.9	17.5	79.8	12.7	55.0	8.7	38.4	293.1
2000-01	57.83	30.37	19.07	86.83	13.85	59.88	9.51	41.32	318.7
2001-02	62.3	32.7	20.57	93.8	14.9	64.6	10.31	44.92	344.1

Source: District Industries Centre, Dindigul, 2002.

Table 4.41 : Empployment Generation of SSI in Dindigul District *(Number of Persons)*

Year	*Food Based*	*Forest Based*	*Animal Husbandry Based*	*Textile Based*	*Chemical Based*	*Engineer-ing Based*	*Electric-Based*	*Miscellaneous*	*Total (%)*
1991-92	5901	3099	1945	8859	1413	6109	971	4221	32518
1992-93	6860	3603	2262	10300	1643	7103	1129	4904	37804
1993-94	7819	4106	2578	11740	1873	8096	1286	5592	43090
1994-95	8779	4610	2894	13180	2103	9089	2392	5329	48376
1995-96	9738	5114	3211	14620	2332	10082	1602	6963	53662
1996-97	10697	5618	3527	16061	2563	11076	1760	7646	58948
1997-98	11294	5931	3724	16956	2705	1693	1858	8073	62234
1998-99	12616	6625	4160	18941	3022	13062	2076	9018	69520
1999-00	13575	7129	4476	20381	3252	14055	2234	9704	74806
2000-01	14535	7633	4793	21822	3482	15049	2392	10387	80093
2001-02	15494	8137	5110	23623	3712	16043	2550	1907	85379

Source: District Industries Centre, Dindigul, 2002.

Table 4.42 : Production Level of SSI in Dindigul District

(Rupees in lakhs)

Year	*Food Based*	*Forest Based*	*Animal Husbandry Based*	*Textile Based*	*Chemical Based*	*Engineering Based*	*Electric-Based*	*Miscellaneous*	*Total*
1991-92	82.34	43.23	27.15	123.62	19.71	85.26	13.54	67.2	462.11
1992-93	117.63	61.77	38.79	176.61	28.17	121.8	19.35	86.68	650.8
1993-94	148.99	78.24	49.13	223.68	35.68	154.28	24.51	125.0	839.5
1994-95	184.28	96.77	60.77	276.68	44.13	190.82	30.31	144.5	1028.3
1995-96	219.57	115.30	72.40	329.67	52.58	227.36	36.12	164.0	1217.0
1996-97	254.86	133.83	84.40	382.65	61.03	263.9	41.92	183.57	1405.8
1997-98	286.23	150.30	94.38	429.75	68.54	296.38	47.08	221.84	1594.5
1998-99	321.52	168.83	106.02	482.73	76.99	332.92	52.89	241.4	1783.3
1999-00	356.81	187.36	117.66	535.71	85.44	369.45	58.69	260.87	1972.0
2000-01	392.1	205.9	129.3	588.7	93.9	406	64.5	280.39	2160.79
2001-02	427.39	224.44	140.94	641.69	102.36	442.54	70.31	299.83	2349.5

Source: District Industries Centre, Dindigul, 2002.

Table 4.43 : Block-wise Performance of SSI in Dindigul District

Block	*No. of Units*	*Investment Rs.*	*Employment (persons)*	*Production Rs.*
Dindigul	5276	157.19	39505	1065.8
Athoor	498	14.85	3732	100.7
Reddiarchatram	329	9.80	2468	66.6
Sanarpatti	498	14.85	3732	100.7
Nilakottai	558	16.62	4177	112.7
Batlagundu	431	12.84	3228	87.1
Plaani	1065	31.74	7676	215.2
Thoppampatti	296	8.82	2216	59.8
Oddanchatram	296	8.82	2216	59.8
Vedasandur	397	11.8	2976	80.3
Vadamadurai	346	10.32	2594	70.0
Gujiliamparai	211	6.29	1582	42.7
Natham	270	8.05	2023	54.6
Kadaikanal	226	6.71	1968	44.4
Total	10697	318.7	80093	2160.79

Source: District Industries Centre Record, Dindigul, 2002.

Table 4.43 reveals that of the total SSI units (10,647) in Dindigul district, the Dindigul block occupied the nearly 50 per cent of the units (5276) in the year 2000-01. It is clear that SSI entrepreneurs concentrated in setting up of the units in the areas where the infrastructure facilities are adequately available. The Dindigul block is a semi-urban area and it is located near the Dindigul Town which has the adequate facilities for the best performance of SSI units. The investment level of SSI was Rs. 318.7 lakhs in Dindigul district in the year 2000-01. Similarly the performance was very significant only in the Dindigul Block of the study district.

Table 4.44 explained the total SSI units in dindigul district The Dindigul (49.3%) and Palani (9.9 %) had good performance in SSI units in 2000-01.

Table 4.45 reveals that the investment level was higher (27.3%) in the Textile based industries of Dindigul district. The investment

Table 4.44 : Block-wise SSI units in Dindigul District

(Number of Units)

Block-wise in Dindigul District	*Food Based*	*Forest Based*	*Animal Husbandry Based*	*Textile Based*	*Chemical Based*	*Engineering Based*	*Electric Based*	*Miscellaneous*	*Total*
Dindigul	957	502	316	1437	229	991	157	687	5276 (49.3)
Athoor	90	47	30	136	22	93	15	65	498 (4.6)
Reddiarchatram	59	31	20	90	14	62	10	43	329 (3.0)
Sanarpatti	90	47	30	135	22	94	15	65	498 (4.6)
Nilakottai	101	53	33	152	24	105	17	73	558 (5.2)
Batlagundu	78	41	26	117	19	81	13	56	431 (4.0)
Plaani	193	101	64	290	46	200	32	139	1065 (9.9)
Thoppampatti	53	28	18	80	13	56	9	39	296 (2.7)
Oddanchatram	53	28	18	80	13	56	9	39	296 (2.7)
Vedasandur	72	38	24	108	17	75	12	51	397 (3.7)
Vadamadurai	62	33	21	94	15	65	10	46	346 (3.2)
Gujiliamparai	38	20	13	57	9	40	6	28	211 (1.9)
Natham	48	26	16	73	12	51	8	36	270 (2.5)
Kodaikanai	47	24	11	65	10	40	6	23	226 (2.1)
Total	1941 (18.1)	1019 (9.5)	640 (5.9)	2914 (27.2)	465 (4.3)	2009 (18.7)	319 (2.9)	1390 (13.9)	10697 (100)

Source: District Industries Centre, Dindigul, 2002.

Table 4.45 : Block-wise Investment of SSI in Dindigul District

(Rupees in lakhs)

Block-wise in Dindigul District	*Food Based*	*Forest Based*	*Animal Husbandry Based*	*Textile Based*	*Chemical Based*	*Engineer-ing Based*	*Electric Based*	*Miscellaneous*	*Total*
Dindigul	28.5	15.0	9.4	42.5	6.8	29.5	4.7	20.7	157.19 (49.4)
Athoor	2.6	1.4	0.8	4.0	0.6	2.7	0.4	2.35	14.85 (4.6)
Reddiarchatram	1.7	0.9	0.5	2.6	0.4	1.8	0.2	1.7	9.80 (3.08)
Sanarpatti	2.7	1.4	0.8	4.0	0.6	2.7	0.4	2.25	14.85 (4.6)
Nilakottai	3.0	1.5	0.9	4.5	0.7	3.1	0.4	2.52	16.62 (5.2)
Batlagundu	2.3	1.2	0.7	3.4	0.5	2.4	0.4	1.94	12.84 (4.0)
Plaani	5.7	3.0	1.9	8.6	1.4	5.9	0.9	4.34	31.74 (9.9)
Thoppampatti	1.6	0.8	0.5	2.3	0.3	1.6	0.2	1.52	8.82 (2.7)
Oddanchatram	1.6	0.8	0.5	2.3	0.3	1.6	0.2	1.52	8.82 (2.7)
Vedasandur	2.1	1.1	0.7	3.2	0.5	2.2	0.3	1.7	11.8 (3.7)
Vadamadurai	1.8	0.9	0.6	2.8	0.4	1.9	0.3	1.62	10.32 (3.2)
Gujiliamparai	1.1	0.5	0.3	1.7	0.2	1.2	0.2	1.09	6.29 (1.9)
Natham	1.5	0.7	0.5	2.2	0.3	1.5	0.2	1.15	8.05 (2.5)
Kadaikanal	1.1	0.6	0.3	1.7	0.2	1.1	0.1	0.92	6.02 (1.9)
Total	57.83	30.37	19.07	86.83	13.85	59.88	9.51	45.32	318.0 (100)

Source: District Industries Centre, Dindigul, 2002.

Tabie 4.46 : Block-wise Employment Level of in SSI Dindigul District

(Number of Persons)

Block-wise in Dindigul District	*Food Based*	*Forest Based*	*Animal Husbandry Based*	*Textile Based*	*Chemical Based*	*Engineer-ing Based*	*Electric Based*	*Miscellaneous*	*Total*
Dindigul	7169	3764	2364	10763	1717	7422	1179	5127	39505
Athoor	677	355	223	1016	162	701	111	487	3732
Reddiarchatram	448	235	148	672	107	463	74	321	2468
Sanarpatti	677	355	223	1017	162	701	111	486	3732
Nilakottai	758	398	249	1138	181	785	125	543	4177
Batlagundu	586	307	193	879	140	606	96	421	3228
Plaani	1393	731	459	2091	334	1442	229	997	7676
Thoppampatti	402	211	132	604	96	416	66	289	2216
Oddanchatram	402	211	132	604	96	416	66	289	2216
Vedasandur	540	283	178	811	129	559	89	387	2976
Vadamadurai	470	247	155	707	113	487	77	338	2594
Gujiliamparai	287	151	95	431	69	297	47	205	1582
Natham	367	193	121	551	88	380	60	263	2023
Kodaikanal	359	192	121	538	83	374	62	234	1968
Total	14535	7633	4793	21822	3482	15049	2392	10387	80093

Source: District Industries Centre, Dindigul, 2002.

Table 4.47 : Block-wise Production Level of SSI in Dindigul District

(Rupees in lakhs)

Block-wise in Dindigul District	*Food Based*	*Forest Based*	*Animal Husbandry Based*	*Textile Based*	*Chemical Based*	*Engineer-ing Based*	*Electric Based*	*Miscellaneous*	*Total*
Dindigul	193.4	101.5	63.7	290.3	46.3	200.2	31.8	138.6	1065.8
Athoor	18.2	9.5	6.0	27.4	4.3	18.9	3.0	13.4	100.7
Reddiarchatram	12.0	6.3	3.9	18.1	2.8	12.5	1.9	9.1	66.6
Sanarpatti	18.2	9.5	6.0	27.4	4.3	18.9	3.0	13.5	100.7
Nilakottai	20.4	10.7	6.7	30.7	4.8	21.1	3.3	15.0	112.7
Batlagundu	15.8	8.2	5.2	23.7	3.7	16.3	2.6	11.6	87.1
Plaani	39.0	20.5	12.8	58.6	0.93	40.3	6.4	36.67	215.2
Thoppampatti	10.8	5.6	3.6	16.2	2.6	11.2	1.7	8.1	59.8
Oddanchatram	10.8	5.6	3.6	16.2	2.6	11.2	1.7	8.1	59.8
Vedasandur	14.6	7.6	4.8	21.8	3.5	15.0	2.4	10.6	80.3
Vadamadurai	12.7	6.7	4.2	19.0	3.0	13.1	2.1	9.2	70.0
Gujiliamparai	7.7	4.1	2.5	11.6	1.8	8.0	1.3	5.7	42.7
Natham	9.9	5.2	3.3	14.8	2.4	10.2	1.6	1.0	54.6
Kodaikanal	8.6	4.9	3.0	12.9	10.8	9.1	1.7	0.5	44.4
Total	392.1	205.9	129.3	588.7	93.9	406	64.5	280.2	2160.79

Source: District Industries Centre, Dindigul, 2002.

level was also low in the Mineral based (18.8%) and Food based industries (18.%1) in the study district. The investment performance shows the highest investment of SSI in the Dindigul block and the Dindigul Municipality areas. It is inferred that the SSI units are most concentrated only in the urban based areas.

The chief causes for idleness in the sector are want of working capital, scarcity of skilled labour and breakdown in the installed machinery. The most potent cause for idleness was lack of skilled labour. The Textile Sector in Dindigul district produces the varieties of spinning items in the Block. Table 4.46 reveals the Animal Husbandry based industry (5.9%) and Chemical based industry (4.3%) are generated low employment level in Dindigul district.

The above performance analysis based on secondary data in Small Scale Industries in Madurai and Dindigul district paved the way for analyzing the primary data in the forth coming sections.

Table 4.48 : Year-wise Number of Units of SSI in Tamil Nadu

Year	*Total Number of Units*	
	Tamil Nadu	*Dindigul*
1991-92	138404	3291
2000-01	387597	10697

Source : District Industries Centre Record, Dindigul, 2002.

The number of units of small scale enterprise for the period from 1990-91 to 2000-01 is given in Table 4.48. Table 4.48 reveals that the numbers of units of SSI during the study period (1991-92 to 2000-01) was increased from 138404 to 387597 in Tamil Nadu. In Dindigul district, three times increase was incurred in registered SSI units from 3291 in 1991-92 to 10697 in 2000-01.

Table 4.49 : Year-wise Investment Level of SSI in Tamil Nadu (*Rs. in crores*)

Year	*Investment Level*	
	Tamil Nadu	*Dindigul*
1991-92	3210.20	88.8
2000-01	11567.22	318.7

Source: District Industries Centre Record, Dindigul, 2002.

Table 4.49 indicates the investment level of SSI after liberalization. Table 4.49 reveals that the investment level of SSI during the study period (1991-92 to 2000-01) was increased from Rs.3210.20 crores to Rs.11567.22 crores in Tamil Nadu. And the investment level of SSI increased from Rs.88.8 lakhs to 318.7 lakhs in Dindigul district.

Table 4.50 : Year-wise Production Level of SSI in Tamil Nadu *(Rs. in lakhs)*

Year	*Production Level*	
	Tamil Nadu	*Dindigul*
1991-92	16747	462.11
2000-01	78,261.66	2160.79

Source: District Industries Centre Record, Dindigul, 2002.

Table 4.50 reveals that the production value of SSI during the study period (1991-92 to 2000-01) was increased from Rs.16747 lakhs to Rs.78,261.66 lakhs in Tamil Nadu and the production level of SSI increased from Rs.462.11 lakhs to Rs.2160.79 lakhs in Dindigul district.

Table 4.51 : Year-wise Employment Level of SSI in Tamil Nadu *(Number of persons)*

Year	*Employment Level*	
	Tamil Nadu	*Dindigul*
1991-92	11,76,700	32,518
2000-01	29,02,212	80,093

Source : District Industries Centre Record, Dindigul, 2002.

Table 4.51 reveals that the employment level of SSI during the study period (1991-92 to 2000-01) was increased from 11,76,700 persons to 29,02,212 persons in Tamil Nadu, and the employment level of SSI was increased from 32,518 persons to 80,093 persons in Dindigul District.

Table 4.52 : Industry-wise Numbers of Units of SSI in Tamil Nadu 2000-01)

Sl.No.	*Industries*	*Tamil Nadu*	*Dindigul*
1.	Food based	70340	1919
2.	Forest based	30995	1041
3.	Animal Husbandry based	20140	614
4.	Textile based	108659	2940
5.	Chemical based	10800	409
6.	Mineral based	88876	2065
7.	Enginnering based	17530	390
8.	Miscellaneous	40257	1319
	Total	387597	10697

Source: District Industries Centre Record, Dindigul, 2002.

Table 4.52 reveals that the share of Tamil Nadu in number of units of SSI has been significant. It holds the first place of SSI in Textile based industries (28%), Mineral based industries (22.9%) and Food based industry (18.1%) are also dominated in Tamil Nadu. At the same time in Dindigul district particularly Textile based industry (27.5%) and Mineral based industry (19.3%) are dominated.

Table 4.53 : Industry-wise Investment of SSI in Tamil Nadu (2000-01)

Sl.No.	*Industries*	*Tamil Nadu (Rs. in crores)*	*Dindigul (Rs. in lakhs)*
1.	Food based	2199	67.83 (21.2)
2.	Forest based	1002.4	20.37
3.	Animal Husbandry based	492.2	9.07
4.	Textile based	3351.6	96.83
5.	Chemical based	402.9	10.85
6.	Mineral based	2273.5	69.88
7.	Enginnering based	745.5	19.51
8.	Miscellaneous	1099.8	24.32
	Total	11567.22	318.7

Source: District Industries Centre Record, Dindigul, 2002.

Table 4.53 shows the investment level of SSI in Tamil Nadu. Similarly the Textile based industry (28.9%) and Mineral based industry (19.6%) are dominated in Tamil Nadu. The Animal Husbandry based industry had the very low investment level (2.8%) in Dindigul District.

Table 4.54 : Industry-wise Employment Level of SSI in Tamil Nadu (2000-01

Sl.No.	*Industries*	*Tamil Nadu*	*Dindigul*
1.	Food based	5,26,668	392.1
2.	Forest based	2,32,074	205.9
3.	Animal Husbandry based	1,50,79	129.3
4.	Textile based	8,13,581	588.7
5.	Chemical based	80,864	93.9
6.	Mineral based	6,65,456	406.0
7.	Enginnering based	1.31.255	64.5
8.	Miscellaneous	3,01,423	280.39
	Total	29,02,122.8	2160.79

Source: District Industries Centre Record, Dindigul, 2002.

Table 4.55: Industry-wise Production Level of SSI in Tamil Nadu (2000-01)

Sl.No.	*Industries*	*Tamil Nadu (Rs. in Crores)*	*Dindigul (Rs. in lakhs)*
1.	Food based	14,202.7	14535 (18.1)
2.	Forest based	6258.3	7633 (7.9)
3.	Animal Husbandry based	4066.5	4793 (5.2)
4.	Textile based	21939.8	21822 (28.0)
5.	Chemical based	2180.6	3482 (2.7)
6.	Mineral based	17945.4	15049 (22.9)
7.	Enginnering based	3539.5	2392 (4.5)
8.	Miscellaneous	8128.5	10387 (10.3)
	Total	78261.66	80093 (100)

Source: District Industries Centre Record, Dindigul, 2002.

The employment level of SSI in Tamil Nadu and in Dindigul District is explained in Table 4.54. It holds the first place in Textile based industry in Tamil Nadu (30.1%) and (25.9%) in Dindigul district.

The production level of SSI shows that the Textile based industry (27.7%) dominated in Tamil Nadu and (24.4%) in Dindigul in the year of 2000-01.

5. IMPACT OF NEW ECONOMIC POLICY ON SMALL SCALE INDUSTRIES

The study district – Madurai is the second biggest city in Tamil Nadu towards its southern tip. The population is around 13 lakhs (2001). It is a tradition bound city. An example may illustrate the levels of tradition. Even in business a man (other than the family members) is not allowed to sit by the side of women even when the bus is crowded with male passengers scarcely populated female passengers! Even the age will not extent any concession!

In such a city women too have started competing within certain entrepreneurial ventures. The District has a very few reputed organization in the private sector like T.V. Sundaram Iyengar & Sons, Madura Coasts, Fenner (I) Ltd., George Oaks Ltd., etc. which are engaged in the production of variety of goods like tyres and tubes, machineries, textile, conveyor belts etc., and also provided employment opportunities. The District offers ample scope for the field of textiles, readymade garments. Bakery units, and floriculture, dairy and cold storage units, Agro and Herbal products, Granite Stones, Blue metal jelly, Chamber bricks, Rubber and Plastic based industries. There is also a very good scope for starting food processing and agro-based industries.

Another study District – Dindigul is popular for the leather industry and lock industry. It has the vast potentials for the generation of employment and income through the Small Scale Industries. Agro-processing industries offer good scope for development among the non-traditional industries. The demand based industries such as dehydrated fruit manufacture, paper cone manufacture, leather goods manufacturing. PVC pipe manufacturing, plastic textile and automobile parts, cattle feed/

poultry feed manufacturing, fruit/vegetable processing near Oddanchatram and oil extraction in Nilakottai are prominent. Natham and Palani taluks are having adequate supply of tamarind, guava and mango.

A field survey was conducted in Madurai and Dindigul districts in order to analyse the impact of New Economic Policy on Small Scale Enterprises. The findings of the micro-level study are divided into five sections, namely, socio-economic status of the respondents, investment level, production and sales level, labour and employment level and problems of New Economic Policy in different SSI sectors of Madurai and Dindigul districts.

Kodaikanal offers very good scope for producing essential medicinal oils like geranium, citronella and lemon grass. Eucalyptus oil and honey processing have a good potential. The district also offers scope for ancillary industries such as leather auxiliaries viz., production of magnesium sulphate, turkey red oil, garlic acid, extract of wattle/balul bate powder, sodium sulphide and lime.

1. Socio-Economic Status of Sample Entrepreneurs:

In order to compare the impact of New Economic Policy on Small Scale Enterprise in Madurai and Dindigul districts, 120 SSI entrepreneurs from each district were interviewed. The findings of the survey are discussed in this section.

It is but natural to presume that an individual is to enter that industry which is not only profitable and permissible by the State, but also that he finds himself capable of handling his own capabilities to large extent, depend upon his family background, academic qualifications and experience.

The sample respondents selected for the study is given in Table 5.1. It is clear that 120 respondents were selected from independent enterprise in each district. Of the total 120 sample respondents in a district, 15 respondents represented from each category of SSI sectors. There are eight categories of Small Scale Industries. They are: Food based industries, Forest based industries, Animal husbandry based industries, Textile based industries, Chemical based industries, Mineral based industries, Engineering based industries and Miscellaneous industries.

The selected 15 small scale enterprises in each category are illustrated in Table 5.1.

Table 5.1: Sample SSI Units in Study Districts

Sl. No.	*Category of Industry*	*Sample Units*	
		Dindigul District	*Madurai District*
I.	**Agro and Food based Industry:**		
	1. Rice and Flour Mill	4	3
	2. Bakery	7	3
	3. Fruit Processing	2	5
	4. Pickless	1	1
	5. Dhal Mill	0	1
	6. Masala Powder	1	1
	7. Coffee Powder	0	0
	8. Appalam	0	1
	Total	15	15
II.	**Forest based Industry:**		
	1. Saw Mill	6	5
	2. Wooden Furniture	4	2
	3. Wooden Packing Cases	2	4
	4. Coir Fibre	3	4
	Total	15	15
III.	**Animal Husbandry based Industry:**		
	1. Leather Foot Wear	7	8
	2. Leather Shoes	3	4
	3. Leather Bags etc.	4	3
	4. Repairing Service of leather goods	1	0
	Total	15	15
IV.	**Textile based Industry:**		
	1. Jacquard Towels	0	2
	2. Twisting of Yarn	1	1
	3. Dying of Yarn Cloth	1	0
	4. Doubling of Yarn	1	1
	5. Screen Printing (cloth)	1	0

(Contd.)

Table 5.1 *(Contd.)*

	6. Lungies, handkerchies dhotis	4	4
	7. Readmade garments	5	4
	8. Knitied fabrics	2	3
	Total	15	15
V.	**Chemical based Industries:**		
	1. Soap, Detergent	4	3
	2. Cleaning Powder	3	3
	3. Camphor	1	1
	4. Poly, print bag, films	2	1
	5. Soapnut Powder	1	1
	6. Plastic Articles	1	1
	7. Rubber Balls	–	2
	8. Rexin Bags	–	–
	9. PVC Chappals	–	–
	10. Tyre Retreading	1	1
	11. Paints/White phynoil	1	1
	12. Vitamin Tablets	0	–
	13. Vitamin Syrups	0	–
	14. Siddha Medicines	1	–
	15. Lime Powder	0	1
	Total	15	15
VI.	**Mineral based Industry**:		
	1.Chamber Bricks	4	3
	2. Country Bricks	0	0
	3. Mosaic Tiles	4	5
	4. Blue Metal Jelly	1	2
	5. Cement Products	0	1
	6. Cement Hallow Blocks	6	4
	Total	15	15
VII.	**Engineering and Allied Industries:**		
	1. General Engineering	4	2
	2. SS Utensil Manufacturing	2	2
	3. Brass and Copper Metal parts		0
	manufacturing	–	0
	4. Steel Furniture	–	1
	5. Jet pumps and parts manufacturing	3	2
	6. Motor Coil rewinding	1	2
	7. Tractor and Two Wheelers Repairing	1	2
	and Servicing		
	8. Auto Mobile Workshop	1	1
	9. TV, Radio Servicing	1	2

Table 5.1 *(Contd..)*

	10. Fridge Servicing	1	1
	Total	15	15
VIII.	**Miscellaneous:**		
	1. Treadle Printing	1	1
	2. Litho Printing (offset)	1	1
	3. Note Book Manufacturing	2	0
	4. Soft Drinks	1	1
	5. Aerated Water (Soda)	1	0
	6. Ice Barlice Candy Fruits	1	0
	7. Cold Storage	0	1
	8. Tailoring on Job works	1	2
	9. Book Binding	1	1
	10. Ornamental and Jewel cut	1	1
	11. Artificial Gemcutting	0	0
	12. Computer, DTP, Xerox	3	3
	13. Computer Software Dev.	0	2
	14. Computer Network Programmes	–	1
	15. Computer Screen Printing	–	0
	16. Typewriting Institute	2	1
	17. Clinical Lab	0	0
	Total	1 5	15
	Total	**120**	**120**

Source: Computed from primary data.

The sample SSI entrepreneurs in two study districts selected from the various blocks and town areas are illustrated in Table 5.2.

Entrepreneurs by Age

The age of the entrepreneur plays an important role in the growth and expansion of industry because the adoption of new methods and techniques of production, progressive outlook related to the age factor of the entrepreneurs. Table 5.3 shows the distribution of entrepreneurs according to age.

Table 5.3 revealed the age-wise classification of the small scale entrepreneurs in Madurai and Dindigul districts. Of the 240

Table 5.2 : SSI Sample Units in various Blocks of Study Districts

Sl. No.	*Dindigul*	*Madurai*
1.	Dindigul	Alanganullur
2.	Authoor	Chellampatti
3.	Reddiarchatram	Kallikudi
4.	Sanarpatti	Kottampatti
5.	Nilakottai	Madurai – East
6.	Batlagundu	Madurai – West
7.	Palani	Melur
8.	Thoppampatti	Sedapatti
9.	Oddanchatram	Thirumangalam
10.	Vedasandur	Thiruparankundram
11.	Vadamadurai	T. Kallikudi
12.	Guijliamporai	Usilampatti
13.	Natham	Vadipatti
14.	Kodaikanal	Madurai Corporation

Source: Computed from Primary Data.

Table 5.3 : Age of the Entrepreneurs of Sample Units

Sl. No.	*Category*	*Below 20*	*21-30 Years*	*31-40 Years*	*41-50 Years*	*Above 51Years*	*Total*
1.	Food and Agro based	5	10	3	9	3	30 (12.5)
2.	Forest based	2	7	9	11	1	30 (12.5)
3.	Animal Husbandry based	4	6	3	7	10	30 (12.5)
4.	Textile based	4	6	5	5	10	30 (12.5)
5.	Chemical based	–	4	12	13	1	30 (12.5)
6.	Mineral based	1	7	6	4	12	30 (12.5)
7.	Engineering based	1	2	7	6	14	30 (12.5)
8.	Miscellaneous	3	10	10	3	4	30 (12.5)
	Total	20 (8.3)	52 (21.6)	55 (22.9)	58 (24.1)	55 (22.9	240 (100)

Source: Computed fıom Primary Data.
Notes: Figures within parenthesis denotes percentages.

samples respondents, 58 respondents (24.1%) are belonging to the age group of 41-50 years. Only 20 respondents (8.3%) are belonging to the age group of the below 20 years. In the case of Food based Industry 10 persons are belonging to the age group of 21-30 years. Similarly, the Forest based Entrepreneurs have dominated in the age group (41-50). But in the case of Chemical based industries, the 31-40 and above 51 age group are dominating in the study districts. It is inferred that the age group of 41-50 years are very much interested in the Small Scale Enterprises.

Sex

Sex is another important social factor influencing the entrepreneurship development in the SSI sector. The female participation and male domination in the development of entrepreneurial skills have to be considered in analyzing the determinants of entreprenenial skill and development. The sex-wise classification of the sample entrepreneurs is exhibited in Table 5.4.

Table 5.4 : Sex-wise Classification of the Small Scale Industries Respondents

Sl. No.	*Category*	*Male*	*Female*	*Total*
1.	Food based	15	15	30
2.	Forest based	25	5	30
3.	Animal Husbandry based	30	–	30
4.	Textile based	28	2	30
5.	Chemical based	29	1	30
6.	Mineral based	30	–	30
7.	Engineering based	30	–	30
8.	Miscellaneous	12	18	30
	Total	199 (82.9)	41 (17.1)	240 (100)

Source: Computed from Primary Data.
Note : Figures within parenthesis denotes percentages.

It is clear from Table 5.4 that a large number of respondents (82.9%) are male SSI Entrepreneurs Only 41 respondents (17.1%) are belonging to the female Small Scale Entrepreneurs in the

Madurai and Dindigul districts. The Animal Husbandry based industry, Mineral based industry and Engineering based industry are dominated by the male entrepreneurship in Madurai and Dindigul districts. It is inferred that the male entrepreneurs and also recently female entrepreneurs are very much interested in the Small Scale Enterprises in Tamil Nadu.

Community

The entrepreneurial development mainly depends on the community of the entrepreneurs. Previously, the communities were categorised based on their own occupation of the households. The community-wise classification of sample SSI entrepreneurs is presented in Table 5.5.

Of the total sample entrepreneurs, a large number of entrepreneurs (38.3 per cent) are beloning to the Backward community and 36.6 per cent of the respondents are most backward community. The Scheduled caste and Scheduled tribes and Forward community entrepreneurs are 18.75 per cent and 6.25 per cent respectively.

It is clear from table 5.6 that the 40.83 per cent of the Small Scale Entrepreneurs are Hindus in the Dindigul and Madurai districts; 30.83 per cent (74 respondents) are Christians and 23.33 per cent (68 respondents) are Muslim respondents in the study districts. It shows that majority of the small scale entrepreneurs are Hindus in the study districts of Tamil Nadu.

Table 5.5: Community-wise Distribution of the Sample Respondents

Sl. No.	*Category*	*FC*	*BC*	*MBC*	*SC/ST*	*Total*
1.	Food based	4	17	7	2	30 (12.5)
2.	Forest based	1	11	10	8	30 (12.5)
3.	Animal Husbandry based	0	12	10	8	30 (12.5)
4.	Textile based	1	14	14	1	30 (12.5)
5.	Chemical based	4	10	13	3	30 (12.5)
6.	Mineral based	2	12	12	4	30 (12.5)
7.	Engineering based	1	9	10	10	30 (12.5)
8.	Miscellaneous	2	7	12	9	30 (12.5)
	Total	15 (6.25)	92 (38.3)	88 (36.6)	45(18.75)	240 (100)

Source: Computed from Primary Data.

Note : Figures within parenthesis denotes percentages.

Religion

The entrepreneurnial skills are influenced by the religion of the entrepreneurs. The religion-wise classification is given in Table 5.6.

Table 5.6 : Religion-wise Distribution of the Sample Respondents

Sl. No.	*Category*	*Hindu*	*Christian*	*Muslim*	*Total*
1.	Food based	14	13	3	30
2.	Forest based	20	10	-	30
3.	Animal Husbandry based	5	5	20	30
4.	Textile based	10	5	15	30
5.	Chemical based	17	8	5	30
6.	Mineral based	8	7	15	30
7.	Engineering based	6	18	6	30
8.	Miscellaneous	18	8	8	30
	Total	98 (40.83)	74 (30.83)	68 (23.33)	240 (100)

Source: Computed from Primary Data.
Note : Figures within parenthesis denotes percentages.

Economic development largely depends on the literacy of the people. This is particularly important in the case of entrepreneurial growth. It affects the decision of a prospective entrepreneurs in the selection of an enterprise, locations and cost of project and application of modern technology. This also arises in day-to-day decision-making as well as in running of a project. Education also helps to understand to aware of various facilities and incentives of the Government. An illiterate person is conservative, superstitious and reluctant to all changes.

From Table 5.7 it is clear that of the 240 sample respondents, only 17 (7.08 %) are illiterate, 29 (12.1%) got diploma level education, 50 (20.8%) are having Degree level literacy in study district. In the case of Small Scale Entrepreneurs, 64 (26.6%) and 80 (33.3%) respondents are having the primary and secondary level education. It is inferred that secondary level education are very high among the respondents in the study districts.

Table 5.7 : Education-wise Classification of the Sample Respondents

Sl. No.	*Category*	*Illiterate*	*Primary*	*Secondary*	*Deegree*	*Dip.*	*Total*
1.	Food based	–	11	19	–	–	(1.25) 30
2.	Forest based	15	10	5	–	–	(1.25) 30
3.	Animal Husbandry based	–	15	10	5	-- 10	(1.25) 30
4.	Textile based	–	5	5	10	2	(1.25 30
5.	Chemical based	1	7	10	10	2	(1.25 30
6.	Mineral based	–	9	12	7	9	(1.25 30
7.	Engineering based	–	3	9	9	6	(1.25) 30
8.	Miscellaneous	1	4	10	9	30	(1.25)
	Total	17 (7.08)	64 (26.6)	80 (33.3)	50 (20.8)	29 (12.1)	240 (100)

Source: Computed from Primary Data.
Note : Figures within parenthesis denotes percentages.

Family Size

Another important factor influencing the entrepreneurial skills is the size of the family. The average family size of the sample respondents is presented in Table 5.8.

From Table 5.8 it is clear that of the 791 family members, 329 (41.6%) are male, 278 (35.1%) are female and 184 (23.3%) are children in the sample respondents household. Similarly the family of the entrepreneurs are having the high level of the male members in the study districts. In the case of children, in the family of the sample respondents in each small scale industry are very low. It is inferred that there is high rate of the male group in the role of entrepreneurial development of the SSI sector. The average size shows that 3.2 persons are living in a SSI entrepreneurs family.

Table 5.8 : Average Family Members of the Sample Respondents

Sl. No.	*Category*	*Male*	*Female*	*Children*	*Total*	*Average No. per Family*
1.	Food based	34	39	16	89 (11.2)	2.9
2.	Forest based	30	36	22	88 (11.1)	2.9
3.	Animal Husbandry based	30	33	30	93 (11.7)	3.1
4.	Textile based	60	40	39	139 (17.5)	4.6
5.	Chemical based	36	39	29	104 (13.1)	3.4
6.	Mineral based	39	32	30	91 (11.5)	3.0
7.	Engineering based	60	31	16	107 (13.5)	3.5
8.	Miscellaneous	40	28	12	80 (10.1)	2.6
	Total	329 (41.6)	278 (35.1)	184 (23.3)	791 (100)	3.2

Source: Computed from Primary Data.
Note : Figures within parenthesis denotes percentages.

It is tried to find out the relationship between the occupation of father and the entrepreneurs. Agriculture is predominant occupation in the Dindigul and Madurai districts. Besides small scale industry like businessman and farmers have developed the entrepreneurs in the district.

The father's occupation-wise distribution of the sample respondents are given in Table 5.9. 82 (34.1%) sample respondent's father are Business man and it shows the highest percentage of entrepreneurs in the small scale industries. The occupation of the 63 sample respondents (26.25%) are agriculture in the study area. The remaining 53 respondents (22.1%) are doing the coolly work and 42 respondents (17.5%) are in the profession in the Madurai and Dindigul districts. It is inferred that the Business family have highy involved in the Small Scale Entrepreneurship.

Table 5.9 : Parents Occupation-wise Distribution of the Sample Respondents

Sl. No.	*Category*	*Cooly*	*Farmer*	*Business*	*Profession*	*Total*
1.	Food based	5	10	10	5	30
2.	Forest based	10	10	10	-	30
3.	Animal Husbandry based	13	10	7	-	30
4.	Textile based	5	8	15	2	30
5.	Chemical based	3	10	10	7	30
6.	Mineral based	7	7	8	8	30
7.	Engineering based	8	3	12	7	30
8.	Miscellaneous	2	5	10	13	30
	Total	53 (22.1)	63 (26.25)	82 (34.1)	42 (17.5)	240 (100)

Source: Computed from Primary Data.
Note : Figures within parenthesis denotes percentages.

2. Sample SSI Units

A few details regarding the year of starting the SSI units and locational aspects of the units are explained in Tables 5.10 and 5.11 respectively.

Table 5.10 : Year of Starting

Sl. No.	*Category*	*Before 1990*	*1991-2000*	*After 2000*	*Total*
1.	Food based	5	19	5	30
2.	Forest based	19	10	1	30
3.	Animal Husbanday based	20	5	5	30
4.	Textile based	10	10	10	30
5.	Chemical based	15	10	5	30
6.	Mineral based	10	10	10	30
7.	Engineering based	7	13	10	30
8.	Miscellaneous	10	15	5	30
	Total	97 (40.4)	92 (38.3)	51 (21.2)	240 (100)

Source: Computed from Primary Data.
Note : Figures within parenthesis denotes percentages.

The study found that most of the industry units were started before 1990 (40.4%).During the economic reforms period (1990-1991 to 1999-2000), the 92 units (38.3%) of the sample SSI units were started in the study districts. After the year, 2000, the newly started SSI units are only 51 sample units (21.2%). The growth of SSI units after implementation of New Economic Policy shows the positive development in the sample study districts.

Table 5.11 reveals that of the total sample SSI units, 28.3 per cent (68 units) are located in the rural areas and 24.2 per cent of the units (58 units) are also located in the semi-urban areas. The urban areas occupied 19.2 per cent (46 units) of the sample SSI units. Despite the Government had provided many concessions to the SSI units located in the industrially backward areas, only 18.7 per cent (45 units) are located in the industrially backward areas. The living areas are also occupied by the SSI units in the study districts. It has 9.9 per cent of the sample units in these two districts.

The nature and type of the SSI organization is presented in Table 5.12. The sole proprietorship type of SSI enterprises are dominated (56.25%) in the study districts. Following the sole proprietorship, partnership type of SSI organization (29.1%) are functioning in the study areas. The remaining 14.5% of the sample units are Joint Stock Companies. The sample SSI enterprises did not cover the Corporation and public sector organization.

3. New Economic Policy and SSI Units

The small scale industries mainly take the necessary steps to mobilize adequate finance both from internal and external sources. Non-availability of sufficient raw materials, break-down of machinery, power cuts and transport bottlenecks are also some of the other causes of under-utilization of capacity. Under-utilization of capacity may lead to lower production and lower profitability. In some cases, under-utilization of capacity may shift the industrial units from profit zone to loss zone. Some of the industrial units are also planning to increase their installed capacities. They should be careful in increasing their capacities. They should first match

Table 5.11 : Region of the Sample SSI Units

Sl. No.	*Region*	*Food*	*Forest*	*Animal*	*Textile*	*Chemical*	*Mineral*	*Engineering*	*Miscell-aneous*	*Total*
1.	Rural	16	20	18	5	5	1	1	2	68 (28.3)
2.	Urban	1	2	5	5	10	10	9	4	46 (19.2)
3.	Semi-Urban	11	1	5	5	11	10	9	6	58 (24.2)
4.	Industrial Backward	1	5	1	10	2	8	10	8	45 (18.7)
5.	Living Area	1	2	1	5	2	1	1	10	23 (9.9)
	Total	30	30	30	30	30	30	30	30	240 (100)

Source: Computed from Primary Data.

Table 5.12 : Type of SSI Sample Entrerprises

Sl. No.	Nature	Food	Forest	Animal	Textile	Chemical	Mineral	Engineering	Miscell-aneous	Total
1.	Sole Proprietor	15	27	28	18	15	13	9	10	135 (56.25)
2.	Partnership	10	3	2	10	10	7	18	10	70 (29.1)
3.	Joint Stock Company	5	–	–	2	5	10	3	10	35 (14.5)
4.	Corporation	–	–	–	–	–	–	–	–	–
5.	Public Sector Undertaking	–	–	–	–	–	–	–	–	–
6.	Others	–	–	–	–	–	–	–	–	–
	Total	30	30	30	30	30	30	30	30	240 (100)

Source: Computed from Primary Data.

the inputs and output. If adequate inputs are available and there is no problem of market, they may increase the capacities.

The performance of SSI units in the selected study districts are analysed in this section. The performance analysis includes the production, sales, investment and employment of the sample SSI units in the study district of Tamil Nadu.

1. *Production*

The locally available raw material has been generally used for the production of small scale industries. The sources of raw materials are: Private, Government and Cooperative.

The sample entrepreneurs are purchasing raw materials mainly from private traders. It is clear that the role of Government and Cooperative sector in supplying raw materials are very poor. The private source of raw materials influenced the higher cost of production due to the higher price of raw materials. The Government may take the necessary steps in supplying raw materials at reasonable rate to the Small Scale Entrepreneurs.

Table 5.13 shows the production value of selected SSI units in study districts. It is clear that the total production value of the 240 SSI sample units was increased from Rs. 3,73,681.35 thousands in 1990-91 to Rs.13,49,417.35 thousands in 2004-05. The change value of the sample units was Rs. 9,75,736.9 thousands. It is inferred that before the implementation of New Economic Policy, Food based industry (4.14%) had dominated in the study area. But after implementation of New Economic Policy the Textile based industry (40.8%) dominated in the production level.

Tables 5.14 and 5.15 revealed that the average production value of a sample SSI unit was Rs.1,18,671.8 thousands under traditional method and Rs. 4,86,852.2 thousands under modern methods of production during the period of 1990-91. But at present the production value of a sample SSI unit had increased to Rs. 5,73,283.1 thousands under traditional method and Rs. 13,86,036 under modern method production. Both the periods, before and after the implementation of New Economic

Table 5.13 : Total Production Value of the Sample SSI Units in Study Districts

(*Rupees in thousand*)

Sl. No. Industry	Before			After			Changes		
	Madurai	Dindigul	All	Madurai	Dindigul	All	Madurai	Dindigul	All
1. Food based	162931.9	146795.1	154863.5 (41.4)	201416.2	235015.2	218215.7 (16.1)	38484.3	88220.1	63352.2
2. Forest based	14421.3	19537.0	16979.15 (4.5)	196121.5	27422.8	111772.15 (8.2)	181700.2	7885.8	94793.0
3. Animal Husbandry based	12617.6	17761.3	15189.4 (4.06)	81623.0	83983.1	82803.05 (6.1)	69005.4	66221.8	67613.6
4. Textile based	137954.2	63616.7	100785.4 (26.9)	272948.3	830046.4	551497.35 (40.8)	134994.1	766429.7	4501711.9
5. Chemical based	4344.4	5017.0	4680.7 (1.2)	16673.8	18682.8	17678.3 (1.3)	12329.4	13665.8	12997.6
6. Mineral based	46611.3	42518.5	44564.9 (11.9)	75939.6	87956.6	81948.1 (6.1)	29328.3	45438.1	37383.2
7. Engineering based	26154.4	27224.2	26689.3 (7.1)	92144.9	126795.1	109470.0 (8.1)	65990.5	99570.9	82780.7
8. Miscellaneous	9019.3	10838.7	9929.0 (2.6)	146259.7	205805.6	176032.65 (13.0)	137240.4	194966.9	166103.6
Total	414054.4	333308.5	373681.35 (100)	1083127.0	1615707.6	1349417.35 (100)	669072.6	1282399.1	975736.9

Source: Computed from Primary Data.
Note: Figures within parenthesis denotes percentages.

Policy, the Food based industry had involved effectively in modern method of production. But the traditional methods are mainly used in Chemical based industry in the study districts of Tamil Nadu.

There are various sources of Capital for small scale industrial units in the district. They are; Own funds, Commercial banks, Development banks, friends and relatives and money-lender. Internal source (Owned funds) in major source of capital.

Table 5.14 : Prodction Value of Sample SSI before NEP

(Rs. in thousand)

Sl. No.	*Category*	*Average Production Value*	
		Traditional Method	*Modern Method*
1.	Food based	60,721.9	2,49,005.1
2.	Forest based	7,569.5	86,388.8
3.	Animal Husbandry based	5,829.5	9,359.9
4.	Textile based	21,834.4	78,951.1
5.	Chemical based	732.9	3,947.9
6.	Mineral based	6,792.9	37,771.9
7.	Engineering based	11,648.7	15,040.5
8.	Miscellaneous based	3,542.0	6,387.0
	Total	1,18,671.8	4,86,852.2

Source: Computed from Primary Data.

Table 5.15 : Production Value of Sample SSI after NEP

(Rs in thousand)

Sl. No.	*Category*	*Average Production Value*	
		Traditional Method	*Modern Method*
1.	Food based	96,731.6	3,39,699.8
2.	Forest based	14,649.2	2,08,895.1
3.	Animal Husbandry based	30,529.1	52,273.9
4.	Textile based	34,691.9	5,16,805.4
5.	Chemical based	8,351.1	9,327.2
6.	Mineral based	18,469.0	63,479.1
7.	Engineering based	3,03,609.5	79,109.0
8.	Miscellaneous based	65,256.7	1,10,775.9
	Total	5,72,288.1	13,80,365.4

Source: Computed from Primary Data.

The cotton textile industry has been growing in importance in recent years because of its valuable contribution to foreign exchange earnings through exports of yarn, fabrics, garments and hosiery products. Dindigul and Madurai districts are equally adopting the traditions as well as modern techonology in producing small scale industries production. The Engineering based industry are mostly using the traditional method. Till now, the modern techniques are mostly used in other industries which are utilising the machineries with power.

Table 5.16 : Changes in Production Value of Sample SSI

Sl. No.	*Category*	*Change in Production Value*	
		Traditional Method	*Modern Method*
1.	Food based	(-) 36,009.7	(-) 90,694.7
2.	Forest based	(-) 7,079.7	(-) 1,22,506.3
3.	Animal Husbandry based	(-) 24,699.6	(-)42,914.0
4.	Textile based	(-) 12,857.5	(-) 4,37,854.3
5.	Chemical based	(-) 7,618.2	(-) 5,379.3
6.	Mineral based	(-) 11,676.0	(-) 25,707.1
7.	Engineering based	(-) 2,91,960.8	(-) 64,068.5
8.	Miscellaneous based	(-) 61,714.7	(-) 1,04,388.9
	Total	4,53,616.2	9,13,513.1

Source: Computed from Primary Data.

2. *Sales*

Small scale industries are facing many problems while exporting their products. To overcome marketing problems in the overseas market, the Export Production Councils for different products make efforts to promote exports of the products of their member units through district marketing, developing vendor relations, opening respective sales outlets abroad as a collective export marketing strategy. It performs the advisory and executive functions. SSI units can access export-related services from the councils. Some council obtains bulk purchase orders from foreign buyers and distribute among member units for supply to council for onward export.

This process ensures export order to every member unit and facilities the timely delivery of goods abroad. The EPCs also provide latest information to the existing as well as new members on export-import policies, customs and excise duty rules etc. Beside trade enquiries, it also circulates tender notices to its member to avail the export opportunities.

To promote and regulate growth and image of readymade garments abroad, the Apparel Export Promotion Council (AEPC) is established in 1978. Its main functions are: to identify and explore export market potential, organizing buyer and seller meets abroad, participating in trade Fairs and Exhibitions abroad, publicity of selected products abroad, advising the Government on matters relating to Export-Import Policy for readymade garments and also to administering and monitoring the export entitlements for readymade garments. Similarity to facilitate the export of chemical based and allied products from India to the overseas market CAPEXIL, formerly known as Chemicals and Allied Products Export Promotion Council was set up in 1958 with the object of providing export assistance to its member through providing trade information.

It also participates in overseas Trade Fairs, Joint Brand publicity programmes and overseas publicity, Individual sales-*cum*-study Tours in the overseas market etc. Being a facilitator, CAPEXIL monitors and analyze the overseas market and disseminates information to members.

The average sales value in domestic market by the sample SSI units is explained in Table 5.17. The table shows that the change in the average domestic sales value was Rs. 57,37,956.1 thousands in Madurai district and Rs. 72,45,447.3 thousand in Dindigul district. After implementation of New Economic Policy there is a tremendous growth in the domestic sales of SSI products in the study districts of Tamil Nadu.

The average sales value of exports of SSI products from the study district, had changed to the extent of Rs. 8,64,770.0

Table 5.17 : Average Sales value Domestic markets

(Rupees in thousand)

Sl. No.	Industry	Before		After		Changes	
		Madurai	*Dindigul*	*Madurai*	*Dindigul*	*Madurai*	*Dindigul*
1.	Food based	3,814.2	4,719.1	1,00,578.5	1,11,540.4	96,764.3	1,06,821.3
2.	Forest based	2,928.5	1,992.7	2,13,107.1	1,48,785.7	2,10,178.6	1,46,793.0
3.	Animal Husbandry based	46,624.1	36,550.9	1,97,842.6	1,74,388.2	1,51,218.5	1,37,837.3
4.	Textile based	7,537.7	42,142.8	35,60,010.2	4,57,146.1	35,52,472.5	45,29,333.3
5.	Chemical based	1,625.4	1,719.0	83,376.1	1,20,161.1	81,750.7	1,18,442.1
6.	Mineral based	4,668.8	6,632.7	56,004.2	70,954.0	51,335.4	64,321.3
7.	Engineering based	15,571.4	17,142.8	11,94,526.0	14,71,099.0	11,78,954.6	14,53,956.2
8.	Miscellaneous	22,804.2	7,950.0	4,38,085.7	6,95,892.8	4,15,281.5	6,87,942.8
	Total	1,05,574.3	1,18,850.0	58,43,530.4	73,64,267.3	57,37,956.1	72,45,447.3

Source: Computed from Primary Data.

Table 5.18 : Average Export Sales Value of SSI Units

(Rs. in Thousands)

Sl. No.	*Industry*	*Before*		*After*		*Changes*	
		Madurai	*Dindigul*	*Madurai*	*Dindigul*	*Madurai*	*Dindigul*
1.	Food based	504.1	809.8	21,217.0	45,307.5	20,712.9	44,497.7
2.	Forest based	914.2	614.4	1,86,428.5	10,614.2	1,85,514.3	10,000.0
3.	Animal Husbandry based	4,294.5	4,067.8	1,56,290.4	1,24,609.2	1,51,995.9	1,20,541.4
4.	Textile based	19,332.8	32,883.5	1,62,190.4	3,71,499.9	2,42,857.6	3,38,616.4
5.	Chemical based	826.1	1,719.0	83,376.1	1,20,161.1	82,550.0	1,18,442.1
6.	Mineral based	3,261.2	6,042.4	39,067.8	47,002.6	35,806.6	40,960.2
7.	Engineering based	4,217.0	5,813.0	91,433.2	1,07,864.2	87,216.2	1,02,051.2
8.	Miscellaneous	2,919.8	2,214.9	61,036.3	50,928.5	58,116.5	48,713.6
	Total	36,269.7	54,164.6	9,01,039.7	8,77,987.2	8,64,770.0	8,23,822.6

Source: Computed from Primary Data.

thousands in Madurai district and 8,23,822.6 thousand in Dindigul district. The average export value of a sample SSI unit in Madurai district was Rs. 36,269.17 thousand during the period of implementation of New Economic Policy and after the implementation, it had increased to 9,01,039.7 thousand. Similarly in Dindigul district the average sales value of a sample SSI unit had also increased, from Rs. 54,164.6 thousand in 1990-91to Rs. 8,77,987.2 thousand in 2003-04.

Table 5.19 explains the average sales value of SSI unit. It is clear that the changes in the average sales value of a SSI unit was Rs. 83,59,232.2 thousand in Madurai district and Rs. 2,12,63,883.1 thousand in Dindigul district. The changes in the total sales value was higher in the case of Engineering based industry in Dindigul district and Textile based industry in Madurai district. It is inferred that the Economic reforms are favourable to Engineering based and Textile based industry in Tamil Nadu.

3. *Investment*

Small Scale Industries are capital light and is suitable to the country like India where capital is deficient. It helps in mobilizing capital. An essentially agrarian economy, people have a tendency to keep their money idle rather than investing in large scale industries. Since the small scale industries are located close to the areas where people stay, mobilization of rural savings is easy. These industries are run with local labour and locally materials. Thus, they help in the proper utilisation of local resources.

Investment is one of the important criteria for evaluate the performance of SSI units in Tamil Nadu. Table 5.20 reveals that the total fixed capital investment level of selected SSI units was Rs. 5,28,338.1 thousand in Madurai district and Rs. 11,72,986.7 thousand in Dindigul district before implementation of Economic Reforms.

After liberalization, the fixed investment capital level of 120

Table 5.19 : Average Sales Value of Sample SSI Units in Study Districts

(Rs. in thousand)

Sl. No.	*Industry*	*Before*		*After*		*Changes*	
		Madurai	*Dindigul*	*Madurai*	*Dindigul*	*Madurai*	*Dindigul*
1.	Food based	4,318.3	5,528.9	1,21,795.5	1,56,847.9	1,17,477.2	1,51,319.0
2.	Forest based	3,842.7	2,606.9	3,99,535.6	1,59,399.9	3,95,692.9	1,56,793.0
3.	Animal Husbandry based	50,918.6	40,618.7	3,54,133.0	2,98,997.4	3,03,214.4	22,58,378.7
4.	Textile based	26,870.5	75,026.3	38,22,200.6	49,44,276.0	37,95,330.1	48,69,219.7
5.	Chemical based	2,451.5	2,716.5	13,08,823.1	1,87,821.2	13,06,371.6	1,85,104.7
6.	Mineral based	7,930.0	12,675.1	9,507.2	1,17,956.6	1,577.2	1,05,281.5
7.	Engineering based	19,788.4	22,955.8	18,85,959.2	1,48,18,963.2	19,66,170.8	1,47,96,007.4
8.	Miscellaneous	25,724.0	10,164.9	4,99,122.0	7,51,914.0	4,73,398.0	7,41,749.1
	Total	1,41,844.0	1,172,293.1	85,01,076.2	2,14,36,176.2	83,59,232.2	2,12,63,883.1

Source: Computed from Primary Data.

Table 5.20 : Fixed Capital Investment Level of Sample SSI Units

(Rs. in thousands)

Sl. No. Industry	*Before*		*After*		*Changes*	
	Madurai	*Dindigul*	*Madurai*	*Dindigul*	*Madurai*	*Dindigul*
1. Food based	49,373.7	18,09.4	1,58,319.4	1,47,072.3	1,08,945.7	1,28,762.9
2. Forest based	1,67,339.9	4,49,007.1	5,75,949.6	13,58,004.2	4,08,609.7	9,08,997.1
3. Animal Husbandry based	86,715.1	84,755.9	3,43,014.3	2,76,365.8	2,56,299.2	1,91,609.9
4. Textile based	26,504.9	63,647.5	1,72,004.5	5,88,073.2	1,45,499.6	48,69,219.7
5. Chemical based	31,767.0	1,10,033.5	1,50,972.9	4,32,186.7	1,19,205.9	5,24,425.7
6. Mineral based	63,501.9	70,627.8	1,33,247.4	1,86,009.1	69,745.5	1,15,381.3
7. Engineering based	49,373.7	18,215.6	3,58,413.2	1,47,072.3	3,09,039.5	1,28,856.7
8. Miscellaneous	53,761.9	3,58,389.9	3,23,089.1	7,75,537.8	2,69,327.2	4,17,147.9
Total	5,28,338.1	11,72,986.7	22,15,010.4	39,10,321.4	16,86,672.3	27,37,334.7

Source: Computed from Primary Data.

SSI units had changed to the level of 16,86,672.3 thousand in Madurai district and Rs. 27,37,334.7 thousand in Dindigul district. At an average, the changes per unit was Rs. 14,055.6 thousand in Madurai district and Rs. 22,811.1 thousand in Dindigul district.

It shows that the liberalization policy helps the SSI entrepreneurs to invest at a higher level in the study districts of Tamil Nadu. The variable capital investment level of SSI units is explained in Table 5.21.

It is clear that the variable capital investment level of 120 sample units was Rs.7,00,228.3 thousand in 1990-91 and it has increased to Rs. 21,81,415.4 thousand in the year 2003-04. The changes in variable capital investment level per unit, at an average, was Rs. 12,343.2 thousand in Madurai district and Rs. 10,442.4 thousands in Dindigul district. Due to inflationary pressure and increasing the price level of raw-material of the SSI units, the variable capital investment level was also increased year by year. So the cost of production was also increased for the SSI, products of Tamil Nadu.

Table 5.22 explains the total investment level of selected 120 units in Madurai and Dindigul districts. The changes in the total investment level of SSI units in Madurai district was Rs. 47,25,756.5 thousands and it was Rs. 60,36,922.9 in Dindigul district. The average change of a selected SSI units in Madurai district was Rs. 39,381.3 thousand and Rs. 50,307.6 thousand in Dindigul district.

The item-wise changes in the capital investment in study districts is exhibited in Table 5.23. From the table, it is clear that the investment level was higher in the case of Forest based industries (9,71,422.6) and Textile based industry (5,04,818.8) in study district of Tamil Nadu. At an average, the changes in the capital investment of a Forest based industry was Rs. 32,380.7 thousand after implementation of New Economic Policy. Similarly there is a tremendous changes in the capital investment of all category of SSI units in Tamil Nadu.

Table 5.21 : Variable Capital Invesiment Level of Sample SSI Units

(Rs. in thousands)

Sl. No.	Industry	Before		After		Changes	
		Madurai	Dindigul	Madurai	Dindigul	Madurai	Dindigul
1.	Food based	1,01,815.1	1,19,542.0	1,49,359.1	1,44,864.1	47,544.0	25,322.0
2.	Forest based	3,29,878.2	3,45,642.6	7,21,851.7	5,98,198.4	39,19,73.5	2,52,555.8
3.	Animal Husbandry based	31,256.0	27,334.4	3,42,430.1	1,75,341.05	31,11,74.1	1,48,006.65
4.	Textile based	1,10,306.6	1,61,684.3	5,61,380.5	6,45,906.9	45,10,73.9	4,84,222.6
5.	Chemical based	11,075.9	47,562.2	1,47,196.8	1,58,444.9	13,61,20.9	1,10,882.7
6.	Mineral based	10,429.7	23,177.6	46,582.3	62,627.2	36,152.6	39,449.6
7.	Engineering based	1,01,815.1	50,035.1	1,71,147.1	2,14,864.1	69,332.0	1,64,829.0
8.	Miscellaneous	3,651.7	2,966.5	41,467.8	30,795.9	37,816.1	27,829.4
	Total	7,00,228.3	7,77,944.7	21,81,415.4	20,31,042.5	14,81,187.1	12,53,097.75

Source: Computed from Primary Data.

Table 5.22 : Total Investment Level of Sample SSI Units.

(Rs. in thousands)

Sl. No.	*Industry*	*Before*		*After*		*Changes*	
		Madurai	*Dindigul*	*Madurai*	*Dindigul*	*Madurai*	*Dindigul*
1.	Food based						
2.	Forest based	1,51,188.8	1,67,668.5	2,77,861.4	2,91,936.4	1,26,672.6	1,24,267.9
3.	Animal Husbandry	4,97,218.1	7,94,649.7	12,97,801.3	19,56,202.6	8,00,583.2	11,61,552.9
	based	1,17,971.1	1,12,090.3	6,85,444.4	4,51,706.8	5,67,473.3	3,39,616.5
4.	Textile based	2,76,097.2	3,71,117.4	24,60,384.9	32,42,551.5	21,84,287.7	30,84,955.8
5.	Chemical based	42,842.9	1,57,595.7	2,98,169.7	5,90,631.6	2,55,326.8	4,33,035.9
6.	Mineral based	73,931.6	93,805.4	1,79,829.7	2,48,636.3	1,05,898.1	1,54,830.9
7.	Engineering based	1,51,188.8	68,250.7	5,29,560.3	3,61,936.4	3,78,371.5	2,93,685.7
8.	Miscellaneous	57,413.6	3,61,356.4	3,64,556.9	8,06,333.7	3,07,143.3	4,44,977.3
	Total	13,67,852.1	21,26,534.1	60,93,608.6	79,49,935.3	47,25,756.5	60,36,922.9

Source: Computed from Primary Data.

Table 5.23 : Changes in Capital Investment in Study District of Tamil Nadu

(Rs. in thousands)

Sl. No. Items	*Food Based*	*Forest Based*	*Animal Husbandry Based*	*Textile Based*	*Chemical Based*	*Mineral Based*	*Engineer-ing Based*	*Miscellane-ous*
I. Fixed Capital								
1. Land and Building	76,388.8	4,05,281.2	2,00,713.4	13,36,392.8	1,34,770.25	53,659.4	1,26,388.8	89,235.0
2. Machinery and Equipment	42,463.2	2,49,314.9	17,517.9	3,88,857.1	77,997.65	37,906.0	92,463.2	48,971.3
3. Furniture and others	2.2	4,207.2	5,723.1	3,34,962.6	7,911.65	997.9	96.0	3,35,212.6
Total	1,18,854.2	6,58,803.4	2,23,954.4	20,60,212.5	2,20,679.5	92,563.4	2,18,948.1	4,73,418.9
II. Variable Capital								
1. Wage	37,510.8	16,088.2	40,839.5	97,157.8	49,464.2	36,563.3	22,510.8	6,374.2
2. Raw materials	2,730.1	1,21,780.5	1,85,777.0	2,45,489.4	28,001.4	620.8	94,074.6	26,223.0
3. Others	6,835.2	1,74,750.5	7,803.7	1,25,001.0	46,036.2	616.9	495.1	225.5
Total	47,076.1	3,12,619.2	2,34,420.2	4,67,648.2	1,23,501.8	37,801.0	1,17,080.5	32,822.7
I & II	1,60,470.2	9,71,423.0	4,58,374.6	25,27,860.7	3,44,181.3	1,30,364.5	3,36,028.6	5,06,241.6

Source: Computed from Primary Data.

Table 5.24 : Average Employment Level of Sample SSI Units

(No. of persons per unit)

Sl. No. Industry	*Before*			*After*			*Changes*		
	Madurai	*Dindigul*	*All*	*Madurai*	*Dindigul*	*All*	*Madurai*	*Dindigul*	*All*
1. Food based	25.4	23.4	24.4 (12.8)	17.1	16.5	16.8 (10.8)	(-) 8.3	(-) 6.9	(-) 7.6
2. Forest based	22.0	18.4	20.2 (10.6)	15.4	12.5	13.95 (9.04)	(-) 6.6	(-) 5.9	(-)17.2
3. Animal Husbandry based	22.1	18.7	20.4 (10.7)	14.9	13.4	14.15 (9.2)	(-) 7.2	(-) 5.3	(-)6.25
4. Textile based	44.5	54.3	49.4 (26.0)	36.4	80.3	58.35 (37.8)	(-) 8.1	(+) 6.0	(-) 2.1
5. Chemical based	22.0	18.5	20.25 (10.7)	17.4	14.5	15.95 (10.3)	(-) 4.6	(-) 4.0	(-)4.3
6. Mineral based	18.2	17.1	17.65 (9.3)	9.3	6.9	8.1 (5.2)	(-) 8.9	(-)10.2	(-)9.55
7. Engineering based	13.8	10.4	12.1 (6.4)	11.1	8.6	9.85 (6.4)	(-) 2.7	(-) 1.8	(-)2.25
8. Miscellanous	22.6	27.2	24.9 (13.1)	17.0	17.3	17.15 (11.1)	(-) 5.6	(-) 9.9	(-)7.75
Total	190.6	188.0	189.3 (100)	138.6	170.0	154.3 (100)			

Source: Computed from Primary Data.

3. *Employment*

SSI units generally provide large number of employment opportunities to the rural poor. It is pertinent to analyse that the impact of New Economic Policy on the promotion of Employment opportunities through SSI units in Tamil Nadu was 154 persons per unit. It was 190 persons before implementation of New Economic Policy and the employment level per SSI unit had declined to 138 in Madurai district. In the case of Dindigul district the employment generation decreased from 198 in 1990-91 to 170 in 2003-04. It is inferred that all category of SSI units generated employment was declined in the study district, except Textile based industry in Dindigul district. The employment generation was higher in the Textile based industry (38.8%). Following the Textile based industry, Chemical based industry, Food based industry and miscellaneous industry had generated around 10 per cent of the total employment by SSI unit.

The category-wise employment generation of selected SSI units are given in Tables 5.25, 5.26, 5.27, 5.28, 5.29, 5.30, 5.31and 5.32 From these tables, it is clear that there is no child labour in small scale industry after the implementation of Child Labour Abolistion Act in Tamil Nadu. It is inferred that male domination in employment opportunities was higher in all category of SSI units in study districts of Tamil Nadu.

Table 5.25 : Average Employment Level (Food based Industry)

Sl. No.	*Period*	*Number of Persons Employed*			
		Male	*Female*	*Child*	*Total*
	MADURAI				
1.	Before	15.8	9.6	—	25.4
2.	At present	9.0	8.1	—	(-) 17.1
3.	Changes	- 6.8	- 1.5	—	8.3
	DINDIGUL				
1.	Before	11.3	12.1	—	23.4
2.	At present	9.5	7.0	—	16.5
3.	Changes	- 1.8	- 5.1	—	6.9

Source: Computed from Primary Data.

Table 5.26 : Average Employment Level (Forest based Industry)

S. No.	*Period*	*Number of Persons Employed*			
		Male	*Female*	*Child*	*Total*
	MADURAI				
1.	Before	14.0	8.0	—	22.0
2.	At present	8.0	7.4	—	15.4
3.	Changes	6.0	0.6	—	6.6
	DINDIGUL				
1.	Before	10.3	8.1	—	18.4
2.	At present	6.5	6.0	—	12.5
3.	Changes	3.8	2.1	—	5.9

Source: Computed from Primary Data.

Table 5.27 : Average Employment Level (Animal Husbandry based Industry)

Sl. No.	*Period*	*Number of Persons Employed*			
		Male	*Female*	*Child*	*Total*
	MADURAI				
1.	Before	14.1	8.0	—	22.1
2.	At present	8.9	6.0	—	14.9
3.	Changes	5.2	2.0	—	7.2
	DINDIGUL				
1.	Before	10.3	8.4	—	18.7
2.	At present	7.3	6.1	—	13.4
3.	Changes	3.0	2.3	—	5.3

Source: Computed from Primary Data.

Table 5.28 : Average Employment Level (Textile based Industry)

Sl. No.	*Period*	*Number of Persons Employed*			
		Male	*Female*	*Child*	*Total*
	MADURAI				
1.	Before	26.1	18.4	—	44.5
2.	At present	20.8	15.6	—	36.4
3.	Changes	5.3	2.8	—	8.1
	DINDIGUL				
1.	Before	30.4	28.9	—	54.3
2.	At present	44.9	35.4	—	80.3
3.	Changes	- 14.5	- 11.5	—	26.0

Source: Computed from Primary Data.

Table 5.29 : Chemical Based Industry (Average Employment Level)

Sl. No.	Period	Number of Persons Employed			
		Male	Female	Child	Total
	MADURAI				
1.	Before	13.9	8.1	—	22.0
2.	At present	10.0	7.4	—	17.4
3.	Changes	3.9	0.7	—	(-) 4.6
	DINDIGUL				
1.	Before	10.3	8.2	—	18.5
2.	At present	8.4	6.1	—	14.5
3.	Changes	1.9	2.1	—	(-) 4.0

Source: Computed from Primary Data.

Table 5.30 : Mineral Based Industry (Average Employment Level)

Sl. No.	Period	Number of Persons Employed			
		Male	Female	Child	Total
	MADURAI				
1.	Before	15.1	3.1	—	18.2
2.	At present	7.2	2.1	—	9.3
3.	Changes	7.9	1.0	—	(-) 8.9
	DINDIGUL				
1.	Before	12.3	4.8	—	17.1
2.	At present	5.8	1.1	—	6.9
3.	Changes	6.5	3.7	—	(-) 10.2

Source: Computed from Primary Data.

Table 5.31 : Engineering Based Industry (Average Employment Level)

Sl. No.	Period	Number of Persons Employed			
		Male	Female	Child	Total
	MADURAI				
1.	Before	9.2	4.6	—	13.8
2.	At present	7.9	3.2	—	11.1
3.	Changes	1.3	1.4	—	(-) 2.7
	DINDIGUL				
1.	Before	7.2	3.2	—	10.4
2.	At present	6.4	2.2	—	8.6
3.	Changes	0.8	1.0	—	(-) 1.8

Source: Computed from Primary Data.

Table 5.32 : Miscellaneous (Average Employment Level)

Sl. No.	*Period*	*Number of Persons Employed*			
		Male	*Female*	*Child*	*Total*
	MADURAI				
1.	Before	14.2	8.4	—	22.6
2.	At present	9.8	7.2	—	17.0
3.	Changes	4.4	1.2	—	5.6
	DINDIGUL				
1.	Before	15.4	11.8	—	27.2
2.	At present	9.5	7.8	—	17.3
3.	Changes	5.9	4.0	—	9.9

Source: Computed from Primary Data.

The above analysis focused the impact of New Economic Policy on SSI in Study districts of Tamil Nadu, based on the changes in the Production level, Sales level, Investment level and the Employment level.

6. Summary, Findings and Conslusion

Small Scale Industry (SSI) has emerged as India's engine of growth. In 2000, the SSI sector accounted for nearly 40 per cent of gross value of output in total exports from the country through over 32 lakh units of the SSI sector provided. The present economic scenario in India has created an excellent climate for the development of SMEs. Although the Indian economy traditionally has been agro based, with a sizeable part of its Gross Domestic Product (GDP) being contributed by agriculture, a notable contributor to the nations gross domestic product in the small scale industrial sector. The SSI sector was dominated in the earlier years by village and cottage industries, and small industrial units with very low capital base, with the increasing pressure of population, which has grown from 350 million in 1947 at the time of Independence to over 985 million as of now there has been a perceptible shift towards industrial economy which provides gainful employment. During the paradigm shift in economy, the small scale sector has remained a very active participant in India's growth.

The New Economic Policy plays a vital role in the economy of our country. The industrial policies announced by the Central and State Governments, have been providing various incentives for accelerating the growth of the SSI sector. However the rationally of state intervention in the promotions of SSI was questioned in some studies. Most of the studies were focused on the performance of SSI at the national level; while the issues related to size, growth, structure and productivity have received inadequate attention at the State level. Under the process of restructuring Indian Economy, liberalization and decontrols has put the small enterprises of a critical juncture of intricacies concerning their future. Therefore, for any change in policy-related to small industries there is a need for elaborate studies on the growth and performance of SSI.

Primary data as well as secondary data were used for the present study. The study period was from 1990-91 to 2003-04 (Fourteen years after liberalization policy in India). Secondary data were collected from the office records and reports of the Ministry of Statistics and Programme Implementation, Ministry of Small Scale Industries and Agro & Rural Industries, Ministry of Industry and Commerce etc.

In order to measure the impact of liberalization on small scale enterprises, certain parameters, namely, number of registered units, production level, sales value, employment generation and earnings were used for the present study. The National level data, State level data and sample study district data were compared for the analysis of impact of economic reforms on small scale industries.

Primary data were also collected from the sample small scale enterprises in Madurai and Dindigul districts of Tamil Nadu. Madurai and Dindigul districts are purposively selected for the study based as the concentration of small scale industries in these study districts. The sample enterprises were selected based on the criteria of large number of enterprises in the study district. The sample enterprises include the textile and garments, wood products and furniture, food processing, motor repair and welding, leather products, metal products, electrical and electronic repairs etc. A sample of 240 small scale enterprises from the study districts were randomly selected and the sample entrepreneurs were administered with a pre-tested questionnaire. The collected secondary and primary data were analysed with the suitable tools like percentage analysis, etc. The findings of the study are summarized below.

Production

The small scale industries sector plays a vital role in the growth of the country. It contributes almost 40 per cent of the gross industrial value added in the Indian economy.

It has been estimated that a million Rupees of investment in fixed assets in the small scale sector produces 4.62 million worth of goods or services with an approximate value addition at ten percentage points.

The small scale sector has grown rapidly over the years. The growth rates during the various plan periods have been very impressive. The number of small-scale units has increased from an estimated 0.87 million units in the year 1980-81 to over 3 million in the year 2000.

When the performance of this sector is viewed against the growth in the manufacturing and the industry sector as a whole, it instills confidence in the resilience of the small-scale sector.

Employment

SSI Sector in India creates largest employment opportunities for the Indian populace, next only to Agriculture. It has been estimated that 100,000 rupees of investment in fixed assets in the small-scale sector generates employment for four persons.

Food products industry has ranked first generating employment, providing employment to 0.48 million persons (13.1%). The next two industry groups were Non-metallic mineral products with employment of 0.45 million persons (12.2%) and Metal products with 0.37 million persons (10.2%).

Per unit employment was the highest (20) in units engaged in beverages, tobacco and tobacco products mainly due to the high employment potential of this industry particularly in Maharashtra, Andhra Pradesh, Rajasthan, Assam and Tamil Nadu.

Next came Cotton textile products (17), Non-metallic mineral products (14.1), Basic metal industries (13.6) and Electrical machinery and parts (11.2). The lowest figure of 2.4 was in Repair services line.

Per unit employment was the highest (10) in metropolitan areas and the lowest (5) in rural areas.

However, in Chemicals and Chemical products, Non-metallic mineral products and Basic metal industries per unit employment was higher in rural areas as compared to metropolitan areas/urban areas.

In urban areas, highest employment per unit was in Beverage, Tobacco products (31 persons) followed by Cotton textile products (18), Basic metal industries (13) and Non-metallic mineral products (12).

Non-metallic products contributed 22.7 per cent of employment generated in rural areas. Food products accounted for 21.1 per cent, Wood products and Chemicai and chemical products shared between them 17.5 per cent.

As for urban areas, Food products and Metal products almost equally shared 22.8 per cent of employment. Machinery parts except electrical, non-metallic mineral products, and chemicals and chemical products between them accounted for 26.2 per cent of employment.

In metropolitan areas, the leading industries were Metal products, Machinery and parts except electrical and Paper products and printing (total share being 33.6%).

Tamil Nadu (14.5%) made the maximum contribution to employment. This was followed by Maharashtra (9.7%), Uttar Pradesh (9.5%) and West Bengal (8.5). Gujarat (7.6%), Andhra Pradesh (7.5%), Karnataka (6.7%) and Punjab (5.6%) together accounted for another 27.4 per cent. Per unit employment was high 17, 16 and 14 respectively, in Nagaland, Sikkim and Dadra & Nagar Haveli. It was 12 in Maharashtra, Tripura and Delhi. Madhya Pradesh had the lowest figure of 2. In all other cases it was around the average of 6.

Export

SSI sector plays a major role in India's present export performance. 45 per cent of the Indian Exports is contributed by SSI sector. Direct exports from the SSI Sector account for nearly 35 per cent of total exports. Besides direct exports, it is estimated that small-scale industrial units contribute around 15 per cent to exports indirectly. This takes place through merchant exporters, trading houses and export houses. They may also be in the form of export orders from large units or the production of parts and components for use for finished exportable goods.

It would surprise many to know that non-traditional products account for more than 95 per cent of the SSI exports. The exports from SSI sector have been clocking excellent growth rates in this decade. It has been mostly fuelled by the performance of garments, leather and gems and jewellery units from this sector. The product groups where the SSI sector dominates in exports, are sport goods, readymade garments, woolen garments and knitwear, plastic products, processed food and leather products. The SSI sector reorienting its export strategy towards the new trade regime being ushered in by the WTO.

Other Findings

Regarding the total number of units, registered SSI units was 28.49 lakhs and unregistered units are 7.23 lakhs of the total number units 35.72 lakhs in 2002-03.

The registered SSI were at higher level (more than 50,000 units) in the States of Punjab, U.P., M.P., Pondicherry in the year 1987-88. But at the time of implementation of NEP (1990), more than 2 lakhs were registered SSI units in Tamil Nadu. At present, the registered SSI units in Tamil Nadu was higher among the various States.

In 1996-97 the fixed investments level of SSI at current price was Rs. 64,839 lakhs and it increased to Rs. 89,276 lakhs in 2001-02 in India.

Through an extensive nation-wide survey of Small Scale Industries, the registered SSI as on March 31, 1988 extremely useful insights came up on their operation, separately for rural and urban areas.

For rural areas, the share of each of the total fixed investment, and investment in plant and machinery, and employment is much lower than their share in the number of units while the reverse is true for metropolitan cities: for urban areas, all the shares generally move in tandem. Consequently, per unit levels are the lowest for rural areas, next higher for urban areas and much higher for metropolitan cities practically for all indicators.

The growth rate of production was only 7.1 per cent in 1993-94 and 8.23 per cent in 2001-02.

All type of small scale industries had generated large amount of employment opportunities to rural people.

The figures of exports for the years 1998-99 and 1999-2000 were Rs.48,979 crores and Rs. 54,200.47 crores respectively, with the increase over the previous years in percentage terms being 11.45 per cent and 10.66 per cent respectively.

The level of exports of SSI products had increased from Rs.17,784 crores (28.11) in 1992-93 to Rs. 59,978 crores (10.66) in 2000-01.

After the implementation of New Economic Policy, there is a tremendous growth in the number of units under DIC in India. The growth rate is 576.6 per cent.

The rate of growth in production and investment is not responding to the growth rate of the SSI units.

In metropolitan cities, it is the reverse while in respect of urban units, there is nodding balance between the two shares.

The modern small-scale industries located in rural areas perhaps under the special development programmes and possibly due to the well-measured economic calculus of urban entrepreneurs, and so on.

The employment level had generated 11,76,700 persons in 1991-92 and 29,02,122 persons in 2000-01 in the SSI sector.

There is a good response in starting of new units and the performance in terms of SSI in Tamil Nadu.

During the ten years period, the growth of the small scale industries was at higher level in Tamil Nadu.

The textile based (Rs. 186.8 lakhs) and Mineral based industry

(Rs.152.6 lakhs) dominated in the investment performance in Madurai district during the ten years.

The 51.8 per cent of the SSI units are located in the rural areas in study districts.

The Chemical based industries had contributed 16.5 per cent to total employment.

The Madurai Corporation (47.8%) and Madurai East (10.2%) had good performance in SSI investment in 2001-02.

The investment level of Textile industry had required the investment of Rs.186.8 lakhs in the year 2001-02 as against Rs.48.4 lakhs in the year 1992-93.

The investment performance shows the highest investment of SSI in the Dindigul block and the Dindigul municipality area.

The 120 respondents were selected from independent enterprise in each district. Of the total 120 sample respondents in a district, 15 respondents represented from each category of SSI sector.

Of the 240 sample respondents, 58 respondents (24.1%) are belonging to the age group of 41-50 years.

The female participation and male dominations in the development of entrepreneurial skills have to be considered in analyzing the deterimants of entrepreneurial skill and development.

Only 41 respondents (17.1%) are belonging to the female small scale entrepreneurs in the Madurai and Dindigul districts.

The 40.83 per cent of the small scale entrepreneurs are Hindus in the Dindigul and Madurai districts, 30.83 per cent (74 respondents) are Christian and 23.33 per cent (68 respondents) are Muslim respondents in the study districts.

The entrepreneurial skills are influenced by the religion of the entrepreneurs.

Of the total sample the small scale entrepreneurs, 64 (26.6%) and 80 (33.3%) respondents are having the primary and secondary level education respectively.

During the economic reforms period (1990-1991 to 1999-

2000) the 92 units (38.3%) of the sample SSI units were started in the study districts.

The remaining 14.5 per cent of the sample units are Joint Stock Companies.

The living areas are also occupied by the SSI units in the study districts. It has the 9.9 per cent of the sample units in these two districts.

The sole proprietorship type of SSI organization (29.1%) are functioning, in the study areas.

The total production value of the 240 SSI sample units was increased from Rs. 3,73,681.35 thousands in 1990-91 to Rs. 3,49,417.35 thousands in 2004-05.

The average production value of a sample SSI unit was Rs.1,18,671.8 thousands under traditional method and Rs. 4,86,852.2 thousands under modern methods of production during the period of 1990-91.

The changes in the average domestic sales value was Rs.57,37,956.1 thousand in Madurai district and Rs. 72,45,447.3 thousand in Dindigul district.

The districts had increased the sales value of exports of SSI products to the extent of Rs. 8,64,770.0 thousands in Madurai district and 8,23,822.6 thousand in Dindigul district.

Economic reforms are favourable to Engineering based and Textile based industry in Tamil Nadu in the performance of average sales value.

At an average, the fixed investment capital level changes per unit was at Rs. 14,055.6 thousand in Madurai district and Rs. 22,811.1 thousand in Dindigul district.

The changes in variable capital investment level per unit, at an average, was Rs. 12,343.2 thousand in Madurai district and Rs. 10,442.4 thousand in Dindigul district.

The average changes in the total investment level of a selected SSI units in Madurai district was Rs. 39,381.3 thousand and Rs. 50,307.6 thousand in Dindigul district.

There is a tremendous changes in the capital investment of all category of SSI units in Tamil Nadu.

The male domination in employment opportunities was higher in all category of SSI units in study districts of Tamil Nadu.

Problems of SSI Entrepreneurs

Extensive discussions held with the officials of various District Industries Centre, Bankers, Non-Government Organizations, SSI Associations, office bearers of Chamber of Commerce and other promoters of small scale units revealed a number of crucial problems confronting the industry. Some of these problems have to be tackled by the Government and others were to be solved by industries themselves. Smallness by itself brings a few problems, and understanding of which is vital for helping development of this sector.

Lack of Awareness

Even 15 years after implementation of New Economic Policy, the SSI entrepreneurs do not have the adequate knowledge about the policy reforms. The policy reforms and the procedural changes would be informed to the entrepreneurs in regional languages.

Manpower Requirement

There has been large-scale movement of agricultural workers from rural areas to semi-urban and urban areas to take up assured wage-works. Most of them found employment in readymade garments, powerloom and spinning units. However, after a period of one or two years, these skilled labour skit their loyalty from one unit to another suddenly, thus placing the industries in a quandary.

Small-scale textile processors encounter peculiar problems with the monitoring and regulating agencies as well. They have deployed causal labour in loading and unloading of goods. Porters are engaged for shifting the yarn as well as cloth manufactured in the small-scale industries. These porters as well as the causal workers employed inside the factory for folding on contract basis are often included in the muster roll of the respective units during the surprise checks carried out by the factory inspectors. The small-scale industrialists are finding it very difficult to digest these actions of the officials. Many a time these units are forced to move courts on account of this, causing great strain and tension.

Power

Power cuts are often hampering the production schedule of many units. Some of the units which have installed sophisticated foreign machines engaged in the manufacture of critical items are the most hit. Uninformed power cuts devour precious raw material in progress besides causing damage to the machines as well. Installation of generator sets is not within the reach of all the industrialists. Even those who have installed the sets are facing high cost production situation.

Finance

There has been a divergent view expressed regarding the availability of credit. Large-scale units express that their financial requirement are met sufficiently by the bankers. Some of the small-scale industrialists have reported that their working capital requirements were not met fully. The insistence on collateral securities at an exorbitant level by bankers has upset many people.

Industries normally have limited sources of funds to meet their working capital requirements and often look to banks to meet a substantial portion of the needs proper assessment by the bankers, followed by effective fund management by the industry and thus ensure that the sales targets are achieved and repayment obligations, if any, are adhered to.

A few other problems are summarised in this sector:

- Diseconomies of scales of production and operations, it must beadmitted that some concern for this aspect has been exercised in the selection and reservation items of SSI as part of the Industrial Policy. Even so, there are number of products that are produced by both SSI and non-SSI sectors with resultant competition.

- Relationship with larger units particularly in the case of ancillaries and sub-contractors. It very often is a question of the big fish swallowing the small.
- Poor resilience due to narrow product range, cheaper or near-obsolete technology and lack of R & D.
- Small scale industries except agro-based have to depend on raw materials from outside and such type of procurement influence the wastage of time and cost in transport.Non-availability of raw materials or prohibitive cost of these industries has weakened the liability of small scale industries. Nearly 80 per cent of the raw materials are purchased from the private concerns in the study district.
- The industrial units may encounter problems of marketing due to lack of marketing information, marketing channel and transport cost. Problems also arise on account of lack of standardization besides marketing on conventional products. There is also practically no marketing research or study of market potentials in the SSI sector
- It is evident from the research that only small proportion of the credit has reached to the small scale entrepreneurs. It is clear that the consultancy unit of the District Industries Centre (DIC) hesitates to attend the problems of small industries in small scale areas. Credit was given under importance by entrusting the task of providing it to commercial banks and cooperatives. But the Government failed to provide infrastructure, education and awareness about the people regarding utilization of credit. The benefits of subsidy and concessional interest rate extent to

rural artisans were nullified by delay in sanctioning of credit, cost of loan by way of grease money, etc.

- Many small scale industries suffer due to lack of skilled labour. Most of the units located in the rural areas find it extremely difficult to get suitable labour. With the work experience in small units, skilled workers tend to turn to large scale units, attracted by their higher emoluments.
- Small scale activity continue to be poorly organized. This is inspite of specialized organization network established exclusively of each industry. Lack of adequate managerial expertise, resource and member confidence continue to plague these Enterprises.

Suggestions

The following are suggestions to be followed for effective functioning of the SSI units located in different parts of the Tamil Nadu.

- There must be a co-ordination and cordial relationship between Government officials and entrepreneur.
- While selecting the entrepreneur to occupy the sheds, priority may be give to qualified unemployed graduates by simplifying the existing procedures.
- A separate industrial estate can be constructed exclusively to allot sheds for women entrepreneurs; particularly some sheds can be reserved for women self-help groups to start their industries.
- There is a linkage between universities engaged with entrepreneurship development and industrial estate, administrative executives.
- Periodical meetings may be conducted by the SIDCO officer to receive the problem of entrepreneurs.
- The Government strictly advice the entrepreneurs to conduct the energy audit, every year as done financial audit.

- The entrepreneurs may also be given an orientation to review the factual informations to Government in order to strengthen our policies and programmes.
- Awareness should be given to entrepreneurs about globalization, liberalization and privatization process, in order to equip the SSI entrepreneurs to become competitive to face products from multi-national industries.
- Efforts may be taken by the NGO's and GO's by organizing industrial motivation campaigns in all Panchayat Unions for identifying the new entrepreneurs.
- The Chamber of Commerce may help the new entrepreneurs in selecting their new projects suitable to the market economy, and issue necessary technical guidance and required other marketing assistance.
- The Government may issue provisional SSI certificate through online with the help of approved browsing centers.
- In order to strengthen the globaliztion, a Export Guidance Cell will be formed to help the exporters in each district.
- The entrepreneurs must be given an orientation to review the factual information to Government in order to strengthen the policies and programmes.
- Awareness should be given to entrepreneurs about the globalization, liberalization and privatization process in order to equip the Indian entrepreneurs to become competitive to face products from multi-national corporations.
- Encouraging adequate infrastructure investment should be the responsibility of the State, as private enterprises are not expected to invest in such infrastructure.
- There is need to develop wide range of intermediate technologies which permit different factor proportions in the productive process. These intermediate technologies offer consider scope for modernization on the one hand and minimizing the impact of industrialization on the

other. Such a pattern of industralization would require the selection of labour intensive industries which will combine the advantages of low capital per worker and per unit of output.

- As an incentive to SMEs, the financial package being offered under project uptech by Banks, could be improved by offering a large dose of assistance under the equity fund scheme beyond the present ceiling of Rs.0.10 million and a concessional rate of interest on the term loan component.
- Time bound concessions such as excise duty exemption for 5-7 years not only gives protection at the start to a particular unit but also enables the Government to help many more units over time. Overhaul of the policy measures should also take into account effective ways of making information and finance available to these units, removal of hurdles like labour legislation and Inspector Raj and provision of basic infrastructure.
- Some of the key areas which require further reform to attain and sustain higher rates of gross domestic product growth are:
  - (a) Greater openness of the economy.
  - (b) De-reservation of items from the reservation list of the small scale sector.
  - (c) Deregulation of India's private sector, including liberalization of labour laws and exit policies.
  - (d) Demonopolisation of infrastructure and decentralization of economic policy-making.
- The neglect of in-house R and D by Indian enterprises in the post-reform period is an issue of concern. This trend needs to be reversed by providing a policy package to encourage R and D.
- In view of the liberal policy on technology imports, enterprises feels less inclined to invest in a rather uncertain

activity like in-house R and D and prefer to meet their technological needs through imports. The imported technology has several commercial attractions over the locally developed alternatives. Hence indigenous innovative effort will need some protection from technology imports.

- The financial sector and various other service sectors need to be liberalized, both with respect to their domestic regulations as well as opening them upto foreign competition. In fact, inefficiencies in the service sectors of a developing economy impact negatively on the export competitiveness of its agriculture and manufacturing sectors through forward linkages.
- The reforms remain incomplete on several fronts, including the distorted excise duty structure, cumbersome procedures of export tariffs on critical inputs, labour market reforms, reservation for small scale sector, and poor banking and insurance services. Further reforms on these fronts should contribute to improvements in all the elements of the value chain, augmenting exports as well as domestic demand.
- Firms are making efforts to improve manufacturing capabilities. This is being done through building alliances as well as through initiatives within the firm. Quality upgradation seems to be their key priority. These efforts as improving manufacturing capability may still prove to be inadequate to meet the competitive challenges. These inadequacies may also adversely affect India's chances of efficiency seeking FDI, the need for which has been emphasized.
- Changes in labour laws are needed in two respects. One, a simplification of laws, such as those concerning ESI is needed which permits modulation of the labour force with varying levels of capacity utilization at least for the small scale sector.

- The Government is also expected to discuss the issue of raising the foreign investment limit in the sector from the 24 per cent to 49 per cent. The above changes are likely to be implemented soon so that SSI sector in the country can brace itself for meeting the situation advising out of the total removal of the quality restrictions on all items.
- People must develop a positive and favourable attitudes towards small scale industries, which would facilitate the last growth of small sector. People have to accept privatisation and globalization by realizing the benefits without opposing it.
- In order to promote R and D in small industry, it is essential to strengthen the technological infrastructure and make it easily accessible to small firms. This has to be done particularly at district level to be more effective.

Conclusion

Economic growth becomes really meaningful when the people participate extensively in the production process. The real challenge of growth is to provide full employment. The small scale sector is the symbol of that fact of our economy which reflects production by masses rather than mass production. In the globalization process we need a cooperative and organized effort to face the products from global market. Hence SIDCO and other agencies engaged their services in the development of small industries should take the responsibility to safeguard our industries in general and home entrepreneurs in particular. This provide collective cooperation of Government public and entrepreneurs is essential to win the globally competitive industrial world. Because the small scale sector one of the major segment, which covers 35 per cent of our total population in providing employment, income and above all social value.

Globalization and change in technology are emerging as the

major forces that will modify and mould the environment for small business and entrepreneurship over the next decade which will witness the emergence of more competitive and efficient SSI sector, the role of the Government will be that of facilitators for providing support to SSI in the era of Globalization. The Government would increasingly focus its energies towards providing human resources development support along with establishing quality certification facilities and dissemination of information.

APPENDIX

QUESTIONNAIRE FOR ENTREPRENEURS

I. General

1. Address of the Industry :
2. Details about the Entrepreneur
   (a) Name :
   (b) Age :
   (c) Sex :
   (d) Community :
      (i) Caste :
      (ii) Religion :
   (e) Education : Illiterate/Primary/Secondary/Degree/Diploma/other
   (f) Family members: Male Female
   Child Total
   (g) Occupation of the parent:

3. Details of the Industry:-Farm/Non–farm/Government/Wage/Labour/other

   (a) Type of the Industrial unit: Food based/Forest based/Animal based/Textile based/Chemical based/Building Material and Ceramics/Engineering and Allied industry/Electrical & Electronic Based/Miscellaneous
   (b) Nature of the activity : Main … … … … …
   Sub ………………
   (c) Year of starting :
   (d) Region of Location : Rural/ urban / Semi-urban industrial/Backward/Living Area.
   (e) Nature of Organization : Sole Proprietor/ Partnership/

Joint Stock Company/
Corporation/Public Sector
Undertakings/others.

(f) Membership in Associations: Yes/No.

(1) Seminars organized by the Associations on the NEP provision & threats. &Yes/No

(2) If yes is there any collective representation or strategy adopted to face the threat and challenges?

1.
2.
3. In the changing context of withdrawal of Government support. How do you prepare to withstand the withdrawal?
4. What do you really expect from the Government or Association or International Agencies?

4. Details of NEP

(a) Do you know the New Industrial Policy/New Economic Policy of Government of India : Yes/No

(b) If yes, What are the Main Content of the policy? : (a)
(b)
(c)

(c) Did you aware of LPG (Liberalization, Privatizatio and Globalization) of the Government? : Yes/No

5. SWOT of NEP

Do you avail any benefit from NEP/NIP? Yes / No

Strength

(1)
(2)
(3)

Weakness

(1)
(2)
(3)

Opportunities

(1)
(2)
(3)

Threat

(1)
(2)
(3)
(1) Do you accept that the NEP after the growth of SSI? Yes?No.

II. Capital and Investment

Sl.No	*Source*	*Amount*	
		Before 1991	*At Presents*
1.	Own fund		
2.	Borrowed from formal institutions		
	(a) Bank		
	(b) Cooperative Society		
	(c) KVIC		
	(d) Other agency (specify)		
3.	From Non-formal institution		
	(a) Private		
	(b) Chit funds		
	(c) Money lenders		
	(d) Others		
	Total		

(a) Do you know the investment limit of SSI? Yes/No
If Yes, How much? Rs.

(b) Have you affected or benefited by raising of investment limit of SSI?
Yes/No

(c) If yes, What one the Impact of increasing investment limit of SSI under
Economic reforms?
(i)
(ii)
(iii)

(d) Whether your unit is considered as SSI? Yes/No
If Yes, When? — Before raising investment limit/ After raising Investment limit.

(a) Fixed capital

Sl. No	*Source*	*Rs. Value*	
		Before 1991	*At Present*
1.	Land		
2.	Buildings		
3.	Machinery & Equipments		
4.	Furniture		
5.	Others		
	Total		

(b) Variable Capital

Sl. No.	*Source*	*Per Day/Week/Month/Product*	
		Before 1991	*At Present*
1.	Rent		
2.	Raw Materials		
3.	Wage		

4. Transport	
5. Packaging & Labeling	
6. Power	
7. Marketing	
8. Other expenses	
Total	

(iii) What are the reason for the increase/decrease of the level of Investment?

(iv) Do you agree that the NEP influence the level of investment ? Yes /No

If Yes, how?

1.

2.

Problems after NEP

(1) Competition
(2) Production
(3) Capacity utilization
(4) Labour/wage
(5) Borrowings
(6) Demand
(7) Profit margin
(8) Technology
(9) Provide variety of goods
(10) Dereservation
(11) Deregulation
(12) Deficiencing

III. Production Level

1. When did you get the licence for starting the SSI Unit?

   ____

2. If before delicensing, what are the difficulties faced by you in getting licence?

(a)
(b)

3. How much you spent for getting license? Rs. ——
4. If after delicensing, what the benefits derived from it?
   (a)
   (b)
5. Benefits in terms of money due to delicensing?
6. Types of goods produced:
   Main :
   Sub :
7. Types of Raw Materials used for the production?
8. Source of Raw Material: Private/Government/Societies/ SSE/Others (Specify)
9. Did you avail any benefits under NEP for the supply of raw materials? Yes/No
   If Yes, what are the benefits?
10. Full capacity of production of the unit:Per day/per week/ per month/per year
11. Did you fully utilize capacity? Yes/No
    If No, Why? (a)
    (b)
    (c)
12. Do you perform the production though out year? Yes/No
13. Total Production level:

Product	*Production*					
	Before Reforms			*After Reforms*		
	Qty.	*Value*	*Rs.*	*Qty.*	*Value*	*Rs.*
Main 1 2						
Main 1 2						
	Total					

(i) What are the reasons for the changes in the production after reforms?

(i)
(ii)
(iii)

IV. Sales

(a) Marketing channels:

(i) Direct consumer
(ii) Wholesales – Retailer-Consumer
(iii) Dealers-Agents – Retailer-consumer
(iv) Other (specify)

(b) Sales level

Sl. No. Method/Source	*Before Reforms*			*At present*		
	Qty.	*Value*	*Rs.*	*Qty.*	*Value*	*Rs.*
1. Direct sales						
2. Through dealers						
3. Through agents						
4. Through show room						
5. Through whole sales						
6. Through Retailers						
Total						

(c) Do you make advertisement for your product? Yes/No
If yes types of advertisement?
Advertisement Expenditure Rs : Per month/ per year
(d) Are you exporting your product? Yes/No
If Yes, How much? Rs. ——Per year
(e) Do you know the current Exim policy? Yes/No
If Yes, what is your opinion about the Exim policy in export Promotion?
(f) In what way the globalization policy promotes the export/ sales?
(i)
(ii)

(g) Do you know the role of the present Foreign Exchange Regulation Act? (FERA) Yes/No
If yes, what is impact of FERA on your business?

(h) What are changes in the export of your product after economic reforms?
(i)
(ii)

(i) What are the benefits received for export promotion?
(i)
(ii)

(j) Do you know the Mono policies Restructed Trade Practies (MRTP) Act? Yes/No

(k) Is there any impact of the liberalization of MRTP Act? If Yes, what are the impacts of MRTP?

V. Employment

(a) No. of administrative staff : Male Female
(b) Hired/Seasonal labours in your enterprise :

Sl.No. Category	*Before reform Family labour*	*No. of worker Hired labour*	*Total*
	M F C T	*M F C T*	*M F C T*
1. Regular			
2. Seasonal			
3. Total			

At Present *No. of workers*

Sl.No Category	*Family labour*	*Hired labour*	*Total*
	M F C T	*M F C T*	*M F C T*
1. Regular			
2. Seasonal			
3. Total			

(c) What are the reasons for the changing conditions of employment after economic reforms?

(i)

(ii)

(d) Do you accept the privatization policy? Yes / No

If Yes, Why?

(i)

(ii)

If No, Why?

(i)

(ii)

VI. Earnings/Profit/loss

Sl. No.	*Category*	*Before Reforms (Rs.)*	*After Reforms (Rs.)*
1.	Profit		
2.	Loss		

(a) Do you agree that the policy changes promote the enterprise for profit earnings? Yes/No

(b) What are the sources of promotion of SSI under liberalization era?

(i) Tax Reforms

(ii) Competition

(iii) Others

4. Quantitative restrictions

1. Quantitative restrictions in your product :
2. Tariff level of Your Industry :

5. Do you like quantitative restrictions? Yes/No

VII. Opinion of SSI Entrepreneurs

1. Do you know of New Economic Policy? Yes/No

2. Do you like new Economic Policy? Yes/No
3. Is the New Economic Policy Useful to You? Yes/No
4. Do you avail any benefit from the New Economic Policy ? Yes/No
5. Do you accept that the delicensing policy promotes SSI? Yes/No
6. Do you know the small scale Industries policy? Yes/No
7. Do you know the New Industrial policy? Yes/No
8. If there any Possibility for sales promotion under globalization policy? Yes/No
9. Do you accept that NEP affect the growth of SSI? Yes/No
10. Did the New Economic policy influence small scale entrepreneurs to improve the skills? Yes/No
11. Is it possible to compete your SSI in the multinational companies? Yes/No
12. Have you satisfied with the implementation of NEP? Yes/No
13. Have you got liberal investment credit under Foreign Direct Investment? Yes/No
14. Do you agree that the small industries influence the self-employment? Yes/No
15. Do you want to continue the NE policy measures in India? Yes/No
16. Do you like the further increase in investment limit for SSI? Yes/No
17. Can you modernize your industry for globalization? Yes/No
18. If there any negative growth in the role of trade unions after NEP? Yes/No

19. Are you interested in the Government intervention before NEP? Yes/No
20. Are you interested in the market competition forces for the growth under NEP measures? Yes/No

Bibliography

Books

B. P. Guha and K.R. Debnath, *Economic Development—India's Status, Growth and Development,* B.R. Publishing Corporation, Delhi, 2002, pp. 125-150.

B. Ramachandran, *Economic Reforms Need Radical Changes,* Kalpaz Publication, Delhi, 2003.

B. S. Nhatia, G.S. Batra, *Entrepreneurship and Small Business Management,* Deep & Deep Publications Pvt. Ltd., Rajauri Garden, New Delhi, 2001.

G. Sarangis, *Central Excise Guide for Small Scale Industry 1996-97,* Centax Publications Private Limited, New Delhi, 1996.

G.S. Batra & Narinder Kaur, *Globalisation Strategies and Economic Liberalisation,* Anmol Publications Private Limited, New Delhi, 2000.

G.S. Batra & R.C. Dangwal (ed), *Entrepreneurship and Small Scale Industries – New Potentials,* Deep & Deep Publications Pvt. Ltd., New Delhi, 2003.

Hina Sidhu, *Structural Changes and Productivity in Small Scale Industries,* Mittal Publications, New Delhi, 1998.

J.C. Verma & Gurpal Singh, *Small Business and Industry,* Sage Publications, New Delhi, 2002.

M. Soundarapandian, *New Economic Policy and Rural Development,* Serials Publication, New Delhi, 2006.

M. Soundarapandian, *Rural Industries in India,* Mohit Publications, New Delhi, 1999.

M. Soundarapandian, *Small Scale Industries - Problem, Vol. 1, Management Vol. 2,* Concept Publishing Company, New Delhi, 2002.

M. Soundrapandian, *Economic Reforms and Employment,* Discovery Publishing House, New Delhi, 2005.

M. Soundrapandian, *Rural Entrepreneurship: Growth and Potentials,* Kanishka Publishers, New Delhi, 2001.

Mcine Pieter Van Dijk, *Innovations and Micro & Small Enterpriser Development in Africa and Asia,* Institute of Small Enterprises Development, Cochin, 2003.

P.M. Mathew (ed), *Finance for Small Enterprises in India,* Institute of Small Enterprises and Development, Cochin, 1998.

P.M. Mathew (ed), *Small Enterprise Development – The Experience of the South and the North,* Oxford & IBH Publishing Co. Pvt. Ltd., New Delhi, 2000.

P.M. Mathew, *The State of Small Enterprise Development in India, 1997,* Institute of Small Enterprises and Development, Cochin 1997.

P.M. Mathew, *Towards a Vibrant Small Enterprise Economy in India,* Institute of Small Enterprises and Development, Cochin, 2000.

R.P. Singh (ed) *New Economic Policy and Perspective to Rural Development,* National Institute of Rural Development, Hyderaband, 1997.

Rakesh Mohan, *Small Scale Industry Policy in India: A Critical Evaluation,* National Council of Applied Economic Research, New Delhi, 2001.

Ruddar Datt, *Economic Reforms, Labour and Employment,* Deep & Deep Publications Pvt. Ltd., New Delhi, 2003.

Ruddar Datt, K.P.M. Sundaram, *Indian Economy,* S. Chand & Company Ltd., New Delhi, 2004.

S. Krishnamurthi, *Small Scale Industries–Policy, Rules and Regulations,* Vinod Law Publications, Lucknow, 1997.

Shuji Uchi Kawa (ed), *Economic Reforms and Industrial Structure in India,* Manohar Publishers, New Delhi, 2002.

Suman Bery, Barry Bosworth and Arvind Panagariya (ed) *India Policy Forum 2004,* Vol. I, Brookings Institution Press, Washingtom, 2004.

Syed Vazith Hussain, *Small Scale Industries in the New Millennium,* Sarup & Sons, New Delhi 2003.

V. Padmanand & V.G. Patel, *Managing India's Small Industrial Economy,* Sage Publications, New Delhi, 2004.

Vijay Joshi & I. M. D. Little, *Indias Economic Reforms 1991-2001,* Oxford University Press, Madras, 1997.

Journals

A. Raghurama and N. Hala Naik, "Marketing Problems of Small Scale Units in Daskhina Kannada," *Southern Economist,* Vol. 42, No. 22, March 15, 2004, pp. 7-11.

A. Raghurama, "Globalisation and Challenges for Small Scale Sector in India," *Southern Economist,* Vol. 43, No. 19, February 2005, pp. 13-18.

A. Reghurama, "Globalisation and Challenges for Small-Scale Sector in India, *Southern Economist,* Vol. 43, No. 19, Feb.1, 2005, pp.13-14.

A.K. Ojha, "Globalisation and Liberalisation", *Third Concept,* Vol. 16, No. 186, August 2002, pp. 13-15.

A.K. Roy, "New Economic Policy and Old Trade Unions," *Economic and Political Weekly,* Vol. XXXI, No. 44, November 2, 1996, pp. 2901-2907.

Abhijit Banerjee *et al.* "Strategy for Economic Reform in West Bengal," *Economic and Political Weekly* , Vol. XXXVII, No. 41, October 12-18, 2002, pp. 4203-4218.

Amarendra Kumar Tiwari, "Economic Policy and Reform Process," *Third Concept,* November 2003, pp. 27-29.

Aminur Rashid Khan & Saby Asachi Das, "Economic Reforms and Rural Development," *Kurkshetra,* January 2003, pp. 31-35.

Anuradha Seth, "Cost-efficiency of Small Manufacturing Enterprises – Implications for Employment Policy", *Economic and Political Weekly,* November 25, 1995, pp. 130-134.

Aravind Panagariya, "Growth and Reforms during 1980 and 1990," *Economic and Political Weekly,* June 19-25, 2004, Vol. XXXIX, No. 25, pp. 2581-93.

Arvind Kumar, G. Nanjunda Gowda, "Impact of Economic Liberalization on the Growth Performance of Indian Rice Exports," T.L. Swamy, "Economic in India Some Issues," *The Asian Economic Review,* Vol. 47, No. 1, April 2005, pp. 116-123, 145-150.

B. Nagaraju and S.C. Narayana, "Impact of Reforms on Handlooms and Powerlooms: A Case Study of Chitoor District Andhra Pradesh," *Journal of Rural Development,* Vol. 22 (3) 2003, pp. 345-362.

Bala Subramanya, "Technological Innovations in Small Enterprises," *Economic and Political Weekly,* Vol. XXXVIII, No. 21, pp. 2067-74.

C. Rangarajan, "Economic Reforms: Some Issues and Concerns," *The Indian Economic Journal,* Vol. 49, No. 2, October-December 2001-02, pp. 1-6.

C. Srinivasalu, "Rural Industralisation Developmental Approach *vessus* Liberalization," *Southern Economist,* Vol. 40, March 1, 2002, pp. 9-10.

C. Srinivasalu, "Rural Industrialisation Developmental Approach versus Liberalization", *Southern Economist,* Vol. 40, No. 21, March 2002, pp. 9-10.

C. Vethirajan, "Rehabilitation of Sick SSI Units in India," *Third Concept,* July 2004, pp. 26-35.

D. Chinnaiyan and R. Nandagopal, "Acccessibility of Bank Finance by SSI: A Case Study," *Southern Economist,* Vol. 43, No. 21, March 1, 2005, pp. 24-26.

D. Namasivayam, "The Role of Subsidies in Investments – Preference of Group Members in Non-farm Projects: An Application of Sensitivity Analysis," *Journal of Rural Development,* Vol. 20, No. 3, July September 2001, pp. 533-574.

D.G. Gohil, "Growth and Development of SSI in Gujarat: A Study," *Southern Economist,* Vol. 44, No. 17, Jan 1, 2006, pp.10-12.

D.J. Mahajan, "Impact of Liberalisation on Employment in India", *Southern Economist,* Vol. 41, No. 3, June 1, 2000, pp. 8-10.

D.M. Nanjundappa, "Small Scale Industry in the Globalisation Era, SSI Sector in India's Growth," *Southern Economist,* Vol. 42, No. 9, July 15, 2002, pp. 5-8.

Danish A. Hashim, "Post - MFA: Making the Textile and Garment Industry Competitive," *Economic and Political Weekly,* Vol. XL, No. 2, January 8, 2005, pp. 117-128.

G. Somayajula and V. Venkataramana, "Impact of EXIM-Policy 2001 – WTO on Small and Medium Enterprises," *Southern Economics*, Vol. 40, No. 23 & 24, April 1-15, 2002, pp. 13-19.

G. Somayajulu & V. Venkatramana, "Impact of EXIM-Policy 2001 – WTO on Small and Medium Enterprises," *Southern Economist,* Vol. 40, No. 23 & 24, April 1 & 15, 2002, pp. 13-19.

G.K. Chadha and P.P. Sahu, "Small Scale Agro-Industry in India: Low Productivity is its Achilles' Heed," *Indian Journal of Agricultral Economics*, Vol. 58, No. 3, July-September 2003, pp. 518-541.

G.K. Chadha, "Impact of Economic Reforms on Rural Employment", *Indian Journal of Agricultural Economics,* Vol. 56, No. 3, July-September 2001, pp. 491-525.

G.L. Gaur, "Impact of Liberalisation and Globalisation on Employment in India," *Southern Economist,* Vol. 43, No. 13, November 1, 2004, pp. 11-14.

G.S. Gupta, A.K.A. Rathi, "Small Scale Chemical Industry in Gujarati Structure, Conduct and Performance," *Economic and Polical Weekly,* Vol. XXXI, No. 48, pp. M.79-M.84.

Gitanjali Mishra, "Small Scale Industries–New Opportunities for Banks," *State Bank of India–Monthly Review,* June 1997, pp. 326-333.

H. Raman, "Economic Reforms: Budget 2002-03", *Southern Economist* ,Vol. 42, No. 9, September 2003, pp. 13-16.

H. Raman, *Challenges facing Industrial Sector Growth of India, Southern Economist*, 41-42. No. 9, Sep. 1, 2003.

Hanumantha Rao and K. Rajayalakshmi "Structure of Employment and Casualisation in Rural India during Pre-and Post-reforms Regime," *Journal of Rural Development,* Vol. 21 (1), pp. 27-42.

Harjeet Ahluwalia, "Financial Sector Reforms in the New Wave Economic Development," *Yojana,* August 2003, pp. 10-13.

J. Mohan Rao, "Economic Reform and Ecological Refurbishment – A Strategy for India," *Economic and Political Weekly* , Vol. XXX, No. 28, July 15, 1995, pp. 1749-1760.

K. Kamalakannan, "Industrial Policies concerning Small Scale Industries, *Kisan World,* Vol. 32, No. 6, June 2005, pp. 14-15.

K. Srinivasulu, "Textile Policy and Handloom Industry Policy Promises and Performance," *Economic and Political Weekly,* Vol. XXXI, No. 49, December 7, 1996, pp. 3198-3206.

K. Sundar, R. Kumar Gandi & G. Gangatharan, "The Role of SIDBI in Financing SSIs," *Southern Economist,* Vol. 4, No.1, May 1, 2002, pp. 27-29.

K.R. Shyar Sundar, "Economic Reforms and Industrial Relations System in India, Some Issues and Discussion", *Economic and Political Weekly,* Vol XXXIII, No. 23, June 6-12, 1998, pp. 1379-1383.

K.V. Ramaswamy, "Globalisation and Industrial Labour Market," *The Indian Journal of Labour Economics,* Vol. 46, No. 2, April1 June 2003, pp. 253-74.

M. Jaya Singh, "SSIs, Small Industries, Big Scope," *Kisan World,* Vol. 30, No. 8, August 2003, pp. 26-27.

M. Soundarapandian, "Labourisation in Small Scale Industries: Need and Issues," *Third Concept,* January 2002, pp. 47-48.

M. Sundara Rao & M. Ramakrishna, "Imriew of the Eghth Plan Employment Strategy," *Economic Affair,* Vol. 40, Qr. 2, April-June 1995, pp. 73-78.

M.H. Bala Subramanya, "Small Industry and Globalisation," *Economic and Political Weekly,* Vol. XXXIX, No. 18, May 1-7, pp. 1826-1833.

M.H. Bala Subrananya *et al.* "Research and Development in Small

Industry in Karnataka," *Economic and Political Weekly,* September 28, 2002, pp. 4010-4017.

Manisha Lodha, "Liberalisation and Trade Policy," *Southern Economist,* Vol. 42, No. 9, September 1, 2003, pp. 19-21.

Montek S. Ahluwalia, "Economic Perfomance of States in Post-Reforms Period," *Economic and Political Weekly,* Vol. XXXV, No. 19, May 6-12, 2000, pp. 1637-48.

Ms. Valasamma Antony, "Rehabilitation of Sick SSI Units – A Few Guidelines," *Southern Economist,* Vol. 42, No.1, May 1, 2003, pp. 7-10.

Mubarak Ali, Mohamed Sindhasha, "IT Based Services to Agriculture and Agro-based Industries," *Kisan World,* Vol. 31, No. 12, December 2004, pp. 35-36.

N. Mahaligam, "Need for Modernisation of Small Scale Industry," *Kisan World,* Vol. 29, pp. 13-14.

N. Namasivayam & K. Kamalakannan, "Financing of Small Scale Industries in Rural Development," *Kisan World,* Vol. 32, February 2005, No. 2, pp. 5-6.

N. Rasul, "Food Processing Industries Overview," *Third Concept,* January 2002, pp. 37-41.

N. Rasul, "Food Processing Industry," *Third Concept,* January 2002, pp. 43-47.

Nagesh Kumar, "Economic Reforms and their Micro-Economic Impact," *Economic and Political Weekly,* Vol. XXXV, No. 10, March 4-10, 2000, pp. 803-812.

Nagesh Kumar, "Liberalisation, Foreign Direct Investment Flows and Development," *Economic and Political Weekly,* Vol. XL, No. 14, April 2, 2005, pp. 1459-68.

Narinder Kaur, "Globalization and Liberalization of Indian Economy": *Indian Economic Panorama,* Vol. 10, No. 2, July 2000, pp. 2-3.

Neela Mukherjee, "World Trade Organisation and Small & Medium Enterprises from a Developing Country's Pesspective: A Study of Indian Small Scale Industries", *The Indian Economic Journal,* Vol. 148, No. 2 Octber-December, 2000-01.

Neelam Jain, "Small Scale Industries in the New Millennium," *Southern Economist,* Vol. 43, No. 10, September 15, 2004, pp. 17-19.

Neelam Jain, "Small-Scale Industries in the New Millienniurn," *Southern Economist,* Vol. 43, No. 10, September 15, 2004, pp. 17-19.

Nilanjan Banik, "An Analysis of India's Exports during 1990s," *Economic and Political Weekly,* Vol. XXXVI, No. 44, November 3, 2001, pp. 4222-4230.

Nimbalkar, "Small and Medium Enterprises Emerging Issues," C-S Prasad, "Indian Small Scale Industries in Merging International Scenario," Pankaj Jain, "Building and International SME Network," *Lagu Udyog,* Vol. XXVII, No. 3 to 5, 2002, October-December, 2002, pp. 10-17, 22-27, 28-35.

O.P. Sharma, "The New Plan and Globalization", *Yojana,* Vol. 47, No.1, January 2003, pp. 29-36.

P.D. Jeromi, "Economic Reforms in Kerala", *Economic and Political Weekly,* July 23, 2005, pp. 3267-3277.

P.K. Vasudeva, "Is Small Industry Ready for a QR – Free Regime", *Economic and Political Weekly,* Vol. XXXVI, No. 1, January 6-12, pp. 22-24.

P.M. Mathew, "Small and Medium Enterprises – Role calls for Relook," *The Hindu — Survey of Indian Industry,* 2004, pp. 331-334.

P.M. Mathew, "Small Industry–Waiting for a New Deal," *The Hindu* , Survey of Indian Industry, 2005, pp. 43-45.

Pankaj Ghemawab, Murali Pafibandla, "India's Exports since the Reforms," *Economic and Political Weekly,* Vol. XXXIII, No. 20, May 16-22, 1998, pp. 1196-1198.

Pardip Singh Shehrawat & N. Laharia, "Strategies for Shaping Future of Small Scale Agro-processing Industries," *Indian Economic Panorama,* Vol. 10, No. 2, July 2000, pp. 46-49.

R. Ravindra Pirabu & C. Thangamuthu, "Non-farm Employment among Scheduled Caste Households in Tamil Nadu: A Study",

Southern Economist, Vol. 42, No. 9, September 1, 2003, pp. 8, 9-12, 13-16.

R. Srinivasan, "Growth of Small Scale Industries", *Southern Economist,* Vol. 42, No. 9, September 1, 2003, pp. 8-12.

R.L. Ayderabad & N.M. Makandar "Food Processing Industries in India", *Third Concept,* January 2003, pp. 41-45.

R.N. Sengupta, "Preparing SMEs in India to meet New Challenges," *SBI Monthly Review,* November 1998, pp. 578-589.

Rajesh Chadha, "Exim Policy Changes," *Economic and Political Weekly,* Vol, XXXV, No. 16, April-15-21, 2000, pp. 1334-40.

Rajkishor Meher, "The Handloom Industries and the Socio-economic Conditions of Weavers in Orissa," *Journal of Rural Development,* Vol. 14, No. 3, July-September 1995, pp.301-320.

Rajshri Jayaraman and Peter F. Lanjaw, "Small Scale Industry, Environment Regulation and Poverty: The Case of Brazil," *The World Bank Economic Review,* Vol. 18, No. 3, 2004, pp. 451-464.

Rajshri Jayaraman and Peter Lanjocew, "Small Scale Industry, Environmental Regulation, and Poverty: The Case of Brazil," *The World Bank Economic Review*, Vol. 18, No. 3, 2004, pp. 443-448.

Rakesh Basant, "Corporate Response to Economic Reforms," *Economic and Political Weekly,* Vol. XXXV, No. 10, March 4-10, 2000, pp. 813-822.

Ramaswamy R. Iyer, "The NEP: The Dangers Ahead", *Economic and Political Weekly,* Vol. XXX, No. 30, July 30, 1995, pp. 1913-1114.

Ramesh Chand, "Whether India's Food Policy? From Food Seurity to Food Deprivation," *Economic and Political Weekly,* Vol. XL, No. 11, March 12, 2005, pp. 1055-1062.

Rana Bijoy Deb, "Employment Generation in Small Units: A Case Study", *Yojana,* Vol. 48, May 2004, pp. 41-44.

Rana Bijoy Deb, "Employment Generation in Small Units: A Case Study," *Yojana,* Vol. 48, May 2004, pp. 41-44.

Ravindra H. Dholakia, Deepak Kapur, "Economic Reforms and Trade Performance Private Corporate Sector in India", *Economic and Political Weekly*, Vol. XXX, No. 30, July 30, 1995, pp. 1913-1114.

Rip Landes, Ashok Gulati, "Farm Sector Performance and Reform Agenda", *Economic and Political Weekly*, August 7-13, 2004, pp. 3611-3619.

Robin Mukherjee etal, "Small - Scale Industries in West Bengal, 1971–97," *Economic and Political Weekly*, Vol. XXXIV, No. 48, November 27 – December 3, 1999, pp. M.157-162.

Romesh Diwan, "Economic Reforms as Ideology", *Economic and Political Weekly*, Vol. XXX, No. 30, July 29, 1995, pp. 73-85.

S. Anburajan, "Performance and Credit Rating for SSI," *Small Industry*, Vol. 14, Issue, No. 06 - October 2005, p. 7.

S. Ganesh, "Indian Textile Industry: Stifled by Warped Policies," *Economic and Political Weekly*, Vol. XXXVII, No. 12, March 23-29, 2002, pp. 1095-1100.

S. Mahendra Dev, "Economic Reforms, Poverty, Income, Distribution and Employment," *Economic and Political Weekly*, Vol. XXXV, No. 10, March 4-10, 2000, pp. 823-835.

S. Nanjundan, "Economic Reforms and Small Scale Industry," *Economic and Political Weekly*, Vol. XXXI, No. 4, January 27, 1996, pp. 191-192.

S. Vaidehi *et al.* "WTO and Small Scale Industries," *Kurukshetra*, Vol. 52, No. 2, December 2003, pp. 30-32.

S.P. Gupta, "Economic Reforms and Its impact on Poor," *Economic and Political Weekly*, Vol. XXX, No. 22, June 3, 1995, pp. 1295-1313.

Sarthi Acharya, Niru Acharya, "Structural Adjustment and Small Producers–Reflection from Case Studies," *Economic and Political Weekly*, Vol. XXX, No. 1, January 7, 1995, pp. 45-50.

Sector and Impact on Credit to SMEs and the Poor", *Economic and Political Weekly*, Vol. XL, No. 12, pp. 1167-1180.

Sheela Bhide, "Development of Small Scale Industries," *Economic and Political Weekly*, Vol. XXXV, No. 50, 2000, pp. 9-15.

Shripad & Boloshetty, "Trade in Indian Higher Education Service Sector: Implications of WTO's GATS Part II," *University News,* Vol. 43, No. 38, September 19-25, 2005, pp. 6-14.

Shripad S. Boloshetty, "Trade in Indian Higher Education Service Sector: Implications of WTO & GATS Part I" , *University News,* Vol. 43, No. 36, September 5-11, 2005, pp.1-8.

Shuji Uchikawa, "Economic Reforms and Foreign Trade Policies," *Economic and Political Weekly,* Vol. XXXIV, No. 48, November 27– December 3, 1999, pp. M.138-148.

Sibghatullah Farooqi, "Small Scale Industries facing Acute Crisis," *Kurkshetra,* Vol. 51, No. 1, November 2002, pp. 39-42.

Sridhar Krishna, "Phasing out of Impact Licensing-Impact on Small-Scale Industries", *Economic and Political Weekly,* Vol. XXXVI, No. 27, July 7-13, 2001, pp. 2545–2550.

Subramanian Swamy, "Political Structure and Economic Reforms, A Comparative Appraisal of India and China," *Economic and Political Weekly,* Vol. XL No. 10, March 5-11, 2005, pp. 934-940.

Subrata Dutfa, "Urbanisation and Development of Rural Small Enterprises," *Economic and Political Weekly,* Vol. XXXVII, No. 30, July 27; 2002, pp. 3181-3189.

Suchitra Mohanty and T. Haque "Regional Disarities in the Flow of Institutional Credit in India," *Journal of Rural Development,* Vol. No. 1, January-March 2003, pp. 79-90.

Sudheesh Kaippachens, "Impact of Economic Reforms on the Banking Sector," B. Krishnamurthey & C.S. Yatanali, "Small Scale Sector – Protection to Competition,", *Southern Economist,* Vol. 41, No. 5, July 1, 2002, pp. 7-10, 17-20.

Sudheesh Kaippachery, "Impact of Economic Reforms on the Banking Sector," *Southern Economist,* Vol. 41, November 1, 2002, pp. 7-20.

Sudip Chaudhuri, "Economic Reforms and Industries Structure in India," *Economic and Political Weekly,* Vol. XXXVII, No. 2, January 12-18, 2002, pp. 155-162.

Sukanta Kumar Sahoo, "Small Scale Manufacturing Industries in

India," *The Indian Economic Journal,* Vol. 51, No.1, June 2003-04, pp. 52-63.

Sukanya, "Economic Policy for Balanced Growth", *Yojana,* Vol. 48, September 2004, pp. 19-23.

Sukumar Mukhopadhyay, "Exim Policy 2002-07," *Economic and Political Weekly,* Vol. XXXVII, No. 15, April-13, 2002, pp. 13-89, 90.

Sumit Roy, "New Institutional Economics, State and Development–Some Conceptual and Empirical Issues", *Economic and Political Weekly,* Vol. XXX, No. 30, July 29, 1995, pp. 65-72.

Sunnada Sen Sowmya Kant Ghosh, Basic Norms, "Indian Banking

Supriya Roy Chowdhury, "Globalisation and Labour," *Economic and Political Weekly,* January 3, 2004, pp. 105-106.

Suresh K. Chadha, "Application of Supply Chaise Management Practices in SSI's and Role of Government," *The Indian Journal of Public Administration,* Vol. XLIX, No. 4, October-December 2003, pp. 739-748.

T. Krishna Murthy, "Globalisation its Impact on Indian Economy," *Sarvodaya,* Vol. 2, No. 6, November-December 2004, pp. 17-20.

T.A. Bhavani, "Small Scale Units in the Era of Globalisation Problems and Prospects", *Economic and Political Weekly,* Vol. XXXVII, No. 29, July 20, 2002, pp. 3041-3052.

T.R. Gurumoorthy, "Recent Trends in India's Textile Exports", *Kisan World,* August 2003, pp. 22-23.

T.S. Papola, "Small and Micro-Enterprises in a Globalising Economy: Some Perspective on Policy Framework for their Integration," *The Indian Journal of Labour Economics,* Vol. 47, No. 4, October-December 2004, pp. 891-900.

Tapan R. Mohanty, "Rural Entrepreneurship in the Era of Globalisation: Challenges and Response", *Khadi Gramodyog,* Vol. XXXXIX, No. 6, March 2003, pp. 137 to 148.

Tirthankar Roy, "A New Textile Policy: Do We need one?", *Economic and Political Weekly,* Vol. XXXIII, No. 40, October 3-9, 1998, pp. 2563-2565.

V. Anbumani, "An Economic Estimation of Policy Shift on the Production Function in Small Scale Basic Metals and Alloys Industries," *Organisational Management*, Vol. XXI., No. 1, April-June 2005, pp. 62-72.

V. Balu, "Personnel Management in Small Scale Units – An Indian Perspective,", *Third Concept*, September 2002, pp. 41-42.

V. Madasamy & A. Joseph Tavier, "Impact of Khadi and Village Industries in Rural Development", *Kisan World*, Vol. 31, May 2004, pp. 23-24.

V. Selvaraj, "Impact of Globalisation on Employment", *Kisan World*, Vol. 30, No. 11, November 2003, pp. 29-30.

V.P. Raghavan, "Globalisation and the Farm Economy of India", *Southern Economist*, Vol. 41, No. 12, October 15, 2002, pp. 7-9.

V.S. Yyas, "Globalisation: Hopes, Realities and Coping Strategy," *Economic and Political Weekly*, Vol. XXXVII, No. 12, March 23-29, 2002, pp. 1109-1114.

Valasamma Antony, "The Prospects and Growth of SSIs in India: An Overiew," *Southern Economist*, Vol. 41, No. 1, May 1, 2002, pp. 23-29.

Vilasini G. Patkar & Sanjay S. Kaptan, "Village Industries–Problems and Propects in the Post Liberalisation Era," *Jagriti*, Vol. 49, No.12, November 2005, pp. 13-15, 16-17, 18-20, 25-27.

Yuko Nikaido, "Technical Efficiency of Small Scale Industry," *Economic and Political Weekly*, Vol. XXXIX, No. 6, February 7-13, 2004, pp. 592-597.

Report

Director of Census Operation, Tamil Nadu, Chennai.

Government of India, Ministry of Small Scale Industries, Annual Report, 2001-02

Indian Economic Sources, 1999, pp. 126-130.

Ministry of Commerce and Industry, Department of Commerce, Auunal Report, 2001-02.

Valasamma Antony, "What ales the SSI Sector", Economic Report on the Indian Institute of Public opinion, Vol. 43, No. 4, October to December 2000, pp. 19-34.

Newspaper

R. Gopalakrishnan, "Industrial Needs: Is KVI an Opportunity for Small Scale Sector? "Don't SSIs "Manufacture?,". *The Hindu*, Sunday, April 24, 2005.

R. Gopalakrishnan, "Industrial-Needs,-"Is' Rating" relevant to SSIs?" *The Hindu*, 2005.

R. Gopalakrishnan, "Industrial Needs–SMEs Bill should be Overhauled", *The Hindu*, Sunday, May 29, 2005.

R. Gopalakrishnan, "Industrial Needs–Steel and SSIs – Hard Options for Future," *The Hindu*, 2005.

R. Gopalakrishnan, "Industrial Needs–Law, not bureaucracy, should define SSIs", *The Hindu*, 2005.

R. Gopalakrishnan, "Industrial Needs–Clear air can be good business,". *The Hindu*, March 21, 2004.

R. Gopalakrishnan, "Industrial Needs–SSIs need facilitation, not Protection," *The Hindu*, June 6, 2004.

R. Gopalakrishnan, "Industrial Needs–Packaging industry a catalyst of economic growth", *The Hindu*, Sunday, May 9, 2004.

R. Gopalakrishnan, "Industrial Needs–Revamp extension services to SSIs," *The Hindu*, July 4, 2004.

R. Gopalakrishnan, "Industrial Needs–Packaging: A Confluence of Technologies", *The Hindu*, Sunday, May 23, 2004.

R. Gopalakrishnan, "Industrial Needs–Make Use of SSI Upgradation Schemes", *The Hindu*, Sunday, June 20, 2004.

Index

and the countless other women who nourish my soul, I adore you. And to Johnny B, the man I love – I promised you my hand in marriage and your name in a book. Consider this a fifty per cent deposit. I love you, my forever diamond.

This mission is dedicated to Rachel Leyshon, who is sometimes my M, sometimes my Q, occasionally my arch-nemesis and always my Super Ed. Five years ago I wrote a book that made you laugh – the joke's been on you ever since. Thank you for offering me a chair at this extraordinary table. I'll work on my table manners. You are the best and I cherish you. No matter what my track changes might say . . .

And finally, to my incredible GodsSquad. Thank you so much for all your support for my Godyssey – I hope you will take Vi and Russell to your hearts like you have Elliot and Virgo. It will always be my mission to write books that make you laugh, make you think and make you happy. Thank you so much for choosing to accept them.

Love, and other coded messages,

Maz

xxx

MISSION REPORT

Well, hello again!

I write these thanks – have written this book, in fact – during The Year the World Stood Still, and this adventure has been a huge help to navigate through it all. I am so grateful for the opportunity to do the thing I love, and my fond thanks go to everyone at Chicken House HQ, along with Jenny and Adamma, for supporting me as I embark on this new operation. I'll try not to go too rogue too often.

To my not-so-secret agent, Veronique Baxter – thank you for always having my back, however crazy my schemes.

To the band of crazy mavericks that surround me – thank you for being the best family and friends I could wish for. To my husbands (past and future) and my kids (my greatest present), you will always be my most accomplished mission. To Authors Assemble and The Skunk Pirates, I thank and value you beyond measure for your wit and wisdom. To Arf, Bo, Scatty, Mollie, Karen, Victoria, Susie, Kiran, Maya, Robin, Lisa, Lucy, Onjali, Mel